Touring At
SOUTHERN AFRICA

MapStudio

CONTENTS

4 & 5
HOW TO USE THIS BOOK

6 & 7
MAP OVERVIEW OF SITES

8 to 11
BEST OF SOUTHERN AFRICA

ROUTES

12 & 13
MAIN ROUTE 1 INTRODUCTION
CAPE TOWN TO GHANZI TOWN

14 & 15
PICTURE ROUTE
CAPE TOWN TO THE CEDERBERG

16 & 17
PICTURE ROUTE
WEST COAST TO WATERBERG
PLATEAU PARK

18 & 19
TOP SITE – CAPE PENINSULA

20 & 21
TOP SITE – WEST COAST
FLOWER ROUTE

22 & 23
PICTURE ROUTE
ETOSHA TO GHANZI TOWN

24 & 25
TOP SITE – OKAVANGO DELTA

26 & 27
MAIN ROUTE 2 INTRODUCTION
AI-AIS TO MUTARE

28 & 29
PICTURE ROUTE
ORANGE RIVER TO AUGRABIES FALLS
SITE – KGALAGADI-KALAHARI

30 & 31
PICTURE ROUTE
GREEN KALAHARI TO KATSE DAM

32 & 33
SITE – FISH RIVER CANYON
& RICHTERSVELD
SITE – MALUTI MOUNTAINS
& SANI

34 & 35
PICTURE ROUTE
BLOEMFONTEIN TO MAGALIESBERG

36 & 37
PICTURE ROUTE
POLOKWANE TO CHIMANIMANI
SITE – EASTERN HIGHLANDS

38 & 39
SITE – NORTHEASTERN FREE STATE
SITE – GREAT ZIMBABWE

40 & 41
MAIN ROUTE 3 INTRODUCTION
CAPE TOWN TO VICTORIA FALLS

42 & 43
PICTURE ROUTE
OVERBERG TO MAPUTO

44 & 45
PICTURE ROUTE
SOUTH COAST TO MAPUTO
SITE – WILD COAST

46 & 47
TOP SITE – GARDEN ROUTE

48 & 49
TOP SITE – ZULULAND, MAPUTALAND
& INHACA

50 & 51
PICTURE ROUTE
MAPUTO TO VICTORIA FALLS
SITE – MANA POOLS

52 & 53
TOP SITE – VICTORIA FALLS

54 & 55
MAIN ROUTE 4 INTRODUCTION
CAPE TOWN TO SWAKOPMUND

56 & 57
PICTURE ROUTE
WORCESTER TO GABORONE

58 & 59
PICTURE ROUTE
FRANCISTOWN TO MATOBO HILLS
SITE – HWANGE

60 & 61
TOP SITE – CHOBE

62 & 63
PICTURE ROUTE
BULAWAYO TO SWAKOPMUND

64 & 65
PICTURE ROUTE
NAMIB TO SESRIEM
SITE – HENTIES BAY &
SKELETON COAST
SITE – SOSSUSVLEI

66 & 67
SITE – CENTRAL KALAHARI
GAME RESERVE
SITE – SWAKOPMUND SURROUNDS

68 & 69
MAIN ROUTE 5 INTRODUCTION
SWAKOPMUND TO VICTORIA FALLS

70 & 71
PICTURE ROUTE
SWAKOPMUND TO SESFONTEIN

72 & 73
PICTURE ROUTE
KAOKOLAND TO KHOMAS HOCHLAND
SITE – KAOKOLAND

74 & 75
TOP SITE – ETOSHA PAN

76 & 77
PICTURE ROUTE
KHAUDOM TO VICTORIA FALLS

78 & 79
SITE – ZAMBEZI RIVER (ZAMBIA)
SITE – CAPRIVI STRIP

80 & 81
MAIN ROUTE 6 INTRODUCTION
DURBAN TO MAPUTO/WINDHOEK

82 & 83
PICTURE ROUTE
DURBAN TO KZN MIDLANDS
SITE – MIDLANDS MEANDER

84 & 85
PICTURE ROUTE
DUNDEE TO SOWETO
SITE – SOWETO

86 & 87
TOP SITE – BATTLEFIELDS &
CENTRAL DRAKENSBERG

88 & 89
PICTURE ROUTE
WINDHOEK TO MAPUTO

90 & 91
SITE – SUN CITY, PILANESBERG &
CRADLE OF HUMANKIND
SITE – KRUGER (SOUTH) & BLYDE
CANYON

92 & 93
MAIN ROUTE 7 INTRODUCTION
HARARE TO GORONGOSA

94 & 95
PICTURE ROUTE
HARARE TO NIASSA RESERVE
SITE – NORTHERN MOZAMBIQUE

96 & 97
PICTURE ROUTE
MAPUTO TO BEIRA
SITE – GORONGOSA NATIONAL PARK

98 & 99
TOP SITE – MOZAMBIQUE COASTLINE

STREETPLANS

100 & 101
ORIENTATION MAP – Southern Africa showing cities and towns covered
Pretoria – South Africa

102 & 103
Cape Town – South Africa
Windhoek – Namibia

104 & 105
Gaborone – Botswana
Maputo – Mozambique

106 & 107
Maseru – Lesotho
Mbabane – Swaziland
Harare – Zimbabwe

108 & 109
Johannesburg – South Africa
Port Elizabeth – South Africa
East London – South Africa

110
Durban – South Africa
Pietermaritzburg – South Africa
Kimberley – South Africa

111
Bloemfontein – South Africa
Polokwane – South Africa
Bisho – South Africa

112
Nelspruit – South Africa
Mafikeng – South Africa
Keetmanshoop – Namibia
Walvis Bay – Namibia

113
Maun – Botswana
Bulawayo – Zimbabwe

Beira – Mozambique
Inhambane – Mozambique

114
Beaufort West – South Africa
Bethlehem – South Africa
Citrusdal – South Africa
Clanwilliam – South Africa

115
Colesberg – South Africa
George – South Africa
Estcourt – South Africa
Graaff-Reinet – South Africa

116
Grahamstown – South Africa
Knysna – South Africa
Kroonstad – South Africa
Ladysmith – South Africa

117
Lamberts Bay – South Africa
Lydenburg – South Africa
Mossel Bay – South Africa
Musina – South Africa

118
Newcastle – South Africa
Oudtshoorn – South Africa
Pilgrims Rest – South Africa
Port Shepstone – South Africa

119
Richards Bay – South Africa
Rustenburg – South Africa
Sishen – South Africa
Springbok – South Africa

120
Stellenbosch – South Africa
St Lucia – South Africa
Strand – South Africa
Swellendam – South Africa

121
Tzaneen – South Africa
Umtata – South Africa
Upington – South Africa
Vryburg – South Africa

122
Vryheid – South Africa
Witbank – South Africa
Worcester – South Africa
Gobabis – Namibia

123
Henties Bay – Namibia
Katima Mulilo – Namibia
Kolmanskop – Namibia

Lüderitz – Namibia

124
Mariental – Namibia
Okahandja – Namibia
Opuwo – Namibia
Oshakati – Namibia

125
Otjiwarongo – Namibia
Rundu – Namibia
Sesfontein – Namibia
Swakopmund – Namibia

126
Tsumeb – Namibia
Francistown – Botswana
Ghanzi – Botswana
Jwaneng – Botswana

127
Kanye – Botswana
Mahalapye – Botswana
Nata – Botswana
Selebi Phikwe – Botswana

128
Chimanimani – Zimbabwe
Chinhoyi – Zimbabwe
Gweru – Zimbabwe
Kariba – Zimbabwe

129
Kwekwe – Zimbabwe
Masvingo – Zimbabwe
Mutare – Zimbabwe
Victoria Falls – Zimbabwe

130
Blantyre – Malawi
Mozambique Island – Mozambique
Nampula – Mozambique

131
Quelimane – Mozambique
Tete – Mozambique
Vilankulo – Mozambique
Xai-Xai – Mozambique

TOURING MAPS

132 & 133
ORIENTATION MAP – Showing pagination of main touring maps

134 to 197
Main touring maps

RESOURCES

198 to 207
Tourism resources

HOW TO USE THIS BOOK

MAIN ROUTE INTRODUCTION

This book covers Southern Africa as 7 driving routes. Each route is shown as a spread containing images, text, a strip route map and a simple location map.
The strip route map indicates main towns and sites along the route, and the distances between them. The locator map shows all the main roads in Southern Africa and highlights the specific route being covered.

These routes appear on the contents page as:

....
26 & 27
MAIN ROUTE 2 INTRODUCTION
AI-AIS TO MUTARE
....

Introductions to the various routes can be found on the following pages:

Pg – **12 & 13** Route 1
Pg – **26 & 27** Route 2
Pg – **40 & 41** Route 3
Pg – **54 & 55** Route 4
Pg – **68 & 69** Route 5
Pg – **80 & 81** Route 6
Pg – **92 & 93** Route 7

PICTURE ROUTE

Each **Main Route** is divided into smaller detailed sub-sections. Each **Picture Route** page contains images, text and contact information for the section.

These routes appear on the contents page as:

....
34 & 35
PICTURE ROUTE
BLOEMFONTEIN TO MAGALIESBERG
....

These sections can be found starting on the following pages:

Pg – **14, 16, 22** Route 1
Pg – **28, 30, 34, 36** Route 2
Pg – **42, 44, 50** Route 3
Pg – **56, 58, 62, 64** Route 4
Pg – **70, 72, 76** Route 5
Pg – **82, 84, 88** Route 6
Pg – **94, 96** Route 7

MAIN ROUTE INTRODUCTION SAMPLE SPREAD

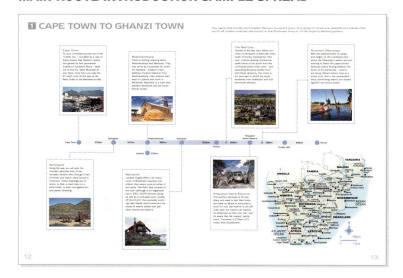

PICTURE ROUTE SAMPLE SPREAD

TOP SITE SAMPLE SPREAD

SITE SAMPLE SPREAD

TOP SITE

Each **Picture Route** includes **Top Sites** for the country or region. They follow the same format as a **Picture Route**, but in more detail and with a coverage map of the area.
See examples on pgs – **18, 24 & 60**

SITE

Each **Picture Route** also includes **Sites** for the country or region. They follow the same format as **Top Sites**, but are usually 2 or 3 columns only.

See examples on pgs – **32, 85 & 97**

CITY & TOWN STREETPLANS

There are 96 **Streetplans** in this book, starting with an orientation map on page 100. This map contains the page numbers of the various **Streetplans**. The **Streetplans** start with the largest cities first, and then work their way down to smaller towns and villages. Where possible, the **streetplans** are in alphabetic order, following country groupings.

Streetplans show detailed information such as police stations, points of interest, hospitals, directionals, one-way streets, scale, information centres, parking areas, post offices and contact details.

Streetplans appear on the contents page as:

....
                                    102 & 103
Cape Town – South Africa
Windhoek – Namibia
....

MAIN TOURING MAPS

There are 64 pages of seamless **Main Touring Maps**, at a scale of 1 : 1,500,000, starting with an orientation map on page 132.

Main Touring Maps show detailed information such as major, main and minor roads, rivers, lakes, dams, pans and marshes, international and provincial boundaries and border crossings, national parks, reserves and conservation areas, toll routes, places of interest, accommodation, cities, towns and villages, airports and airfields.

TOURISM RESOURCES

Starting on page 198 are 10 pages of up-to-date information. They have been listed in order of routes 1 – 7, with telephone, e-mail and website information.

If you would like to be listed, kindly forward your details to:
tourist@mapstudio.co.za

CAPITAL OR MAJOR CITY

OTHER TOWNS AND VILLAGES

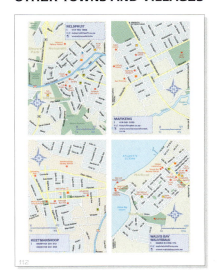

MAIN TOURING MAP SAMPLE SPREAD

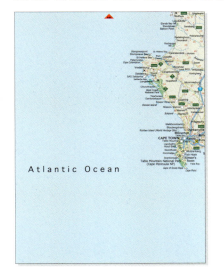

TOURISM RESOURCES SAMPLE SPREAD

MAP OVERVIEW OF SITES

HOW TO USE THIS MAP

This page can be used to locate any route, top site, site or streetplan. Each entry on the map has a number which corresponds with a page number in the book.

Locate **main route introductions** and **picture routes** using the quick reference page numbers below:

MAIN ROUTE INTRODUCTION
Pg – **12 & 13** Route 1
Pg – **26 & 27** Route 2
Pg – **40 & 41** Route 3
Pg – **54 & 55** Route 4
Pg – **68 & 69** Route 5
Pg – **80 & 81** Route 6
Pg – **92 & 93** Route 7

PICTURE ROUTE
Pg – **14, 16, 22** Route 1
Pg – **28, 30, 34, 36** Route 2
Pg – **42, 44, 50** Route 3
Pg – **56, 58, 62, 64** Route 4
Pg – **70, 72, 76** Route 5
Pg – **82, 84, 88** Route 6
Pg – **94, 96** Route 7

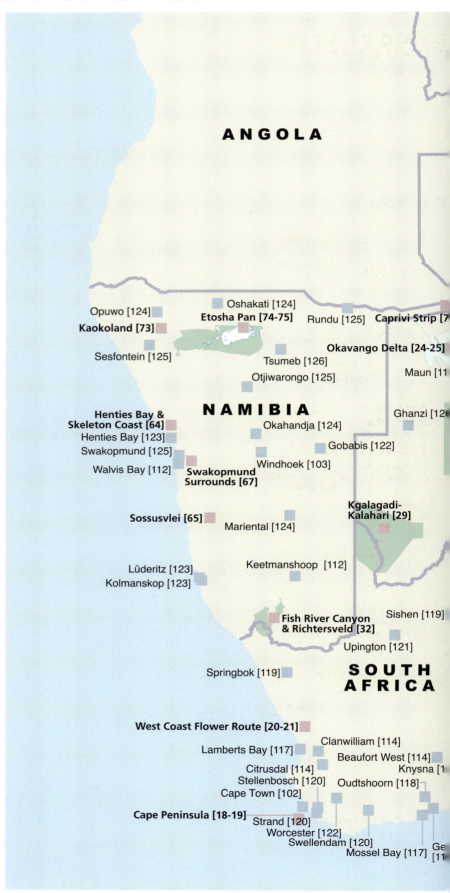

BEST OF SOUTHERN AFRICA

SOUTH AFRICA

1 CASTLE OF GOOD HOPE
South Africa's oldest (fully intact) colonial structure. Built by Jan van Riebeeck from 1666–79 to protect Table Bay, it replaced the very first clay-and-timber fort, which was constructed in 1652.

2 TABLE MOUNTAIN
The world's most famous, flattest, mountain-tabletop profile. Composed of sedimentary sandstone and rising to 1086m (3563ft) at its highest point, visitors can get to the top of this National Monument in 2 minutes via state-of-the-art cable cars.

3 ROBBEN ISLAND
South Africa's most historically significant island. Its status as a World Heritage Site (1999) recognises this tiny (6km²; 2 sq miles) island's importance in humanitarian terms (visit anti-apartheid leader Nelson Mandela's prison cell) and in ecological terms (the island is a rare seabird breeding colony).

4 CAPE FLORAL KINGDOM
One of only six floral kingdoms in the world. However, unlike the others, the Cape Floral Kingdom – comprising mainly fynbos and represented by 350 species – is endemic to the southern tip of Africa. *Fynbos* accounts for 80% of the plant species on Table Mountain's slopes. It covers an area of less than 4% of the Southern African land surface.

5 GARDEN ROUTE
The longest garden in Africa. An elongated band stretching for some 200km (125 miles) between Mossel Bay and the Storms River mouth, the Garden Route encompasses the last remaining stands of indigenous hardwoods – yellowwood, ironwood, stinkwood, Knysna boxwood, white alder and blackwood.

6 KNYSNA'S FOREST ELEPHANT
The last of the Cape's forest elephants. Only one solitary, shy female out of the original group remains in Knysna's indigenous forest. Nonetheless, visitors can check out the elephant skeleton, with its giant tusks, in the window of Knysna's Information Centre on Main Street!

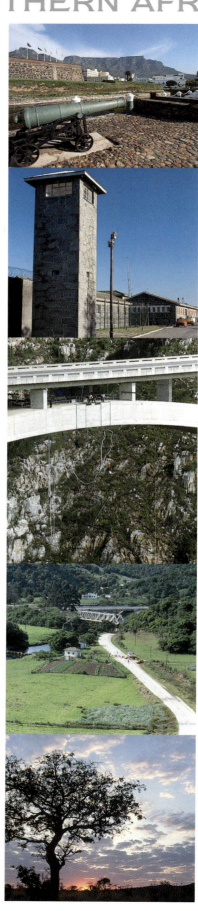

7 BLOUKRANS BUNGEE
The world's highest commercial bungee jump. Outside Tsitsikamma forest village, bungee jumpers leap off the 216m (709ft) Bloukrans bridge in a terrifying 7-second free fall before bouncing back up again.

8 THE RICHTERSVELD
South Africa's only true desert. In a loop of the Orange River dividing Namibia from South Africa, the seared rock and sunbaked soils of this region receive only 50mm (2in) rainfall a year.

9 KIMBERLEY
The world's largest manmade depression. Extending 500m (1640ft) across, with a circumference of 1.6km (1 mile), the Big Hole is presently 800m (2620ft) deep. Initially, an amazing 240m (780ft) was dug with pick and shovel. Later, an underground shaft took the mine depth to 1098m (3600ft).

10 SANI PASS
The country's highest mountain gateway. From Himeville at the foot of the Drakensberg, it climbs 1000m (3280ft) in just 7km (4 miles). This pass is the only access from KwaZulu-Natal into Lesotho. It tops 2865m (9400ft) at its highest point.

11 KWAZULU-NATAL BATTLEFIELDS
South Africa's most concentrated collection of battlefields. To the west of the country's Zulu heartland, there are 50 sites of interest, among them 10 major battlefields commemorating bloody battles waged between Zulus, Boers and British soldiers.

12 ST LUCIA WETLANDS
South Africa's largest and most pristine inland body of water. Accorded World Heritage status in 1999, these wetlands extending for 80km (50 miles) feature five ecosystems: marine, shore (between lake and sea), reed and sedge swamps, lake, and western shores (fossil corals, sand forest, bushveld and grassland).

13 CRADLE OF HUMANKIND
Most historically significant site (perhaps in the world) tracing humankind's origins. Hominid finds at

Sterkfontein Cave, part of the Kromdraai Conservancy (a World Heritage Site in the Magaliesberg), prove that ancient man walked here 3.3 million years ago.

14 MARAKELE NATIONAL PARK
South Africa's newest reserve. In the heart of the Waterberg near Thabazimbi, 130km (80 miles) north of Rustenburg, this 600km² (235-sq-mile) sanctuary harbours some of the rarer wildlife species such as tsessebe and red hartebeest.

15 KRUGER NATIONAL PARK
The country's largest wildlife reserve (and also one of the biggest in the world). Covering 19,633km² (7657 sq miles), this park protects 147 mammal, 507 bird and 114 reptile species.

NAMIBIA

16 FISH RIVER CANYON
Africa's second-largest gorge. The Fish River Canyon, next in size to the Blue Nile gorge, dates from 1800 million to 50 million years ago, with signs of Stone and Iron Age habitation in its valley. It runs for 160km (100 miles), and in places towers to 600m (1968ft).

17 KOLMANSKOP
Southern Africa's best preserved ghost town. Inland of Lüderitz, the first diamonds were found here in 1908, but by 1956 the thriving mining town had been deserted. Leaning telephone poles, eaves shored up by desert sand and ghostly sweeping staircases are an eerie sight.

18 SOSSUSVLEI
The world's highest and oldest dunes. At times rising 200m (656ft) high, these parabolic dunes are the most stable, and therefore most vegetated, dunes because changing wind directions keep them immobile.

19 GIANT'S PLAYGROUND
Namibia's largest playpen. North of Keetmanshoop, a collection of giant, haphazardly balanced, dark basalt rocks has been pummelled by wind and rain into a bizarre playground for Herculean beings.

20 NAMIBIA'S FORTIFIED CASTLES
The most German-influenced fortified castles in a Southern African country. Windhoek's Alte Feste was built in 1889 for protection against the Namas and Hereros; Etosha's Fort Namutoni, built in 1899, warded off the Owambos; while Heinitzburg, constructed in Windhoek in 1914, had more peaceful aims – to house the German Count von Schwerin's fiancée.

21 ETOSHA PAN
One of the most prolific wildlife reserves in the world. Its most impressive feature is its salt pan sprawling for 5000km² (1950 sq miles) and comprising 23% of the national park.

22 TSUMEB
The world's fifth-largest lead mine. It is also the source of 180 other minerals, including copper ore, zinc, silver, gold, germanium and cadmium.

23 HOBA METEORITE
The world's largest meteorite. Lying outside Grootfontein, on the road to Tsumeb, this celestial fragment weighs 54,000kg (119,000 lb). Discovered in 1920, it is protected today from vandalism through its National Monument status.

24 SKELETON COAST
The world's largest graveyard of ships. Because mist can obscure this desert coastline for days, over 100 vessels have foundered along its desolate shores. Today there are but sad rusty remains of the shipwrecked vessels.

25 THE HIMBA
Namibia's most photographed people. The Himba preserve their beautiful features against the harsh elements with a copper-coloured clay made of fat, ochre and ash, which is also smeared into hair that has been wound into ringlets.

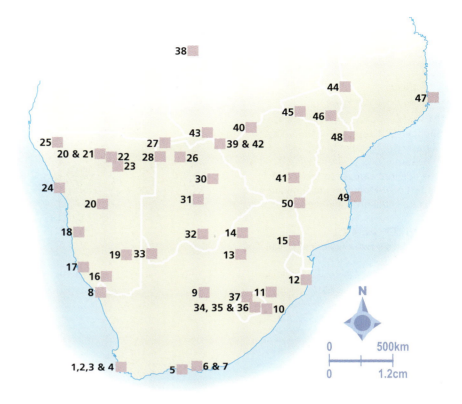

BEST OF SOUTHERN AFRICA

BOTSWANA

26 OKAVANGO DELTA
The world's largest delta. Spreading across 15,000km² (5840 sq miles) in dry years and swelling to 22,000km² (8600 sq miles) after high rains, this delta contains 95% of all Botswana's water. Only around 1800km² (700 sq miles) constitutes dry land.

27 OKAVANGO RIVER
One African river that never reaches the sea. Rising in the eastern Angolan highlands as the Cuito, this river becomes the Okavango in Botswana. Its length of 1430km (890 miles) peters out and dies in Botswana's arid desertland.

28 TSODILO HILLS
One of Southern Africa's wealthiest rock art sites. Sometimes called the Louvre of the Desert, as many as 3500 individual rock paintings chart 25,000 years of habitation in the quartzite Tsodilo Hills west of the Delta panhandle.

29 MAKGADIKGADI & NXAI PANS
The world's largest natural salt pan. Measuring roughly the length and breadth of Portugal, this saline desert covers 12,000km² (4680 sq miles).

30 KALAHARI DESERT
The largest continuous stretch of sand in the world. Desolate, dry and flat, the Kalahari takes up more than 80% of Botswana's land area. Its 1.2 million km² expanse (4.7 million sq miles) also penetrates six other countries: eastern Namibia, Angola, Democratic Republic of the Congo, Zambia, Zimbabwe and a northern segment of South Africa.

31 KALAHARI SAN
Southern Africa's most endangered people. Originally protected by the establishment of the Central Kalahari Game Reserve, the last members of these nomadic hunter-gatherers have since been relocated to settlements on the reserve fringes. Dwindling water and natural resources are seriously threatening their existence.

32 JWANENG
The world's single largest producer of gem-quality diamonds. Botswana supplies 30 million carats to world markets every year and Jwaneng is the country's biggest and richest diamond mine.

33 KGALAGADI TRANSFRONTIER PARK
Africa's first formally gazetted transboundary reserve (1999). Having set a precedent for the future, the combining of Botswana's Mabuasehube–Gemsbok park and South Africa's Kalahari-Gemsbok park has created a 28,400km² (11,00-sq-mile) pristine wilderness.

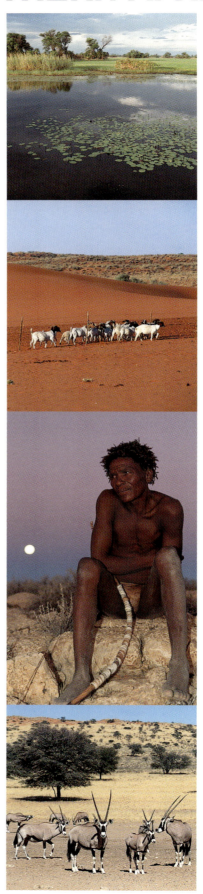

LESOTHO

34 THABANA NTLENYANA
Southern Africa's highest peak. Soaring to an impressive 3482m (11,424ft) in the Drakensberg mountains in the northeast of Lesotho, this basalt lava peak is, in geological terms, over 150 million years old.

35 MALOTI–DRAKENSBERG PARK
Richest repository of San rock art in a transfrontier park. Initiated in 1982, this transfrontier park will incorporate the uKhahlamba-Drakensberg (a World Heritage Site) and Lesotho's Maluti mountains – an area containing 600 rock art sites with over 40,000 individual paintings.

36 LESOTHO HIGHLANDS WATER PROJECT
One of Southern Africa's most important hydroelectric-power projects. A plan to harness Lesotho's abundant water resources will by 2020 supply water and electricity to a large sector of Southern Africa. Once construction is finished (Katse Dam is already complete), the system will link up with South Africa's Vaal Dam and will comprise 5 major and a series of smaller dams, with roughly 200km (125 miles) of tunnels.

37 THABA BOSIU
Site of greatest spiritual significance to the people of Lesotho. East of Maseru, this steep, flat-topped mountain (a World Heritage Site) was the capital from which Moshoeshoe I first ruled in 1824. His grave and the remains of his fortifications lie here.

ZIMBABWE

38 ZAMBEZI RIVER
The country's mightiest and Africa's fourth-longest river. Rising in the highlands of eastern Angola and northwest Zambia, the 2650km (1650-mile) course of this river fans out on the Mozambican coast in the great Zambezi delta. Along the way, the Zambezi accumulates the run-off waters of five other countries.

39 VICTORIA FALLS
In scale, one of the world's most impressive falls. The sheer escarpment edge over which the Zambezi gushes to form the falls measures 1.7km (1 mile) in length. During high rainfall, some 545 million litres (144 million gal) crash over every minute.

40 LAKE KARIBA
At the time of construction, the world's largest manmade lake. It is also Africa's third-largest dam and is the site of a hydroelectric-power plant. With a length of around 280km (175 miles), Kariba takes up 5200km² (2028 sq miles).

41 GREAT ZIMBABWE
The most impressive 13th-century ruins in sub-Saharan Africa. The sophisticated building techniques of these 'great stone houses', *dzimba dza mabwe*, near Masvingo feature interlocking, mortarless stone work incorporating geometric patterns. Nearly a million stone pieces went into the walls of the Great Enclosure.

ZAMBIA

42 LIVINGSTONE ISLAND
The island with the most heart pounding view in Africa. Perched in the middle of the Zambezi, right at the edge of the Victoria Falls on the Zambian side, visitors can cross to the island in low rainfall months to peer over the lip into the thundering, spray-filled abyss, some 100m (330ft) below.

43 ZAMBEZI VALLEY
The hottest zone in Southern Africa. In October, Livingstone town sweats it out at 38°C (100°F) coupled with 90% humidity – although, at Lake Kariba, also fed by the Zambezi, the hottest temperature ever recorded was 46°C (115°F).

MALAWI

44 LAKE MALAWI
Africa's third-largest inland body of water. This lake along the southern Rift Valley swallows up one-fifth of Malawi, taking up 23,000km² (8900 sq miles) along most of its eastern border. Malawi shares its waters with two other countries – Mozambique (Lake Niassa) and Tanzania (Lake Nyasa).

MOZAMBIQUE

45 CAHORA BASSA DAM
Mozambique's answer to Kariba dam. The thundering waters of the Kebrabassa rapids, which funnel through a narrow gorge on the Zambezi River, were harnessed to create this 270km-long (168-mile) dam to supply the country with hydroelectric power.

46 TETE
Hottest town in Mozambique. Windless midsummer days on the blistering banks of the Zambezi can push the mercury in Tete, southeast of Cahora Bassa, to 50°C (122°F).

47 MOZAMBIQUE ISLAND
Mozambique's largest concentration of historic architecture in a confined space. Although crumbling and dilapidated, visitors can gain a good feeling for the country's Portuguese heritage in buildings such as the San Sebastian fort, the chapel of Nossa Señhora do Baluarte, and Saint Paul's palace and chapel.

48 DONA ANA BRIDGE
Africa's longest (converted) railway bridge. North of the Caia ferry which is one of the few means of crossing the Zambezi, the 3.7km (2½-mile) road bridge connects Villa de Sena with Mutarara, but is served by extremely poor roads to either side.

49 DUGONGS IN BAZARUTO
Last of the increasingly rare dugongs along the Mozambican coast. These aquatic herbivores, which feed on sea grasses, algae and crabs, are sometimes likened to sea cows. They have flippers for steering and tadpole-shaped tails for propulsion.

50 INHAMBANE
The greatest number of dhows in one port. Possibly the largest working fleet of dhows on the entire East African coast is based here, strengthened by Inhambane's trade-wind-protected location and boat-building skills. Dhow ferries constantly ply the waters between Maxixe and Inhambane.

51 NEW TRANSFRONTIER PARK
The world's largest conservation area. The recently established Gaza–Kruger–Gonarezhou Transfrontier Park has done away with boundaries between Mozambique, South Africa and Zimbabwe. It is planned to span an impressive 100,000km² (40,000 sq miles). Operation Ark succeeded in translocating around 1000 elephants from Kruger to Mozambique and Zimbabwe.

1 CAPE TOWN TO GHANZI TOWN

Cape Town
For your northward journey out of the 'mother city' – so-called as it was on these shores that Western civilisation gained its first permanent foothold in Southern Africa – head out on the N1, Table Mountain at your back. From here, you take the N7 which runs all the way up the West Coast to the Namibian border.

Keetmanshoop
There is nothing inspiring about Keetmanshoop and Mariental. They only serve as crossroads for southern Namibia – evident in their plethora of petrol stations! From Keetmanshoop, main arteries lead west to Lüderitz and north to Windhoek; Mariental is a main stop between Windhoek and the South African border.

Cape Town — 535km — Springbok — 417km — Keetmanshoop — 390km — Rehoboth

Lüderitz — 332km

Springbok
Along the way, you will spot the rounded, igloo-like huts of the nomadic herders who, through a lack of timber and thatch, were forced to improvise. These dwellings are of stone, or hide or reed mats on a stick frame, or even corrugated iron and plastic sheeting.

Rehoboth
Located roughly 65km (40 miles) south of Windhoek, travellers can refresh their weary souls at either of two spots. The Reho Spa complex in the town (although a bit neglected) has a 39°C (102°F) thermal spring as well as a cold-water pool; nearby, off the D1237, the scenically soothing Lake Oanab resort overlooks the bluest of waters dotted with pelicans, herons and darters.

The name Aha (unlike Archimedes' famous 'eureka!') given to a range of limestone, dolerite and marble hills south of Tsodilo matches the sound, in the Bushman tongue, of the region's barking geckos.

The Red Line
Tsumeb is the last town before you cross a checkpoint (130km/80 miles south of Rundu) marking the 'Red Line', a fence dividing commercial cattle farms of the south from the communal lands of the north – and separating Etosha's wildlife from both these divisions. The intent in the past was to shield the south farmlands from rinderpest and foot-and-mouth disease.

Northern Okavango
With the establishment of camps and lodges on the riverbanks here – where the Okavango's waters are just starting to bleed into papyrus-lined wetlands before flowing between the faults of the panhandle – visitors are being offered *mokoro* trips at a lesser cost. And in the panhandle's deep, fast-flowing waters lurk striped tigerfish and silvery bream.

Khaudom Game Reserve
This territory seriously is for travellers who want to test their limits and have no desire to encounter a soul! For now, the reserve is not officially open but visitors can explore its wilderness at their own risk. Just be aware that the nearest 'settlement', Tsumkwe, is 275km (170 miles) from Grootfontein.

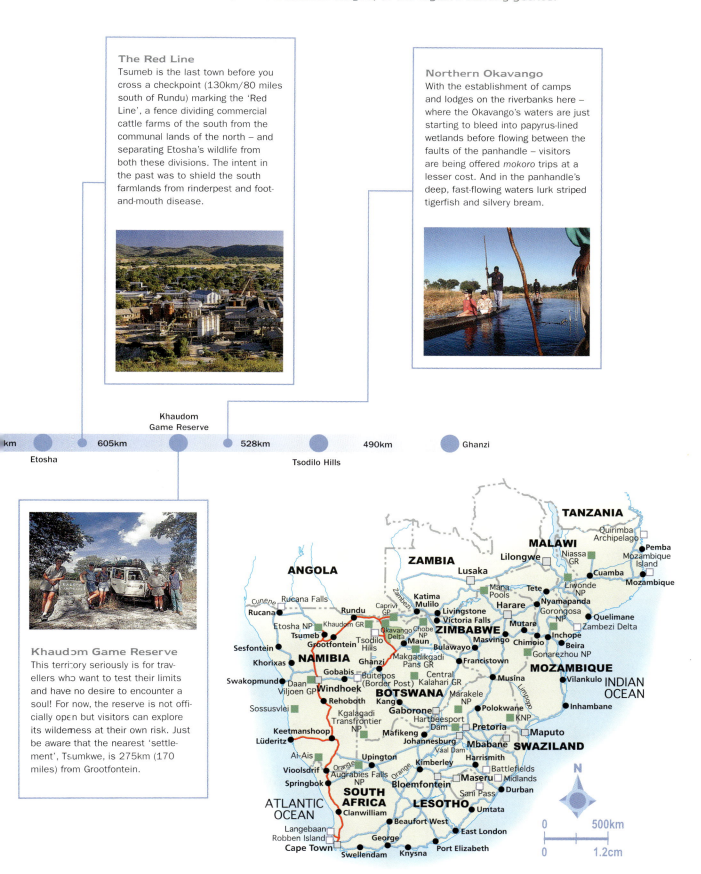

Cape Town to the Cederberg

CAPE TOWN

South Africa's fourth-largest (and scenically, its loveliest) city began life in 1652 as a watering station for the Dutch East India Company, to aid the passage of its ships to the East. Cape Town's people are an interesting mix – descendants of indigenous Khoisan and Xhosa clans, the Dutch and the British, and slaves who were brought in from Asia and Africa. Added to the melting pot were the original Malays, many of them Muslim political exiles from Sri Lanka, the Indonesian Islands and India. The city's character reflects this colourful heritage in its Smartie-hued, flat-roofed Cape Malay houses, Cape Dutch gables, and 19th-century Victorian and Georgian facades.
Tel: 021 426 4260
Email: info@cape-town.org
Website: www.tourismcapetown.co.za

In 1963, in the famous Rivonia Trial, Nelson Mandela and seven other political activists were condemned by the South African government to life imprisonment. Mandela spent 18 years of his sentence in the Robben Island maximum security prison.

MALMESBURY

A key town to the Swartland – the heart of South Africa's wheatland – Malmesbury has some of the country's largest flour mills. Over 20% of South Africa's wheat is grown here, making Malmesbury a major distributor. Whether you travel here in spring, summer or winter, there is a certain beauty to the precise symmetry of wheat country, be it manicured squares of acid-green shoots, rippling waves of golden corn, or shaved stubbles punctuated by rolled wheat bales ever so neatly stacked. If you're into architecture, Malmesbury's historic town walk reveals Gothic Revival, Georgian, Edwardian and Victorian styles.
Tel: 022 487 1133
Email: swartlandinfo@westc.co.za
Website: www.capewestcoast.org

TABLE MOUNTAIN

This sedimentary sandstone monolith, rising to 1086m (3563ft) at Maclear's Beacon, dominates the city bowl and the life of every Capetonian. People negotiate by it, gauge the weather by its tablecloth – sometimes cottony and impenetrable, sometimes wispy and ephemeral – or simply feel reassured by its overwhelming presence. Visitors can glide to the mountain summit in two minutes in a state-of-the-art Swiss-designed cable car. Installed in 1998, it has a revolving floor that turns 360 degrees for stupendous views over Table Bay, and on the icy Atlantic coastline, from Sea Point to palm-treed Camps Bay.
Tel: 021 424 8181
Email: info@cape-town.org
Website: www.tablemountain.net

ROBBEN ISLAND

Visible from Green Point, this 6km² (2-sq-mile) island lying 11km (7 miles) offshore was a place of confinement for early slaves, convicts, lepers and the mentally unstable as early as the mid-17th century. Its first recorded prisoner was indigenous Khoikhoi leader Autshumato, banished there in 1658 by Jan van Riebeeck; its last inmates were political activists, among whom the most famous was, of course, Nelson Rohihlahla Mandela. The last of them were finally released in 1991. Robben Island is today a UN World Heritage Site, proclaimed in 1999 for both its historical and ecological significance.
Tel: 021 419 1300
Email: events@robben-island.org.za
Website: www.robben-island.org.za

The 'swart' from Swartland ('black' in both Dutch and Afrikaans) comes from the hardy renosterbush which covers the uncultivated turf; in winter it turns dark, and across sweeping expanses gives the impression of a grey-black landscape.

Postberg Nature Reserve, attached to Langebaan's shores and part of the West Coast National Park, is opened to the public each spring (August to October) for its flower-bececked aprons that cover the earth – daisies, gazanias, mesembryanthemums as far as the eye can see.

CLANWILLIAM DAM

This vast expanse of water, stretching for 18km (11 miles) in good rainfall years, is fed by the Olifants River and irrigates the surrounding farmlands and citrus groves. If drought hasn't struck, water can often be seen gushing from its sluice gates. Clanwilliam is also the headquarters of the rooibos tea industry, a caffeine-free tea that's low in tannin and high in medicinal properties. It's made from a wild, *fynbos*-like shrub whose reddish-coloured leaves give it its name, 'red bush'. The dam is what draws most visitors; water-skiers rise early to skate over the water's mirrorlike surface before the wind comes up.

Tel: 027 482 8012
Email: cederberg@lando.co.za
Website: www.clanwilliam.info

LANGEBAAN

The magical distilled turquoise waters of this roughly 15km-long (9-mile) lagoon support up to 25 million waterbirds at particular times of the year. Part of the West Coast National Park, it is one of South Africa's most important wetlands. Its most flamboyant inhabitants (depending on the season) are the flocks of prettily crimson lesser flamingos and a breeding colony of white pelicans scooping up fish in large yellow pouches hanging from their beaks. High winds and water are a magnet for kite- and windsurfers, parasailers, Hobie Cats and catamarans, as well as speedboat enthusiasts.

Tel: 022 772 1515
Email: lbninfo@mweb.co.za
Website: www.langebaaninfo.com

CEDERBERG

The Cederberg, the ancient, eroded range that provides Clanwilliam dam with its mountain backdrop, is a magical, spiritual rocky wilderness. Part of the Cape Folded Mountains, its layers of sandstone, shale and quartzite have been subjected to eons of abrasion by whistling winds and dissolving rain, creating an otherworldly rocky habitat peopled by gargoyles and goblins. Various hikes take in natural pinnacles, arches and fissures with names like the Maltese Cross, Wolfberg Arch and the Wolfberg Cracks. San paintings can be viewed (permits necessary) at spots with names like the Amphitheatre and the Stadsaal.

Tel: 027 482 2024/2812
Email: cederberg@lando.co.za
Website: www.clanwilliam.info

West Coast to Waterberg Plateau Park

WEST COAST
The windswept, rocky stretch of the West Coast unofficially begins with Melkbosstrand, beyond the long white beaches of Bloubergstrand, and extends all the way to the Orange River and the border with Namibia. Some call it inhospitable, but there's a certain beauty about the sun-baked sandveld, trees leaning sharply under the wind's furious onslaught, and the wild black-rock coastline. It's the terrain of hardy fisherfolk, who lure crayfish, linefish, perlemoen and mussels to eke out a living. But it's also full of surprises. In August/September, after good rains, the land comes alive with the rainbow hues of a myriad springflowers.
Tel: 022 433 2380
Email: tourism@capewestcoast.org
Website: www.capewestcoast.org

THE GIFBERG
The Gifberg region, a rugged, rocky wilderness cut by the Doring River, is accessed between Klawer and Vanrhynsdorp. High rock cliffs and eroded, wind-carved formations are the playground for hikers, mountain bikers and 4x4 adventurers. Once the roaming grounds of the San people, they've left behind some very fine rock art. Hikers can feast their eyes while walking a handful of one- to nine-hour trails. Populating the rocky mountain slopes is the shrubby tree, *gifboom* ('poison tree' in Afrikaans). Its leaves are highly toxic; so are its wood and bark – in the past the San used both as arrow-poison.
Tel: 027 201 3376
Email: tourism@matzikamamun.co.za
Website: www.tourismmatzikama.co.za

LÜDERITZ
A town distinctly marked by German colonial influences, Lüderitz backs onto the shifting sand dunes of the Namib desert. It still operates as an offshore diamond-extraction concern under the control of a British-Canadian company, after De Beers relocated to the richer deposits of Oranjemund in 1944. The port also focuses on the fishing industry: crayfishing, oyster, mussel and prawn farming, and seaweed and seagrass harvesting. Architecturally, the elaborately decorative influences of the German Imperial and *Jugenstil*, or Art Nouveau, styles are sandwiched between the more pedestrian buildings of this fishing port. Lüderitz is dominated by the 1912 Lutheran church (Felsenkirche) perched on Diamond Hill.

INLAND ISOLATION
Immediately north of Vanrhynsdorp, the bleak (that is, out of flower season), stony Knersvlakte run for 100km (60 miles). Loosely translated as 'plains of gnashing teeth', the name derives from the sound of wagon wheels, belonging to the early Afrikaans settlers, crunching over the harsh terrain. As you head for Springbok, spot the Karoo settlements of white-washed beehive-like homes (dictated by a lack of timber). Isolated, slowly creaking windmills stand sentinel over tough merino sheep or a solitary antelope.
Tel: 027 219 1552/01 3376
Email: vanrhynsdorp@matzikamamun.co.za
Website: www.tourismmatzikama.co.za

KOLMANSKOP
Some 15 minutes outside Lüderitz lies the enigmatic ghost mining town of Kolmanskop. In 1908, a worker on the railway line handed a glinting pebble he'd picked up to supervisor August Stauch. Wise man that he was, Stauch got himself a prospecting licence before spreading the word! Diamond boomtime followed, until World War I and De Beers' move to more lucrative territory. By 1956, the shifting sands had slowly and inexorably crept into the eerily deserted buildings. An absolute treat for photographers, buildings such as the hospital, the restored mine manager's home and the recreation hall with its skittle alley and theatre/ballroom recall an era of heady opulence.
Tel: 09264 63 202 719/1 250 558
Email: office.nacobta@iway.na
Website: www.nacobta.com.na

BRUKKAROS VOLCANO

While driving between Keetmanshoop and Mariental, look out for the extinct Brukkaros volcano dominating the otherwise featureless skyline in the west. Its name evolved from the Afrikaans 'broek' (shorts) and the Nama 'karos', a leather apron traditionally worn around the waist by the women, obviously alluding to the crater's dark apronlike slopes. Those travellers wanting to wring out every experience of this trip can undertake the 4km (2½-mile) trudge from the parking area to the lip of the crater. Options then are to skirt the rim to the northern edge or descend into the crater along a path. Be warned: shade and water are nonexistent!
Tel: 09264 63 221 266/1 255 977
Email: office.nacobta@iway.na
Website: www.nacobta.com.na

OKAHANDJA TO OTAVI

The small, drab town of Okahandja is a crossroads for the main route west to Swakopmund and north to Otavi – launch-point for Etosha. As the administrative centre for the Herero people, a number of their former leaders are buried here. The Herero began migrating southward from the Kaokoland at the end of the 18th century, causing clashes with the Nama people and German missionaries. The area's drabness is spiked only by the vivid primary colours of the Herero women's Victorian-influenced traditional dress, crowned with elaborate cloth headgear. Open-air markets with an impressive array of skilful wood carvings could captivate some travellers.
Tel: 09264 62 501 051/1 255 977
Email: office.nacobta@iway.na
Website: www.nacobta.com.na

QUIVERTREE FOREST AND GIANT'S PLAYGROUND

Around 3km (2 miles) north of Keetmanshoop, it is worth briefly turning off the B1 onto the D29 to see the Quivertree 'forest' – actually, grouped clumps of Aloe dichotoma, whose light-weight, scaly branches were once hollowed out by the San and Nama peoples to use as quivers for their arrows. The trees' 'cabbage-top' crowns and spiky leaves are quite fascinating. Some 5km (3 miles) further is the Giant's Playground, a collection of massive dark basalt rocks eroded into weird shapes and perched precariously as if carelessly lobbed by gargantuan fingers. Both spots are magical in the setting sun – a photographer's delight.
Tel: 09264 61 290 6000
Email: info@namibiatourism.com.na
Website: www.namibiatourism.com.na

DAAN VILJOEN GAME PARK

Only 25km (15 miles) west of Windhoek, in the Khomas Hochland, this game park has no predators, so wildlife lovers are allowed to walk freely through the rolling, thorn-scrub hills. Elevated at 1700m (5580ft), the views over Windhoek are wonderful, especially when sitting at the bar of the park restaurant, watching the twinkling night-time pinpricks of civilisation. Three hiking routes traverse the desert hills, and wildlife viewing – including birdlife – is good. Try spotting gemsbok, hartebeest, kudu, eland and mountain zebra.
Tel: 09264 61 285 7000/232 393
Email: ero@nwr.com.na
Website: www.nwr.com.na

WATERBERG PLATEAU GAME PARK

Heading for Otavi, if you turn off onto the C22 just south of Otjiwarongo, you reach this plateau rising some 150m (490ft) and stretching for 50km (30 miles). Created as a wildlife sanctuary to nurture endangered species, visitors can join game-viewing drives organised from the rest camp. These could yield sightings of black and white rhino, roan and sable antelope bearing stately curved horns and, just maybe, the gorgeous but elusive leopard. Rainwater is thirstily absorbed by the plateau's permeable soils and Etjo sandstone till it trickles to the impenetrable base, where it collects and seeps out as a series of springs – hence the Waterberg's name.
Tel: 09264 61 285 7000/7 305 002
Email: info@nwr.com.na
Website: www.nwr.com.na

CAPE PENINSULA

ROBBEN ISLAND
This island earned its name from the many seals that call it home. Mid-17th-century Dutch settlers coined it 'robbe eiland' after the shiny, sleek creatures. Boat tours leave from the Nelson Mandela Gateway at the V&A Waterfront. It's crucial to book ahead for this three-and-a-half-hour round trip. Catamarans take 30 minutes to the island, from where a 45-minute bus tour circuits the island, with commentary on a leper church and graveyard, the home of Robert Sobukwe, ex-leader of the PAC, and the lime quarry where the white, blinding light permanently affected Mandela's eyesight. Visitors then enter the B-section of the Maximum Security Prison, often hanging onto the words of the ex-warder or former inmate guiding the tour at the time. Mandela's cell has been preserved in the state it was when this famous prisoner inhabited its tiny, sparse space.

KIRSTENBOSCH NATIONAL BOTANICAL GARDEN
The estate land of Kirstenbosch was bequeathed by Cecil John Rhodes to the state way back in 1902. Its role today is to preserve and propagate rare indigenous plant species, although many more flourish in the luxuriant gardens whose truly beautiful high mountain slopes tower protectively over them. Around 9000 of southern Africa's 22,000 indigenous plant species grow here. Seven per cent of the gardens are cultivated while a whopping 90% remains pristine natural *fynbos* and forest. Most prominent is the tall glass conservatory with a baobab as its centrepiece, but more importantly, all the floral regions of

The length of coastline from the Mouille Point lighthouse to Surfers' Corner in Muizenberg, extending for at least 10km (6 miles) out to sea, is officially a marine protected area. This forms an extension of the Table Mountain National Park.
Tel: 021 701 8692
Email: capepeninsula@parks-sa.co.za
Website: www.tmnp.co.za

The "Cell Stories" exhibition in the A-section of the prison – not part of the regular island tour – is a poignant representation of the solitariness of life in the cells. Each of the 40 tiny cubicles contains a story woven around a personal artefact – scraps of paper with drawings or quotations, letters, photographs, hand-crafted objects.

South Africa have been recreated, from arid and alpine to fertile coastal forest. In the gardens themselves, some special spaces are a braille trail filled with the most fragrant plants, a medicinal and herbal plant tract featuring multiple healing shrubs used by *sangomas*, and a magical, dark, shady bower of tall overhanging trees populated by giant gorilla effigies.
Tel: 021 799 8899
Email: info@sanbi.org
Website: www.kirstenbosch.co.za

TABLE MOUNTAIN NATIONAL PARK
Relatively new as a protected area, this national park encompasses various special natural features that once fell into separate categories such as National Monument (Table Mountain), nature reserves and protected natural environments. In May 1998, the entire Peninsula mountain chain from Signal Hill to Cape Point became the Table Mountain National Park. It has a linear distance of some 60km (37 miles). The astonishing fact is that this crooked finger of land, which experiences both warm and cold water currents from the Indian and Atlantic oceans respectively, has the richest biodiversity in the world – and almost entirely within a metropolitan area! The Cape Floral Kingdom (the world has only six such kingdoms) exists in its entirety in South Africa – the only country in the world where this actually happens. The *Fynbos* family is a major part of this fabulous floral kingdom.

CHAPMAN'S PEAK DRIVE

This famous road, which connects Hout Bay with Noordhoek, cuts into the mountainside, tightly hugging the coastline as the road edge disappears in a sheer, breathless drop to the sea below. The cliff face rises so sharply above the road that in September 1999, one too many rockfalls forced its closure. After an estimated cost of R15 million to repair damage and stabilise the cliff face, extensive work was done, including the erection of powerful safety nets above sections of the roadway (around 4km; 2 miles). The road has since officially reopened, giving visitors the chance to soak in spectacular views, particularly those across to Hout Bay and the imposing Sentinel.

Five deaths as a result of rockfalls have occurred on Chapman's Peak Drive since 1987. If you crunch the numbers, there is a probability of 1 in 2.4 million of a motorist being killed by a rockfall.

WEST COAST FLOWER ROUTE

SPRING FLOWERS

Namaqualand, the arid, scrub-covered land stretching roughly north of Darling to the Orange River, is where life unfolds in the desert like colourful butterfly wings emerging from their chrysalis. Spring usually happens over August and September, although it can arrive late, and could extend into October. At this time, thousands of multi-hued daisies, gazanias and mesembryanthemums turn their faces to the sun (cloudy days are no good for flower-viewing), which are their prettiest between 11:00 and 16:00. You get the best flower (and photographic) views by keeping the sun behind you while driving so you face the opened petals.
Tel: 027 712 2011
Email: namakwaland@intekom.co.za
Website: www.northerncape.org.za

WHERE TO SEE THE DAISIES

Most popular excursion – because it's only an hour and a half out of Cape Town – is the Postberg Nature Reserve on Langebaan's shores, opened to the public only in spring. Pretty blooms blanket the earth way into the middle distance, and there is seldom disappointment at this spot. Darling prides itself as the nub of the annual wildflower frenzy, and holds much-visited springflower and orchid shows. Nearby is the Tienie Versveld Reserve with its own pretty petalled carpets. Much further north near Kamieskroon, the Skilpad Wild Flower Gardens are closer to the coast and refreshed by a higher rainfall. Its *Ursinia* daisies and gazanias are simply the best!
Tel: 083 910 1028 – Flowerline

Wildflowers close to protect their pollen from blowing away in the wind. When there is no direct sunlight – or if temperatures drop below 16°C – this mimics the conditions of a cold wind blowing, and nature's programming kicks in; the petals naturally close in a gesture of self-protection.

The seeds of hardy, drought-resistant wildflowers lie dormant in dry, stony soils and rely on good first rains in the early Cape winter, usually March and April. If all goes according to plan, they burst into bloom in the August spring.

IN SEARCH OF SUCCULENTS AND GEOPHYTES

The Biedouw Valley, north of Clanwilliam, is famous for its violent pink and orange *vygies* (mesembryanthemums), as is Vanrhynsdorp, together with its *Ursinias* and yellow *botterblom*. Bulbs, corms and tubers, known as geophytes, bloom in the Nieuwoudtville Wildflower Reserve – look out for irises and bulbinellas.

RICHTERSVELD IN BLOOM

If you're travelling as far as Springbok, the Goegap Nature Reserve's flowering succulents put on their display in granite koppies and at the foot of hardy quiver trees. Beyond, venturing into the terse grey rocky landscapes of wind-sculpted pillars and spires that characterise the Richtersveld, water-conserving fleshy mesembryanthemums dominate. One-third of all known species of mesems grow here, together with quirky *halfmens* trees.

Tel: 027 718 2985/6
Email: tourismsbk@namakwa-dm.co.za
Website: www.northerncape.org.za

The Khoikhoi tell a story of how their people were driven south after conflict with another cultural group. Individuals who turned to gaze longingly at the land lost to them were metamorphosed into trees, which is why *halfmens* trees – transmogrified figures of their own people – always appear to face toward the north.

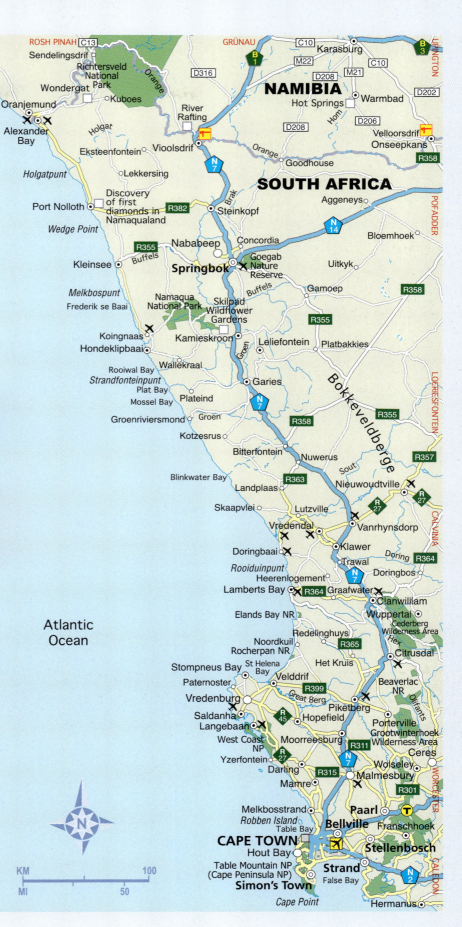

Etosha to Ghanzi Town

TSUMEB

As mining towns go, the only exciting element about Tsumeb is its wealth of around 180 minerals. Deposits include copper ore, silver, germanium and cadmium. Tsumeb is also the world's fifth-largest lead mine. The most fun part is its coat of arms displaying mining tools and two frogs. Tsumeb's name is a weird amalgamation of the San word '*tsomsoub*' meaning 'to dig a hole in loose ground' and the Herero word '*otjitsume*' for 'place of frogs'. The latter refers to copper and lead ore streaks in surrounding rock which actually look as if frog spawn has been scooped up and splattered across it.
Tel: 09264 67 220 728/1 290 6000
Email: travelnn@tsu.namib.com
Website: www.namibiatourism.com.na

ETOSHA (NAMUTONI FORT)

This whitewashed German fort (see also p74), built originally in 1899 by the German cavalry to ward off Owambo retaliatory action, is Etosha's most atmospheric park accommodation. In 1958, after restoration, it was opened as a tourist facility, and rituals still in practice today are the lowering of the flag each evening and a bugle call at sunrise and sunset. The tower rooftop is a favoured sunset rendezvous; you can even spot wild animals by training your binoculars on the vast 360-degree views spread out below.
Tel: 09264 61 285 7000/7 229 300
Email: reservations@nwr.com.na
Website: www.nwr.com.na

HOBA METEORITE

Driving from Tsumeb to Grootfontein, a turnoff 3km (2 miles) before hitting the second town leads (follow the signs) to the world's biggest meteorite. Weighing in at 54,000kg (119,000 lb) and believed to have fallen 80,000 years ago, hunter Jacobus Brits came upon it in 1920. By 1955, thoughtlessly acquisitive visitors had begun chipping at it, and the meteorite was declared a National Monument to protect it. It consists of 82% iron, 16% nickel and 0.8% cobalt.
Tel: 09264 67 240 360/1 255 977
Email: office.nacobta@iway.na
Website: www.nacobta.com.na

DROTSKY'S CABINS

Within the narrower confines of the northern Okavango delta area, before it splays into the delta proper, Drotsky's Cabins are perched beside a channel of the river, some 5km (3 miles) south of Shakawe. A-frame huts and chalets nestle into luxuriant riverine forest while looking out onto reeds and papyrus. It goes without saying that you drift into sleep and awaken to the chattering and twittering of myriad feathered friends.
Tel: 09267 687 5035
Email: drotskys@info.bw
Website: www.botswanatourism.org

WEST AND EAST CAPRIVI

The Okavango River and the surrounding expansive floodplains it feeds dominate the Kavango region of northeastern Namibia. Here, desert sands of the Kalahari encounter the wet swampland of Okavango. Further eastward is the flat, 500km-long (300-mile) Caprivi Strip, jammed in-between Angola, Zambia and Botswana. Its odd shape is the result of political wrangles between British and German colonial powers, where Germany was intent on maintaining access to the Zambezi and the Indian Ocean. Along the Caprivi's banks, local people grow vegetables, sorghum and maize. You will also see them catching fish using their woven, funnel-like fish traps. This zone of forested tracts, swamps and channels crammed

TSODILO HILLS

About 50km (30 miles) west of Sepupa village on the Okavango Panhandle, the quartzite cliffs of the Tsodilo Hills rearing unexpectedly from the featureless desert create that much more of a surprise. These 'mountains of the gods', reached only by 4x4, are revered by San and Mbukushu alike, and closer inspection reveals precious rock paintings – over 3000 and counting. Storytellers recount how the hills were named Male, Female and Child, leaving the smaller fourth one nameless – but whisperings intimate that this was actually Male Hill's first wife, who was passed over for the taller Female Hill.
Tel: 09267 395 3024
Email: botswanatourism@gov.bw
Website: www.botswanatourism.org

LAKE NGAMI

In times past, this body of water used to be a superlake covering much of northern Botswana. Today it is among the world's most prolific sites for waterbirds. In the dry months, the crowded reedbeds flanking the lakeshores become brittle, dry and then disintegrate, but the regenerating rains revive them again. This rotting vegetation creates highly nutritious waters, attracting zillions of bird species. A fascinating phenomenon here is the spontaneous combustion of peat and papyrus. Fires suddenly flare up along the banks, with the tightly packed vegetation smouldering for months until extinguished naturally by rain and the rising waters.
Tel: 09267 318 0774/97 1405
Email: dwnp@gov.bw
Website: www.botswanatourism.org

with water lilies was turned into the Bwabwata National Park in 1999. It is made up of the vast West Caprivi triangle, the Mahango Game Park on its western fringe, the Buffalo core area on the river opposite Mahango, and the Bagani/Omega agricultural areas in the northwest corner of the Strip.
Tel: 09264 285 7000/66 253 048
Email: reservations@nwr.com.na
Website: www.nwr.com.na

The Okavango River rises in the Angolan highlands. After entering Botswana, it remains the country's only perennial river and hereafter never reaches the sea. Instead, the river dries up in northern Botswana's desert sands.

GCWIHABA HILLS AND CAVES

Only well-equipped 4x4 vehicles should attempt the 10–12-hour journey into the remote wilderness roughly 150km (90 miles) south of Tsodilo. Here, the limestone and dolomite Aha Hills rise up from the barren Kalahari to form a plateau straddling the Namibia/Botswana border. The Gcwihaba caves, part of the same upland, mean 'hyena's lair' in the !Kung language, but are also known as Drotsky's Caves after Bushmen led Martinus Drotsky there in 1934. Eons ago, an ancient river carved out great caverns while dissolving, percolating rain and abrasive wind and weather produced spellbinding stalagmites, stalactites and flowstone formations.
Tel: 09267 395 3024
Email: botswanatourism@gov.bw
Website: www.botswanatourism.org

GHANZI

This town is commended only for its role as the largest urban settlement existing midway along the southern Trans-Kalahari Highway, connecting Maun and Gaborone with the desert road to Windhoek. Travellers should make sure they stock up on petrol and essential supplies here. For all its remoteness, Ghanzi is the administrative centre for vast tracts of what's considered to be very fine cattle ranching country. This region is also the domain of the traditional Kalahari San people.
Tel: 09267 395 3024/754 0833
Email: botswanatourism@gov.bw
Website: www.botswanatourism.org

OKAVANGO DELTA

THE DELTA
The Delta is the largest in the world, spreading over 15,000km² (5850 sq miles) in dry years and expanding to 22,000km² (8600 sq miles) during years of high rainfall. Surrounded by the parched Kalahari, an astounding 95% of all surface water in Botswana is concentrated in this Delta. From its panhandle it spreads out like a fan with Maun, gateway town to the Delta, centrally located at the edge of the fan. The length from apex to outer curve is roughly 175km (110 miles). Of the main Delta area, about 10% is dry land.

Fishing, game-viewing, taking photographs and island bush walking can all be done from the surprisingly stable comfort of your mokoro, with your poler as well-informed guide.

ELEPHANT-BACK SAFARIS
The Inner Delta extends from the base of the panhandle to Chief's Island, which is part of the Moremi Game Reserve. West of Chief's Island, the upmarket and pricey Abu's Camp offers unique elephant-back safaris (initially the first of its kind in Africa, so they say. . .). Conceived by a certain Randall Moore, he arranged for the return of three African-born, circus-trained elephants from the USA. As a result, visitors gain a considerably elevated perspective on wildlife as they amble in among the unconcerned animals.
Tel: 011 465 3842
Website: www.moremi-safaris.com

WHAT TO DO, WHERE
Because the northern and central zones of the Okavango Delta feature huge concentrations of permanently and seasonally flooded areas, camps based here tend to focus on aquatic activities such as fishing and *mokoro* safaris. Camps in the southern Delta, on the other hand, put their energy into terrestrial pursuits such as game drives and guided walks.

MOKORO TRIPS
The original *mekoro* (note the plural form of *mokoro*) – shallow dugout canoes used for centuries by the local people – are made from the hollowed trunks of slow-growing hardwoods such as ebony or sausage tree. To make them is slow and time-consuming as each canoe needs to be soaked in water for several weeks to prevent the wood from drying out. In efforts to keep up with modern needs, fibreglass *mekoro* are being manufactured. A single canoe usually takes the poler (who poles standing up), two people and their food and equipment.

GUNN'S CAMP
Also based in the Inner Delta area, Gunn's Camp finds itself on its own palm-treed island, Ntswi, near the southern tip of Chief's Island and just across the Boro River channel. It offers camping facilities and luxury tents. Island walks and one- to six-day *mokoro* trips can be arranged, mainly from June to December, depending on the water levels.
Tel: 09267 686 0023
Email: gunnscamp@dynabyte.bw

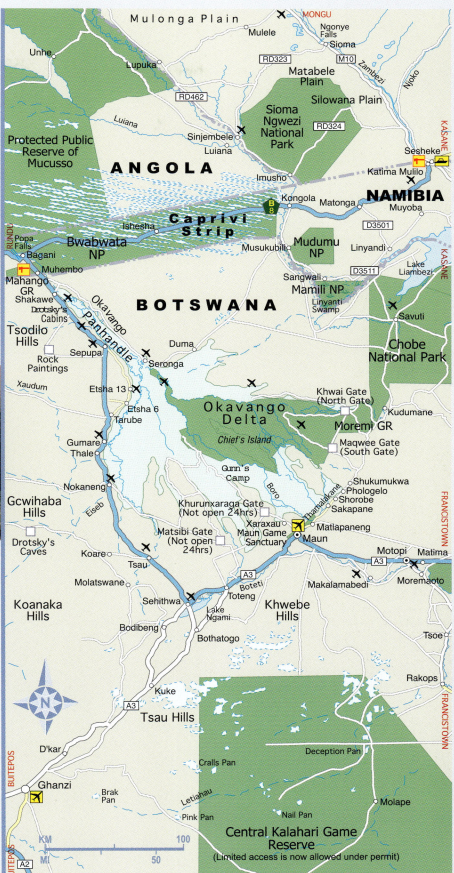

WHERE DOES THE WATER GO?

Of the Okavango Delta's surface water, 96% disappears through evaporation, 2% sinks into the underground water table and 2% drains into the Thamalakane River. Angola and Namibia claim rights to the Okavango's waters too. An oddity is that, in the Delta's parched southern reaches, the seasonal flood is at its highest during the dry winter. This is so because of rainfall happening in Angola, which then takes six months to wash down and permeate the Delta. By May, the water has reached the panhandle, it then slows considerably on reaching the Delta, and around August whatever hasn't evaporated reaches Maun. Environmentalists have shown that the slightest reduction in the Delta's average flow will drastically affect unique flora and fauna in the southern floodplains. Conservationists are now lobbying for the wetland areas to be proclaimed a World Heritage Site.

2 AI-AIS TO MUTARE

Ai-Ais
Don't leave these hot springs before having gazed over the deeply gouged maze of the Fish River Canyon from the two viewpoints lying roughly 80km (50 miles) north of Ai-Ais. The first is the main viewpoint, with thatched picnic tables; further along is Hikers' Viewpoint, start of the testing hiking trail.

Upington
Between Springbok and Upington are hot, dusty *dorpies* with names like Pofadder and Kakamas, disdainfully used to describe the back end of beyond. Klaas Pofadder, in fact, was a raider who would hole up on an island in the Orange in the 1800s – with a hideout in Pofadder!

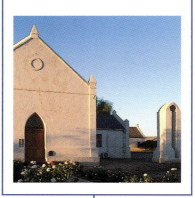

Ai-Ais — 177km — Vioolsdrif — 492km — Upington — 468km — Kimberley — 164

Vioolsdrif
Before crossing the border, stop to take stock of the broad, stony flood-plain of the Orange, which has opened up here to a great, shallow, open valley backed at either end by towering, shadowed, biscuit-coloured mountains.

Kimberley
The first diamond find was a glinting stone (later named 'Eureka') picked up near Hopetown by a young boy in 1866; the second was the 'Star of Africa', shown by a Griqua shepherd to Hopetown resident Schalk van Niekerk. Most famous diamond of all was the 'Cullinan'.

Maseru
If the latent gambler in you is lusting to make a little extra for your road-trip, you can stop by the Lesotho Sun casino (off Nightingale Road). If you're in a hurry, simply try your arm on the slot machines at the Maseru Sun.

At the discovery of the 83.5-carat 'Star of Africa' diamond near Hopetown, southwest of Kimberley, the presiding British colonial secretary referred to it as the "rock on which the future success of South Africa will be built". If only he knew . . .

Bloemfontein

For a fee of the city's stately architecture, try out President Brand Street. You'll pass the 1929-built Appeal Court standing opposite the brick and sandstone Fourth Raadsaal (1893), the National Museum for Afrikaans Literature and the Old Presidency (1861).

Masvingo

This little town is the gateway to Great Zimbabwe, an ancient granite and stone complex of walls and conical towers constructed by the wealthy ancestors of today's Shona people. During the 15th century, however, its inhabitants began withdrawing and by the time the Portuguese arrived, the city was deserted.

Mutare

Close to the border with Mozambique, Mutare nestles prettily in the valley of the Bvumba, a mountainous promontory jutting into the land of its neighbour. It is a forested zone of indigenous woodland and rainforest – luxuriant, verdant and often mist-cocooned.

Maseru 151km — Bloemfontein — 398km — Johannesburg — 809km — Masvingo — 300km — Mutare

Eastern Highlands

Johannesburg

The new three-span Nelson Mandela Bridge connecting Braamfontein with Newtown has revitalised the cultural heart of the city. With 52 asymmetrical diagonal cable-stays, the bridge stretches for 284m (932ft) – the longest of its kind in southern Africa.

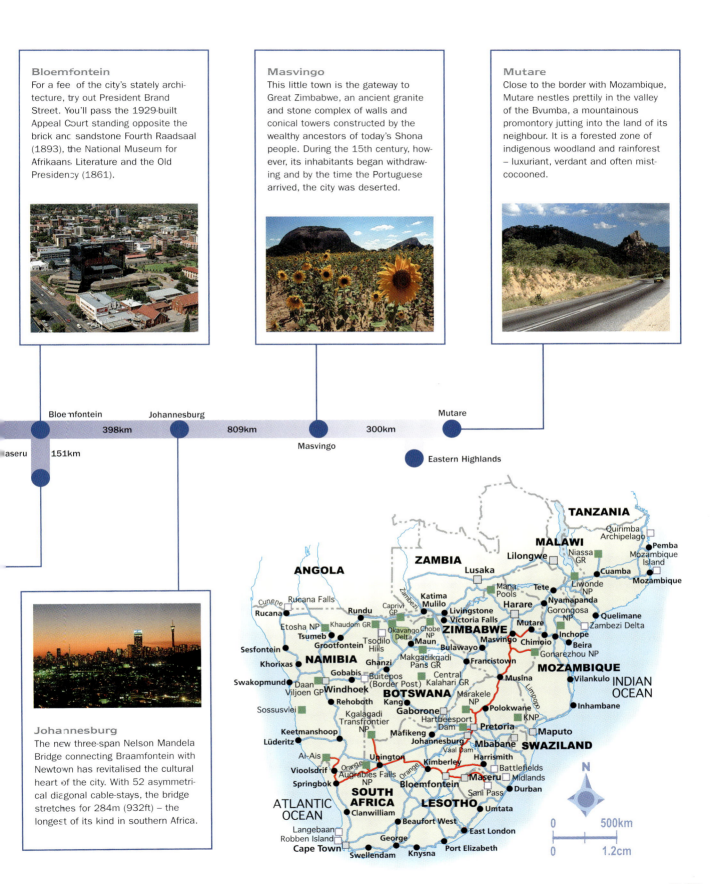

Orange River to Augrabies Falls

ORANGE RIVER
Known as the Gariep in Namibia, the Orange creates a natural border with South Africa, the official border crossing occurring at Vioolsdrif. South Africa's greatest river, its 2450km-long (1520-mile) journey begins in the mighty Drakensberg, but from such lofty beginnings it crosses an inordinate length of arid, inhospitable terrain. The Orange drains 47% of the country and supplies life-giving irrigation to a multitude of crops, among them citrus orchards, grapevines, lucerne, wheat and cotton. Its sheer volume and power is also loved by river-rafting enthusiasts, who flock to ride its waters.
Tel: 011 895 3000
Email: info@southafrica.net
Website: www.southafrica.net

AI-AIS
Not the most magic resort – accommodation is basic, no frills attached – but the attraction here is, after all, the thermal springs – rich in chloride, fluoride and sulphur. Bubbling up at a steamy 60°C (140°F), Ai-Ais is the Nama word literally translated as 'fire water' but alluding to its scalding hot qualities. The water is piped to a series of baths, jacuzzis and an outdoor swimming pool, and is believed to alleviate rheumatism and nervous disorders. The settlement serves mainly as a starting point for the backpackers' trail through the Fish River Canyon.
Tel: 09264 63 262 045/7
Email: reservations@nwr.com.na
Website: www.nwr.com.na

UPINGTON
Again, not the most exciting of places, Upington's significance is its central position. From here it's north to the Kgalagadi Transfrontier Park, and west to Augrabies Falls, and to Namibia via Ai-Ais. Most of the towns north of the Orange River are separated by more than 200km (125 miles) with a dearth of petrol and refreshment stops, so Upington offers a welcome break. The surrounding vast, shrubby plain it lies in is interrupted only by the green swathe of the Orange River's watered strip. Flourishing under irrigation are cotton, wheat, lucerne and vines – for table grapes and raisins as well as winemaking.
Tel: 054 337 2804/2 6064
Email: tourism@kharahais.gov.za
Website: www.kharahaismunicipality.co.za

RIVER RAFTING
An adventure playground when water levels are high from summer rains, the Orange River's rapids are less testing during low waters, usually in winter. Experienced water guides accompany rafting parties over rapids graded in difficulty from 1 to 5, serving up easy-paced paddling to turbulent, adrenaline-pumping white water where sections carry names like Rollercoaster, Crunch and Crusher. Trips for novices and diehard rafters alike range from one to five days. The best time is during the summer rains (November to January).
Tel: 021 712 5094
Email: info@riverrafters.co.za
Website: www.riverrafters.co.za

FISH RIVER CANYON
From Ai-Ais, visitors can enter the Fish River Conservation Area at Hobas, where a series of viewing points give onto sights usually the sole privilege of eagles in their secret eyries. Water and the forces of nature have over millions of years spectacularly eroded this snaking, sheer-walled canyon and its switchback bends. Second in size to Africa's Blue Nile Gorge, the Fish River Canyon is the site of a challenging 4- to 5-day hiking trail, during which trailists carry all their own food, clothing and equipment. Starting at Hiker's Point, one of the viewsites, it ends 85km (53 miles) later at Ai-Ais.
Tel: 09264 63 693 007/6
Email: frgf@canyonnaturepark.com
Website: www.canyonnaturepark.com

Upington's Schröder Street features, at one end, the Kalahari–Oranje Museum, based in the mission church (1875) that helped establish the original settlement. At the other end is a statue of a patrolman mounted on a camel, in memory of fractious earlier times when Griqua rebels, bands of San hunter-gatherers and German forces were warded off by police who were often mounted on sturdy, desert-adapted camels.

Kgalagadi–Kalahari

The edge of the rocky canyon looking onto the maelstrom of the falls has been buffed and polished over time to a smoothly curved parabola. It has deceived many an unsuspecting visitor – more than 20 people have slid uncontrollably into the thrashing waters since the park was created in 1996. So... watch out!

AUGRABIES NATIONAL PARK
Upington is a good central point from which to do a day trip (120km; 75 miles) to the Augrabies National Park. What the Augrabies Falls don't quite achieve in staggering height or extent, they make up for in their desert setting, frothing wildly out of a harshly barren landscape as the waters funnel through a narrow granite channel. The atmosphere is magic, and always noisy – particularly at peak flow, bearing out the falls' Khoikhoi name, 'Aukoerebis' meaning 'the place of great noise'. The main falls plunge for 56m (184ft), while the smaller Bridal Veil fall drops 75m (246ft). The rocky Augrabies National Park, punctuated with spiky quiver trees, camelthorn and Namaqua fig, extends for 184km² (72 sq miles) to either side.
Tel: 054 452 9200, 012 428 9111
Email: reservations@parks-sa.co.za
Website: www.parks-sa.co.za

KALAHARI DESERT
In South Africa, the semi-desert of the Kalahari extends north of the Orange River, west to Namibia and north to Botswana's Okavango Delta. From the river, tall orange-red sand dunes undulate like the waves of an inland sea. It's no wonder that the name derives from 'kgalagadi' meaning 'thirsty land' – no permanent rivers have coursed this ancient landscape for thousands of years. Searingly hot in summer and characterised by cracked and dry crazy-paved saltpans shimmering in midday heat, its main human inhabitants are tiny hardy communities largely descended from San hunter-gatherers and nomadic Khoi herders. A surprising array of wildlife has learned to adapt to this harsh environment. Besides larger species such as gemsbok, others like bat-eared foxes, barking geckos, puff adders and powerfully winged raptors trawl its thinly vegetated sands.
Tel: 012 428 9111
Email: reservations@parks-sa.co.za
Website: www.parks-sa.co.za

KGALAGADI TRANSFRONTIER PARK
In 1999, South Africa's Kalahari-Gemsbok National Park and Botswana's Mabuasehube–Gemsbok National Park were combined to create this transfrontier zone which, impressively, is nearly twice the size of Kruger National Park. The absence of fences leaves wildlife to roam freely. Darker maned Kalahari lion, rapier-horned gemsbok, ponderous-looking wildebeest, brown hyena and jackal share the ancient migration routes. Also forming part of the sanctuary is land inhabited by local indigenous communities who, together with SA National Parks, manage this transfrontier park. Self-guided game drives trace the course of two dry riverbeds, the Auob and Nossob, which are well-frequented by wildlife. Look out for the endearing quizzical suricates, or *meerkats*, standing ramrod straight on their hindlegs to check out their surrounds.
Tel: 054 561 2000, 09267 318 0774
Email: reservations@parks-sa.co.za
Website: www.parks-sa.co.za

Green Kalahari (Upington) to Katse Dam

THE 'GREEN' KALAHARI
Its location on the oasis-resembling irrigated land tract flanking the Orange River makes Upington the kingpin of the area stretching southwest to Kakamas, sometimes labelled the 'green Kalahari'. What characterises it are the old-fashioned wooden waterwheels along the irrigation canals, an old-time technique still used today in which the water is elevated so that, through gravitational action, it is redirected into the vineyards. As you head in the opposite direction to Sishen, you may nevertheless spot one of these old wheels, relentlessly turning in the life-giving waters of the Orange.
Tel: 054 337 2826/04
Email: greenkal@bodr.gov.za
Website: www.greenkalahari.co.za

SISHEN
The iron-ore mining town of Sishen is sometimes also spelled Sesheng, meaning 'new place' since it was established expressly to house mine workers in 1953. Enough said. Today, all emphasis is being placed on a major expansion project by mine owners, Kumba Resources. Beginning in 2006 and estimated to cost around R2 billion, it aims to increase iron-ore production at the giant open-cast mine by an extra 10 million tons by 2008. From Sishen, travellers heading for Barkly West can get there southward via Postmasburg or northward via Kuruman.
Tel: 053 723 2391/332 3642
Email: Info@mokala.co.za
Website: www.mokala.co.za

BARKLY WEST
Poverty is evident in this town which once was the first hub of the heady diamond rush. Up to and during mining magnate Cecil John Rhodes' time as prime minister of the Cape Colony, he was also an MP for Barkly West. Today, a handful of older diggers continue, believe it or not, to prospect by hand in alluvial beds still being worked at the town's fringes. Licensed buyers frequent the Diamond Market on Saturday mornings to inspect (and maybe buy) the week's findings. For the curious, Diamond Tours Unlimited takes visitors through the alluvial diggings.
Tel: 053 531 0673/1
Email: dikgatlong@lantic.net
Website: www.northerncape.org.za

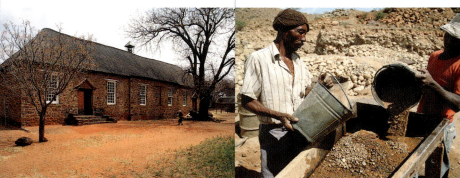

Of the country's table grape crop, 80% of sultanas are cultivated in the Northern Cape. Dried golden sultanas are a major export item for South Africa. Around Upington, look out for fields of trays bearing different fruits spread out in the sun to dry.

POSTMASBURG
The only diversion Posmasburg offers (it's named after Dirk Postma, a founder of the town's reformed church) is a detour to tune into the phenomenon of the Roaring Sands in Witsand Nature Reserve, 100km (60 miles) southwest of the town. In very dry weather, the silky-smooth dune sands vibrate, creating a low hum that swells to a 'roar'.
Tel: 054 337 2804/26
Email: greenkal@bodr.gov.za
Website: www.greenkalahari.co.za

KURUMAN
Travellers wanting to break their journey could stop awhile at the weaver-nested picnic spot which marks the Eye of Kuruman, a natural spring (simply a moss-covered rocky slab with water seeping over it) out of which bubbles 18–20 million litres of water a day!
Tel: 053 712 1001/2502
Email: info@kalahari.org.za
Website: www.kurumankalahari.co.za

Diamonds began in the earth's mantle as carbon particles which, through extreme high temperatures and pressure, crystallised into their hard, clear, shiny form. Molten rock, or magma, was ejected through a weak point in the earth's crust in volcanic eruptions millions of years ago. Kimberlite diamonds (named after our very own Kimberley) are found in the pipes of cooled magma – around 20 carats (4g) of diamonds are extracted per 100 tonnes.

KIMBERLEY

This is not a pretty town, although there is a quaint charm about its authentically reconstructed museum village. Following the first diamond rush in 1869, prospectors camped out at the base of a hill to the northwest in 1871. It became the New Rush tent town, and by 1873 had earned its name Kimberley – home to 50,000 miners. Its riches were the flashpoint of a major power struggle between giant personalities Cecil John Rhodes and Barney Barnato. In the end, in 1889, Rhodes of De Beers Consolidated Mines bought out Barnato, paving the way for De Beers' sole control of the diamond industry, effective still today.
Tel: 053 832 7298
Email: francoisbasson@fbdm.co.za
Website: www.northerncape.org.za

MASERU (LESOTHO)

This capital of the independent mountain kingdom, Lesotho, which was founded in the 1800s by King Moshoeshoe, is named after the local sandstone that's used prolifically in both old and new buildings. It was established by the British as an administrative centre in 1869, and today it also carries the scars of modern historical times in the charred shells of its downtown buildings. Looted and destroyed in 1998 riots after the elections were disputed, redevelopment has created new shopping malls – but there is more vibrant energy in the surrounding hawkers and noisy street stalls. What you can do here is heartily stock up on supplies.
Tel: 09266 22 312 427/3 034
Email: touristinfo@ltdc.org.ls
Website: www.lesotho.gov.ls/lstourism

KATSE DAM

The rough track that once led from Hlotse to Katse Dam has become a very decent tarred stretch thanks to the magic wand waved by the Lesotho Highlands Water Project. The plan is that by 2020, southern Africa will benefit in terms of water and electricity from Lesotho's massive dam. The powerful wall, up to 60m (197ft) thick, curves inward for extra strength and towers to 185m (607ft). The road from Hlotse to the dam navigates several passes – at one point it climbs to over 3000m (9850ft) in less than 30km (20 miles) – on a scenic excursion with dramatic twists, sheer drops that plunge into nothingness and routes barrelled through the mountain.
Tel: 09266 22 312 427/42
Email: itouristinfo@ltdc.org.ls
Website: www.seelesotho.com/travel/info/waterproject

THE BIG HOLE

The old Kimberley mine (known as the Big Hole), which forms part of the Kimberley Open Air Mine Museum, is the largest manmade depression in the world. Unbelievably, the early miners' only implements were picks and shovels, with the hole's depth eventually hitting 800m (2620ft). Its rim extends 500m (1640ft) across and the hole itself takes up almost as much land area as the CBD. When De Beers closed the mine in 1914, some 22.6 million tonnes of earth – the secret trove for over 14.5 million carats of diamonds – had been removed.
Tel: 053 832 7298
Email: francoisbasson@fbdm.co.za
Website: www.northerncape.org.za

If you look for the cleft that is Khubelu Pass in Maseru's backdrop of cliffs, to the east of this is a cone-shaped mountain topped by a large nodule called Qiloane. The story goes that it was this natural feature that inspired the shape of the grass-woven Basotho hat.

WHAT TO DO IN LESOTHO

Lesotho, the 'kingdom in the sky', certainly lives up to its name. Rough, jagged mountains rearing out of an untamed landscape hold the unmistakable promise of exhilarating hikes and pony treks. The sure-footed Basotho ponies are the best means of travel, and organised trails through Lesotho's Maluti mountains are a major tourist industry for the kingdom. Peaks blanketed in winter snow guarantee a distinctly icy wind-chill factor, while summer carpets the open veld and grasslands with indigenous flowers. Trails are sometimes extremely tough (hence the advantage of ponies) but views are stupendous. Keep an eye out for woven Basotho hats and rainbow-coloured wool and mohair rugs and blankets.
Tel: 09266 22 312 427
Email: touristinfo@ltdc.org.ls
Website: www.lesotho.gov.ls/lstourism

FISH RIVER CANYON & RICHTERSVELD

FISH RIVER CANYON

The Fish River rises in the Khomas Hochland mountains southwest of Windhoek. For the last 160km (100 miles) of its course (it joins the Orange River thereafter), it winds through a deep-sided canyon – site of the physically trying hiking trail. Rock layers and geological formations within the gorge date from 1800 million to 50 million years ago and there are Stone and Iron Age sites along its course. A phenomenon of the Fish River Gorge is that it is actually a canyon within a canyon. Some 500 million years ago, an eroded sedimentary basin split and tilted along faults in the crust, creating a large canyon with a level of terraces near its base. The foot of this 'V' became a watercourse which, over time, snaked its way into the sharply twisting gorge of today.

RICHTERSVELD NATIONAL PARK

If you like your landscape fierce and unrelenting, look no further than this dramatically austere, sunburnt terrain stretching across a vast 1600km^2 expanse (625 sq miles). Nudging into a looped curve of the Orange River, it is South Africa's only true desert because of its meagre rainfall of 50mm (2in) a year. Only lizards, klipspringers and some wonderful birds share the blinding heat with the weird *Halfmens* ('half-human') succulent trees. Believe it or not there are several hiking trails (not for sissies!), but the jagged mountainscapes and wild, weathered rock formations make it all worthwhile. For those on wheels, this is high-clearance 4x4 territory. With names like Helskloof and Gorgon's Head, you'd better believe it!

Tel: 027 831 1506
Email: andy@sanparks.org

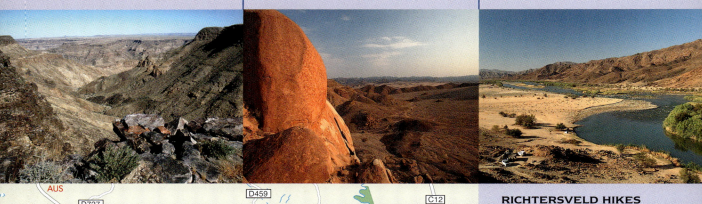

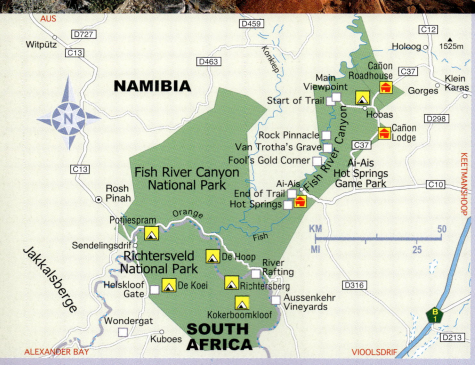

RICHTERSVELD HIKES

You need to enjoy roughing it before you venture out on any of the two- to five-day Richtersveld hikes. There is a limited water supply only at the Sendelingsdrif park headquarters and you rest overnight in the *matjieshuise* that the local Nama herders construct for themselves of branches covered with hides or reed mats. Because of the searing summer heat, hikes take place in the winter/spring months of April to September, accompanied by a local guide. Each trail has a specific focal feature, be it a giant rock amphitheatre and a waterfall, desert mountainscapes or bizarre wind-eroded formations.

MALUTI MOUNTAINS & SANI

MALUTI MOUNTAINS

This impressive range cuts a great swathe from the Golden Gate Highlands in South Africa's Eastern Highlands to Katse Dam in neighbouring Lesotho. Its dramatic lofty heights invite sudden changes in temperature that bring swirling mists and storms in summer and shrouds of snow in winter. The Golden Gate Highlands Park, which sprawls across the foothills of the Malutis, was created to protect the majestic sandstone cliffs rearing up into the sky. The gold glow of reflected sunsets is embodied in the park's name. Hiking trails on both sides of the border reward walkers with truly awesome views.

SENTINEL TRAIL

The advantage of this 10km (6-mile) hike is that it deftly negotiates foothills belonging to both the Maluti and the Drakensberg mountains, and once you're breathing the refined air at 3000m (9800ft) on the escarpment-top, you can actually trek up to Mont-aux-Sources. Atop the Drakensberg in a day! Roughly 3km (2 miles) from the Sentinel carpark, you get to the base of a daunting 30m (98ft) chain ladder. Those not quite ready to match the agility of a monkey can take a detour along The Gulley up to Beacon Buttress. Needless to say, the views are stupendous. Here, words fail.
Tel: 036 488 1207
Email: cdta@futurenet.co.za
Website: www.cdic.co.za

Once only a rough bridle path forged mainly by the local people on sturdy ponies, the stupendous scenery of Sani Pass is a magnet for hikers, trailists and pony trekkers led by the blanket-clad Basotho.

SANI PASS

This breathtakingly high pass (over 20km/ 12 miles it ascends to 1300m/4265ft) starts just beyond the tiny village of Himeville in the Drakensberg's Mkhomazana River valley and snakes its way up to Sani Top. It is the only access road from KwaZulu-Natal into Lesotho. Whipped by winds that emit a ghostly wail as they batter the rugged slopes, pummelling every nook and crevice, this is definitely 4x4 territory. It absolutely warrants the generally overused superlatives when trying to capture natural beauty. A jaw-dropping mountain gateway with hairpin bends gouged out of the rock, it's the highest in the land and its views are unsurpassed.

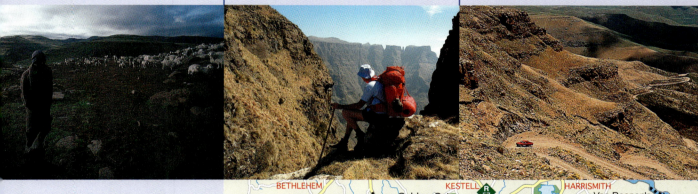

Even if you're not planning to set off on a hike into the mountains, the drive up to the Sentinel hiking trail carpark follows a road that twists and curves along the mountain ridgetops, rising to an altitude of 2540m (8335ft). The views are breathtaking.

Bloemfontein to Magaliesberg

BLOEMFONTEIN
The judicial capital of South Africa and seat of the Free State's parliament, Bloemfontein is at the hub of six major routes dissecting the country. It's natural, then, that most long-distance travellers will stop here awhile to catch their weary breath. Early trekkers used to rest at a fountain near here to refresh themselves before continuing to forge a path across the interior – giving this capital city its name. The main thoroughfare, President Brand Street, reflects its heritage in some late 19th- and early 20th-century stately public buildings, constructed in pale sandstone. Modernity gets a look-in at the city's Waterfront, created in 1998 at the edge of Loch Logan.
Tel: 051 405 8489
Email: information@bloemfontein.co.za
Website: www.bloemfontein.co.za

JOHANNESBURG
More often today called Jozi or eGoli, 'place of gold', Johannesburg's primitive mine camp beginnings transformed swiftly into high-powered metropolis. But in modern times major business has migrated from the city centre to the leafy, moneyed suburbs. Downtown Jozi is now a true slice of Africa: a noisy hustle and bustle of minibus taxis, street vendors, traditional herb and *muti* shops, and tiny stores spilling out wares, from plastic buckets to blankets. The inner city is being revived with the completion of a new interchange linking Braamfontein with Newtown via the new, impressively designed Nelson Mandela bridge.
Tel: 011 327 2000
Email: tourism@gauteng.net
Website: www.gauteng.net

Foreign visitors to Jozi find themselves compelled to visit Soweto, scene of historical political uprisings, a passion for change, and today, an upwardly mobile black sector. Jimmy's Face to Face Tours is still among the best guided trips, taking you to shanty towns, shebeens and some very upscale homes.

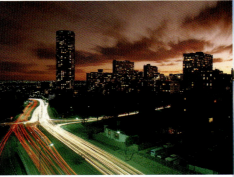

Famous writer of all things fantastical, wonderful and weird, JRR Tolkien – author of Lord of the Rings *– was born in Bloemfontein. He left as a very young child, however, to live in the United Kingdom.*

NEWTOWN CULTURAL PRECINCT
The central focus of this new precinct is the Market Theatre complex with, opposite, MuseumAfrika. The aim is that through art galleries, a stimulating theatrical nightlife, fine dining and conversations over coffee the inner city will be enlivened and revitalised. This is also the home of jazz, recalling the musically rich and atmospherically electric black Sophiatown era. The story of onetime mining city and business hub eGoli, and the people that made it buzz, is told in MuseumAfrika.
Tel: 011 688 7834/327 2000
Email: info@jda.org.za
Website: www.jda.org.za

JOHANNESBURG SURROUNDS
Gold Reef City, because it embodies the foundations on which Jo'burg flourished, is one of the city's most-visited sites. And a worthwhile reconstruction of an 1890s gold-mining town it is, with its authentic olde-worlde buildings and shopfronts, and energetic miners' gumboot dances. The obvious wealth of the northern suburb residential areas is flaunted in the sophisticated and lavish shopping centres of Sandton and Rosebank, and the entertainment centre of the Randburg Waterfront. For walks and picnics in leafy tree-shaded surrounds, Jo'burgers go to Zoo Lake, north of Parktown. If visitors want more, the Sterkfontein Caves northwest of Jozi are where nearly 40% of hominid fossil discoveries in the world have been made.
Tel: 011 327 2000
Email: tourism@gauteng.net
Website: www.gauteng.net

Pretoria's most famous face is when its 70,000 jacaranda trees put on their deep lilac mantle. First imported from Rio de Janeiro in 1888, these trees line the city's avenues, dropping their pretty blooms to carpet the streets in soft purple.

PRETORIA SURROUNDS
To the southwest of Pretoria, and south of Hartbeespoort Dam, the Lesedi Cultural Village is made up of the authentic *kraals* of the Zulu, Pedi, Xhosa, Ndebele and Basotho cultures. Guided tours twice a day entertain visitors with singing and dancing, traditional dress, and the flavours of African cooking. You can also take up the invitation to overnight in a grass hut with a local Lesedi-based family. About 50km (30 miles) west of Pretoria, and just north of Hartbeespoort Dam, the De Wildt Cheetah Research Centre is a highlight for out-of-town visitors. In the face of scepticism, the centre successfully bred the highly rare king cheetah – previously thought to be extinct – in captivity. The cheetahs, distinguished by black bands along the length of

HARTBEESPOORT
Gautengers with a lust for nature flock to this manmade dam, west of Pretoria in the Magaliesberg mountain range. Both the Crocodile and Magalies rivers flow into it, keeping it wet and well-watered for yachtsmen, boardsailors, water-skiers and noisy, overzealous jet-skis. It's a hectic zone of holiday and retirement homes, campsites and picnic spots, arts and crafts vendors. Fishermen also manage to get in some quiet time along the dam's banks – and there's even a freshwater aquarium here to ogle at.
Tel: 012 253 1567
Email: blackeagle@mweb.co.za
Website: www.hartbeespoortdam.co.za

PRETORIA
Pretoria (see also p89), South Africa's administrative capital, counts among its most famous architectural sights the Union Buildings and the Voortrekker Monument. The former landmark designed by Sir Herbert Baker is a Renaissance building influenced by Italian and Cape Dutch styles, and was built to serve as administrative offices for the Union of South Africa. The Voortrekker Monument, erected between 1938 and 1949, honours the Trek Boers who rejected British rule and undertook the arduous journey from the Cape in the 1830s. In its Hall of Heroes, a stab of sunlight falls on an engraved motto at exactly 12:00 on 16 December – the day of the Battle of Blood River.
Tel: 012 337 4430
Email: andrewm2@tshwane.gov.za
Website: www.tshwane.gov.za

their spines and their unusually large dark spots, can be watched at feeding time. The centre is involved in the breeding of other endangered animals, and visitors will also see wild dog and brown hyena on their tour.
Tel: 012 337 4430
Email: andrewm2@tshwane.gov.za
Website: www.tshwane.gov.za

Pretoria's National Zoological Gardens are internationally recognised for their conservation efforts (they are rated 10th in the world). Much time and energy has been spent on breeding programmes for rare or endangered species – among these Arabian oryx, Malayan tapir and, recently, a number of Alaskan Kodiak bears.

MAGALIESBERG
The Magaliesberg mountains (see also p90), named after the 17th-century chief Mogale of the once-local Kwena clan, form a sweeping boomerang-like curve between Hartbeespoort and Rustenburg to the west. Its rolling hills, narrow rocky ravines and mountain streams are a welcome relief sandwiched in-between the trafficked frenzy of Johannesburg and the vast North West bushveld. Hikers spend a lot of time exploring its many trails. The Magaliesberg range also encompasses a number of nature reserves.
Tel: 014 577 1733
Email: maginfo@mweb.co.za
Website: www.magaliesburg.co.za

Polokwane to Chimanimani

POLOKWANE (PIETERSBURG)
Lying slap-bang in the middle of Limpopo, or the Northern Province, is Polokwane, its capital city. Huge volumes of traffic shift through as the N1 forges its route (the Great North Road) to Musina and South Africa's border with Zimbabwe. And from Polokwane the R71 connects up with Tzaneen and Kruger. As an administrative and industrial centre, Polokwane is not hugely exciting (be prepared for all the one-way streets) but there are lots of chain restaurants for the famished. For some light entertainment, check out the higgledy-piggledy assortment of outdoor sculptures on Civic Square.
Tel: 015 295 7300/5 0483
Email: info@golimpopo.com
Website: www.limpopotourism.org.za

MARAKELE NATIONAL PARK
In the heart of the Waterberg, northeast of the hunting and mining town, Thabazimbi, Marakele is the country's newest national park. Covering 600km² (235 sq miles), it lives up to its Tswana name 'place of sanctuary' as it protects less-often spied animals such as tsessebe, red hartebeest, roan and sable antelope and hundreds of breeding pairs of the endangered Cape vulture. Elephant and rhino have been introduced from Kruger. The rocky Kransberg's altitude with its cliffs, plateaus and ragged peaks allows verdant ferns, ancient cycads and exotic orchids to flourish. Mainly 4x4 territory, day visitors in sedan vehicles can drive in restricted areas.
Tel: 015 288 9000, 014 777 1745
Email: matibeke@mweb.co.za
Website: www.limpopotourism.org.za

Indigenous people love to weave stories around the dishevelled, roots-in-the-air appearance of the mighty baobab. One legend goes that an angry God flung it head-first into the soil, deliberately planting it upside down. Its hard brown pods, resembling castanets, contain seeds in a powdery pulp known as cream of tartar, which can be eaten.

BAKONE MALAPA MUSEUM
If it's indigenous culture you're interested in, 9km (6 miles) southeast of Polokwane on the R37 is an open-air museum focusing on the traditions of the local Bakone cultural group of the Northern Sotho. People live in the traditional show village and are engaged in pottery and leather crafts. On site is evidence of Ndebele iron and copper smelting, and paintings dating to AD1000. A local guide will recount legends, history and architectural aspects of the complex. It's a simple place but it has heart.
Tel: 015 290 7300/5 2432
Email: info@golimpopo.com
Website: www.golimpopo.com

EASTWARD TO TZANEEN
Heading east of Polokwane, Letaba is an eternally green, forested mountain zone offering a touch of coolness between bushveld to the west and hot lowveld to the east. Here, the start of the Drakensberg escarpment rises dramatically across Mpumalanga. Letaba offers swathes of pine forest, rivers and valley lakes – sometimes cool and eerily misted. As you descend to subtropical Tzaneen, roadside stalls are piled high with avocados and macadamia nuts. Tzaneen is reached over Magoebaskloof Pass or via Haenertsburg, and from the highveld escarpment edge, roads drop to Tzaneen through tea plantations and indigenous forest.
Tel: 015 307 6513/7244
Email: reservations@tzaneeninfo.co.za
Website: www.tzaneeninfo.co.za

MUSINA (MESSINA)
On either side of the N1 to Musina is hot, dusty bushveld interspersed with fat, grey baobabs. Don't expect much of this mining town; its importance lies essentially in the fact that it's the last outpost of civilisation before hitting the Beitbridge borderpost. The border doesn't remain open 24 hours a day, so the 18km (11 miles) to Musina is useful for overnight stopovers. The only sight to get halfway excited about is the Baobab Tree Reserve that surrounds the mining settlement.
Tel: 015 534 3500
Email: musinatourism@limpopo.co.za
Website: www.limpopotourism.org.za

GONAREZHOU NATIONAL PARK

After the wide-scale destruction of wildlife and habitat from searing drought (temperatures of up to 50°C; 122°F) and civil war in Mozambique (guerillas regularly crossed the border for food and refuge), Gonarezhou reopened in 1994. At its southernmost point, this hot baobab wilderness is virtually an extension of Kruger and Mozambique – separated by the Limpopo – creating a natural migratory triangle. In the Shona tongue, *ghona-rezhou* translates as 'place of elephant', and the will of these pachyderms to survive surprised everyone when, in the early 1990s, 200 had to be translocated to Madikwe in South Africa because the park was unable to support them. Gonarezhou's most striking feature is its towering sandstone Chilojo Cliffs which turn ochre, orange and pink at sunset.
Tel: 09263 4 706 077/8, 707 624/9
Email: natparks@africaonline.co.zw
Website: www.zimparks.com

Eastern Highlands

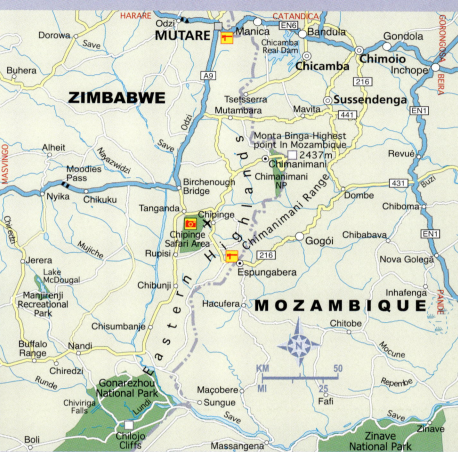

MASVINGO

Travellers generally pass through this lazy little town to get to the Great Zimbabwe ruins lying some 30km (20 miles) away. The name Masvingo is derived from the Shona word '*rusvingo*' meaning 'walled-in enclosures'. The only fame the town can claim is that the pioneer column headed up by hunter Frederick Courteney Selous stopped here in 1890 after successfully traversing the Matabeleland stronghold of Lobengula. The permanent base eventually established nearby made it the first white settlement in then-Rhodesia.
Tel: 09263 39 62643
Email: mgpa@webmail.co.za
Website: www.zimbabwetourism.co.zw

The Great Zimbabwe dry-stone complex is believed to be the largest ancient city in sub-Saharan Africa.

CHIMANIMANI NATIONAL PARK

The village of Chimanimani looks onto a seemingly-impregnable great granite wall that smoulders in the early morning sun. Beyond this is a natural landscape of sandstone towers cut by flowing water, stone forests, slopes of tangled vegetation, and savanna valley. The park can only be explored on foot – a paradise for hikers – and a plethora of caves and rock overhangs in the Bundi valley offer shelter and protection for camping. Chimanimani in the local language describes narrow openings that can only be negotiated in single file, and one such gap occurs in the mountain where the Msapa River flows through.
Tel: 09263 4 706 077/8, 707 624/9
Email: natparks@africaonline.co.zw
Website: www.zimparks.com

HIKING IN THE MOUNTAINS

A series of one- to five-day walks present some serious hiking, starting with the first stretch straight up and over the massif face. On the higher peaks and in the backcountry, hikers need to be aware of the Mozambican border, which is marked only at Skeleton Pass and the Saddle. By straying too far, there's still a vague possibility of stumbling on unexploded land mines. Getting to the highest point at Mount Binga takes a two- to three-hour climb from the mountain hut, but on a clear day you can literally see for ever – right across Mozambique to the Indian Ocean.
Tel: 09263 4 758 730/12/24/34
Email: info@ztazim.co.zw
Website: www.zimbabwetourism.co.zw

NORTHEASTERN FREE STATE

WINBURG
Heading northeast on the N1 from Bloemfontein to Winburg, local tourist centres are working hard to create some interest for travellers along the length of the N5 between Winburg and Harrismith. Winburg is a sleepy town which belies the fact that it was the first capital of the former Boer republic, Orange Free State. The Ford's Hotel, no longer in existence, was where leaders of the five Voortrekker groups decided to form a government headed up by Piet Retief. Some 3km (2 miles) south of the town, a Voortrekker monument in the form of five columns represents each of the parties.

WILLEM PRETORIUS NATURE RESERVE
About 20km (12 miles) north of Winberg, this reserve along the shores of the Allemanskraal dam opens on to lovely waterscapes with, beyond the northern shore, a series of hills providing a pretty backdrop. Chalets of the Aventura Aldam Resort maximise the scenic setting. For its low-key profile, a surprising number of animals – white rhino, buffalo, giraffe, kudu and eland – roam the reserve's hills, while gazelle species nibble on the grasslands around the dam.
Tel: 057 651 4003
Email: butim@dteea.ff.gov.za
Website: www.freestatetourism.gov.za

BETHLEHEM TO HARRISMITH
Distractions vary according to preferences: bird-lovers could be sidetracked by the Pretoriuskloof Bird Sanctuary outside Bethlehem (a Voortrekker stronghold in the 1840s); Anglo-Boer War buffs could head for Fouriesburg, under 50km (30 miles) south of Bethlehem, which, among its sites, counts Surrender Hill, Snymanshoek and Dunblane, as well as a monument, blockhouse, and war graves; or simply continue to the top red-meat-producing town, Harrismith, for a whopping great steak. The town has a couple of its own war memorials (and its flat-topped landmark, the 9km/6-mile-long Platberg). The turnoff to the splendid Golden Gate Highlands park, meriting a longer stay, is off the N5 before Harrismith. About 25km (15 miles) southwest of Harrismith is Sterkfontein dam and nature reserve backed by rugged peaks. Expect yellowwoods, exotic tree ferns – even vultures at feeding time at one of the viewpoints.

As travellers move progressively eastwards, the dry Free State's rainfall increases and herds of indolent cattle and woolly sheep spread out across the sweeter grasslands. Fields of maize and, in season, blazing butter-yellow sunflowers prettify the landscape.

GREAT ZIMBABWE

The distinctive soapstone birds unearthed at Great Zimbabwe are believed to be Rozvi dynasty totems, holding mythological significance. The suggestion has been made that they represent fish eagles. They are the country's national emblem.

HILL COMPLEX & GREAT ENCLOSURE
Sprawling over 2km² (1.5 sq miles), the stone settlement consists of the Hill Complex, and a little further on the Valley Enclosures, of which the Great Enclosure embraces the much-photographed Conical Tower. Resembling a symbolic grain store, it has been carbon dated as one of the last structures to have been built, and archeologists digging beneath it found it to be solid rock and stone. The Hill Complex, the oldest of the stone structures, is speculated to carry religious and spiritual significance.

STONE ARCHITECTURE
Architecturally, the 70m-long (230ft) Parallel Passage running northeast from the Conical Tower reveals the most sophisticated building methods of the entire complex. The outer wall tapers from its 6m (20ft) base to a thickness of 4m (13ft) at the top, with each dry stone course itself tapering for stability. Along the upper edge of the 11m-high (36ft) wall the stones interlock to form three geometrically patterned lines. Swahili glass and porcelain artefacts, soapstone birds and other archeological finds are displayed in the site museum.

GREAT STONE HOUSES
The site on which Great Zimbabwe stands shows that the first signs of inhabitation date to the 11th century. The complex itself, constructed of granite boulders and mortarless interlocking stones decorated in places with chevron and herringbone patterns, was built from the 13th century onward by wealthy Shona-speaking cattlemen. It became a powerful capital involved in the Swahili gold trade, its influence permeating an empire that extended through much of southeast Africa. It is speculated to have supported a population of anything between 10,000 and 40,000. The most credible origin of the name Zimbabwe is the Shona 'dz'mba dza mabwe', meaning 'great stone houses'.

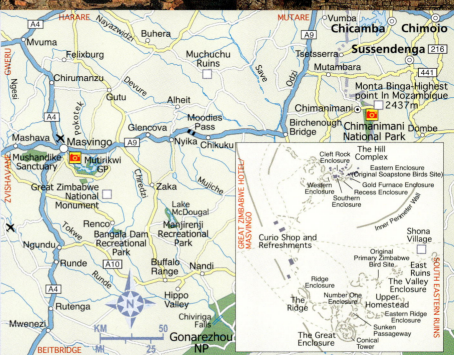

3 CAPE TOWN TO VICTORIA FALLS

Cape Town
As the N2 cuts inland across the Southern Cape, wheatlands stretch to distant mountain horizons on either side – but boring they aren't. Depending on the season, landscapes can vary from tender apple green shoots, gold rippled velvet or graphic lines of stubble dotted with rolled hay bales. After Mossel Bay, travellers enter early explorer François le Vaillant's 'enchanted abode' of the Garden Route.

Harare
If your priority is a place to stay, the Harare Sheraton on Samora Machel Avenue West could fleece you of your holiday bank notes even more than Meikles – standing on its very own block – while the Crowne Plaza, fronting onto the peaceful parklike surrounds of the Harare Gardens, probably has the nicest setting.

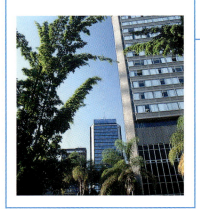

Cape Town — 1753km — Durban — 620km — Maputo — 1464km — Harare

Durban
From Port Shepstone, the N2 hugs the balmy, tropical Indian Ocean coastline as far as Richards Bay, with glimpses through lush banana and palm groves of the blue waters beyond. This stretch encompasses Durban's South and North Coast zones, crammed to the hilt with holiday resorts.

Maputo
As travellers approach this Mozambican city, they can almost start to taste the bounty from the sea that Maputo's so well known for – giant pink prawns, spiky langoustines, shrimps, calamari and gamefish. As powerful is the mental image of that first cold Portuguese beer served with piri-piri cashew nuts and spicy seafood snacks.

Less oft quoted than Dr David Livingstone on the subject of the Victoria Falls, Frederick Selous in 1881 described them as "one of the most transcendentally beautiful natural phenomena on this side of Paradise".

Livingstone
This town started on Constitution Hill as a settlement of hunters, traders and missionaries after Cecil John Rhodes had the Zambezi River bridge built in 1905 to create a rail link between Zambia and then Rhodesia.

Victoria Falls
Although the falls were long called Mosi-oa-Tunya – 'smoke that thunders' – by the Mokololo people, David Livingstone's name, which honoured his queen, Victoria, has stuck over the years.

| 481km | Lusaka | 473km | | 10km | Victoria Falls |

Livingstone

Lusaka
Orientate yourself in this confusing city via the north–south Cairo Road, running past the busy shopping area near the railway station and bus terminal, and Independence Avenue which is crossed by Cairo to the south and runs east towards the embassies and international hotels.

Overberg to Umtata

The chiselled rock cliffs of Meiringspoort, Schoemanspoort, Swartberg and Seweweekspoort – making up the 'four passes' – are a grounding experience when it comes to man vs. nature.

THE OVERBERG REGION

In earlier times, it was impossible for European settlers to penetrate the rugged barrier of the Hottentots Holland mountains beyond today's Somerset West and Gordon's Bay. Only when the circuitous Sir Lowry's Pass cut across the forbidding heights could they pass into the coastal interior, known as the Overberg, which in Dutch means 'over the mountain'. Winding slowly to the top of the pass, the views over False Bay are expansive and the sea at times a breathless turquoise, at others a white shimmering sheet. Descending to the Overberg, itself bounded to the north by the Riviersonderend, Langeberg and Outeniqua mountain ranges, the region stretches to the Breede (Breë) River mouth just north of De Hoop Nature Reserve. Along the coast are the fishing and nature-oriented weekend playgrounds of Onrus, Hermanus, Arniston, and De Hoop. Inland, via the relatively new tourist-oriented R62, visitors head out to ostrich capital Oudtshoorn and the stupendous scenery of the Four Passes, hacked through the vast, towering walls of the Swartberg range.
Tel: 028 214 1466
Email: info@capeoverberg.org
Website: www.capeoverberg.org

BONNIEVALE

Before motorists reach Swellendam, a turnoff takes them northwest to Bonnievale in the Breede River valley. Its fame hinges more on its nearby bigger cousin, Robertson, whose serrated rows of vineyards in searingly hot, dry country produce richly flavoured white wines that pack quite a punch. Bonnievale has its own fair collection of wine farms, but most wine-tasting action happens in and around Robertson. The entire valley encompasses some 10% of the country's vines, and its setting at the foot of the Langeberg make it a pleasure to drive through.
Tel: 023 616 3753/422
Email: info@bonnievale.co.za
Website: www.bonnievale.co.za

SWELLENDAM

This historic little town must have the best setting in the entire Western Cape. Nestled at the base of the Langeberg, the giant mountain seems to rise vertically above it with an imposing tangible presence. The centre expanded from the humble beginnings of the Drostdy, founded by a commissioner of the Dutch East India Company (built 1746–47), and it's now the pivotal building of a really fine historic country museum on Swellengrebel Street. Displaying Cape Dutch architecture typical of the 18th century, there is also the Old Gaol, the jailer's cottage, and a collection of 18th and 19th-century farming implements.
Tel: 028 514 2770
Email: infoswd@sdm.dorea.co.za
Website: www.swellendamtourism.co.za

DE HOOP NATURE RESERVE

Heading out of Bredasdorp, a turnoff leads onto a dirt road to this reserve. For those wanting to get away from it all for some unadulterated peace and quiet, this 50km (30-mile) stretch of pristine shoreline is for you. Part of it undulates into magical 90m-high (295ft), sugar-white sand dunes. Bird-watchers can repair to the lagoon, whose populations vary according to water levels; nevertheless, 260 different species have been recorded. Migrant waders spend time here from September to April. On a short circular drive to Tierhoek you could meet up with Cape mountain zebra, bontebok, rhebok and mountain reedbuck.
Tel: 028 425 5020
Email: capenature@tiscali.co.za
Website: www.capenature.org.za

For those who have energy to expend, a series of mountain biking trails in the Potberg mountain section of De Hoop reserve will keep them well occupied. Watch out for – but don't disturb – the breeding colony of rare Cape vultures. You could also embark on the 5-day walking trail over 70km (43 miles) through the reserve.

THE GARDEN ROUTE

Overflowing descriptions that have famously filled the notebooks and diaries of early 17th- and 18th-century travellers have, over time, been honed to the present epithet, Garden Route. Beginning with Mossel Bay and ending at the Storms River mouth, this section of coastline is accompanied all the way by the Outeniqua, Tsitsikamma and Langkloof mountains. Well-watered by rivers, lakes, lagoons and foamy waves it certainly is, but to properly appreciate it, you need to get off the N2 and explore the byways. Once-pervasive indigenous forests of yellowwood, ironwood and stinkwood have been greatly reduced through felling by early settlers, but wooded tracts remain and pine and bluegum plantations have been planted.

Tel: 044 873 6314
Email: info@gardenroute.org.za
Website: www.capegardenroute.org

The disdain surfers have for non-surfers is evident in their surfspeak, which includes 'shark biscuit' for boogie boarders and 'egg whippers' or 'deck chairs' for paddle-skiers.

JEFFREYS BAY

More popularly referred to as Jay Bay, this spot has built its reputation on the quality of its waves and the surfers who flock here. The town itself doesn't have too much going for it, but the surf pumps and the perfect rollers keep coming in. Jam-packed over the holidays, it thrives on its surfing culture where talk centres on wave sites called Magna Tubes, Albatross and the legendary Supertubes. Dolphins love riding the waves too!

Tel: 042 293 2923
Email: Jbay-tourism@agnet.co.za
Website: www.infojeffreysbay.com

GRAHAMSTOWN

Starting its life as a military post (under Colonel John Graham) where 4500 British families were encouraged to make a new home, the early settlement grew into a lively trading centre. This was the birth of the 1820 settlers, and their heritage permeates this artistically oriented, erudite university town. Arts and culture mesh with history at the 1820 Settlers Monument, a fort-like edifice in the shape of a ship on Gunfire Hill. It's here, in the modern Monument Theatre, that the annual Grahamstown National Arts Festival is staged in early to mid-July – an extravaganza of local talent expressed in art, music, dance, theatre, and street stalls.

Tel: 046 622 3241
Email: info@grahamstown.co.za
Website: www.grahamstown.co.za

GARDEN ROUTE HIGHLIGHTS

If you choose to stop awhile in Mossel Bay, don't miss the Dias Museum complex with its life-size replica of Bartolomeu Dias's 25-ton lateen-sailed wooden caravel. Stop at Dolphin's Point viewsite just before reaching Wilderness for a stunning view of this holiday spot's long, lazy, white rollers. Check out the chain of salt- and freshwater Wilderness lakes, linked by the snaking Serpentine channel. Slide down a few fresh oysters from Knysna's 17km-long (11 miles) lagoon, protected at the sea entrance by the two sandstone Knysna Heads. Have lunch (or a drink) on Plettenberg Bay's Lookout deck overlooking the sea's edge at Lookout Beach.

Tel: 044 873 6314
Email: info@gardenroute.org.za
Website: www.capegardenroute.org

PORT ELIZABETH TO GRAHAMSTOWN

South Africa's fifth-largest city looks out across Algoa Bay, and it's mainly sea, sand and sun that pull people to the city. PE's once well-preserved historic buildings are suffering neglect – but the pounding surf is exhilarating and the wide white beaches are expansive. Humewood Beach, paralleled by Marine Drive, is where it all happens – the Oceanarium, Tropical House, the dolphin and seal shows, and snake park all beckon. You get more for your money by pushing on to Grahamstown, whose 60 national monuments include beautifully restored Georgian and Victorian homes lining the city streets.

Tel: 041 585 8884
Email: info@nmbt.co.za
Website: www.nmbt.co.za

UMTATA

The former capital, and today the Transkei's largest town, Umtata was founded in 1871 when Europeans agreed to settle on the Umtata River at the request of the Themba clan, who needed a buffer against raiders from the Pondo clan (ironically, both clans belong to the Xhosa nation). Today it is noisy, chaotic and dirty, but is useful as a gateway to the Wild Coast for last-minute banking, supplies and fuel. If you're forced to stay awhile, a new Nelson Mandela Museum in the old parliament building illustrates his 'long walk to freedom' with photographs and visual material. Also displayed are gifts he's received from all corners of the world.

Tel: 047 531 5290/2
Email: infomtata@ectourism.co.za
Website: www.ectourism.co.za

South Coast to Maputo

THE SOUTH COAST
This stretch of coastline from Margate north to Durban, lapped by the warm(ish) Indian Ocean and drenched in abundant rainfall, is the quintessential subtropical holiday playzone. Think sugar cane, banana plantations, palms and pecan nut trees, splashed with the hot, tropical hues of hibiscus, frangipani and canna lilies. For 160km (100 miles), hotels, resorts and holiday apartments – from the supremely elegant to the brashly tacky – are the life and soul of the wave-washed coastline. Sunshine all year round brings humidity in summer and mild gentle days in winter, with a constant gravitation of holidaymakers to lively resort towns mostly based on river mouths.
Tel: 039 316 6139/2 2322
Email: margate@venturenet.co.za
Website: www.hibiscuscoast.kzn.org.za

DURBAN
There is plenty of cultural flavour in the mix of Zulu, Indian and white communities of South Africa's third-largest city and largest port (see also p82). The Indian influence, particularly, is pervasive in the mosques (visit the Juma Musjid, or Grey Street, mosque), the vibrant colours and heady scented spices of the elaborately domed (11 of them) Victoria Street Market, and the exotic temples (don't miss the awe-inspiring marble temple room of Chatworth's Temple of Understanding). Durban's marine promenade, in earlier days dubbed the Golden Mile, has all the

THE NORTH COAST
This 80km (50-mile) stretch from Umhlanga Rocks north to the Tugela River mouth has somehow evaded the overcrowded fate of the South Coast, and the sheltered bays and estuaries are more tranquil. A bonus is the shallower and therefore warm waters which are loved by bottle-nosed dolphins – they feed here year-round. Around Umhlanga Rocks, less than half an hour from Durban's centre, hotels and timeshare resorts keep busy with visitors drawn to the banana palm shores, steep sandy beaches, crashing surf – and protection from shark nets! For greater luxury and a more upmarket experience, look no further than Ballito, Salt Rock and Shaka's Rock further north.
Tel: 032 946 1997/2434
Email: info@dolphincoast.kzn.org.za
Website: www.dolphincoast.co.za

COASTAL RESORTS
Amanzimtoti ('the water is sweet') has a lovely 3km (2-mile) beach just north of the Manzimtoti River, Scottburgh on the mouth of the Mpambonyoni is nestled in lush sugar plantations, and Port Shepstone has the Oribi Gorge Nature Reserve some 25km (15 miles) away. Cut to depths of 300m (985ft) by the Umzimkulwana River, this wide, luxuriantly forested ravine has some dizzying views. Great for picnics accompanied by the sounds of the samango monkeys. Uvongo's spit of white sand separating a lagoon from the restless sea is intensely pretty. Here, the Vungu River plunges into the lagoon, protected by wild-banana-clad high cliffs, before meeting the sea. Tourist havens Margate, Port Edward and nearby Wild Coast Sun keep families happily occupied and entertained.
Tel: 039 316 6139/2 2322
Email: margate@venturenet.co.za
Website: www.hibiscuscoast.kzn.org.za

trappings of traditional family seaside entertainment: piers, paddling pools, amusement parks, and ice cream parlours. The arrival of petty crime has since tarnished its reputation, but this doesn't deter the crowds who continue to find distraction and entertainment here. The Sea World aquarium and dolphinarium has moved to the ra-ra extravaganza of uShaka Marine World (see p82) but FitzSimons Snake Park will keep the kids happy. The harbour area of the Victoria Embankment is the focus of a dockside art and music scene, and superb views over the harbour can be had from the pub and restaurant there.
Tel: 031 366 7500/04 7144
Email: tkzn@zulu.org.za
Website: www.zulu.org.za

RICHARDS BAY
This modern industrial town is out of place on this pristine slice of coast. Its port is second in size to Durban's but it handles the greatest volumes of cargo in the country. It also holds the dubious title of the world's largest coal terminal. Better to spend more time at Mtunzini, just before Richards Bay, on an unspoiled tract of coastal forest in the Umlalazi Nature Reserve. Walking trails lead you through the forest to the beach, and on a circular walk through mangrove swamps you can inspect the lively crabs and mudskippers. If you're stopping awhile, a boat trip to the river mouth gives you the chance to perhaps hear the quintessential fish eagle call or catch the nosedive antics of the kingfishers.
Tel: 035 901 5018/408
Email: rbtour@ughungulu.co.za
Website: www.tourismassociation.org.za

Wild Coast

KOSI BAY

Lying not far from the Mozambique border, Kosi Bay is reached from Mkuze, just south of Pongolapoort dam. This is generally 4x4 territory and the experience is 'back to nature' in its fullest sense (no tar roads, no electricity). The name 'bay' is in actual fact a system of four interconnecting lakes and estuary mangrove swamps which make their way to the sea at Kosi mouth; the only way to get to the sea is via the four-day guided circular trails around the lakes. Visitors stay in a campsite or thatched chalets in pristine surrounds of cycads, and fig tree and raffia palm forests. Boating, fresh- and saltwater fishing, and hippo, crocodile and leatherback turtle spotting keep naturalists supremely content.

Tel: 035 562 0966
Email: res@elephantcoastbookings.co.za
Website: www.elephantcoast.kzn.org.za

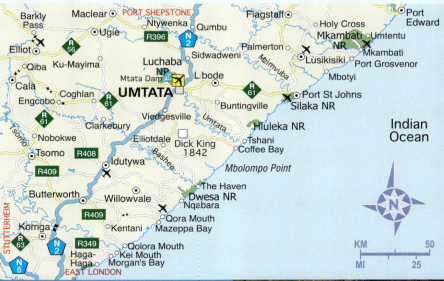

MAPUTO

Situated on a small cliff overlooking Maputo Bay, this city – known as Lourenço Marques in its heyday – is rebuilding its life after the civil war. A bustling centre, it is dilapidated in parts, lifted in others by its sidewalk cafés, interesting architecture and (slow-paced) renovation. There is irrepressible energy in the noisy colourful markets and lively late-night bars that spill out into the sultry air on Rua do Bagamoio. A squat, mid-19th-century stone fort, now a museum of colonial history, is a reminder of Maputo's Portuguese heritage.

Tel: 09258 1 307 320/3
Email: info@futur.org.mz
Website: www.futur.org.mz

MORGAN'S BAY TO QOLORA MOUTH

The Wild Coast shoreline connecting Morgan's Bay, Kei Mouth and Qolora embraces the Transkei's best resorts, greatly favoured by families. An estuary created by two converging rivers carving their way through forested dunes is where Morgan's Bay finds itself, overlooking vast sweeps of white beach. From here, a short bumpy ride to Kei Mouth village gets visitors (and their cars) onto a small pontoon. This crosses the Kei River to Qolora Mouth where Trennery's Hotel, another favourite holiday stamping ground, is perched above a steep beach. Walking, canoeing, rowing or pure, sleep-inducing inaction quickly drains all the stress from wound-up city dwellers.

COFFEE BAY TO PORT ST JOHNS

The hilly, lushly tropical coast intersected by craggy cliffs and steep, narrow ravines between Coffee Bay and Port St Johns draws a constant stream of local and foreign nature-seekers. Its entire length can be hiked but people generally tackle sections at a time, staying either in designated local villages or in hotel accommodation along the way. Naturalists can also absorb the wild beauty on horseback on guided trails led by the Pondo people. Descending into ravines, trailing clifftops and fording rivers are all part of the experience. A distinctive landmark not far from Coffee Bay is the rock arch Hole in the Wall – 'place of sound' to the Xhosa people because high waters give rise to giant waves thundering through the opening.

Tel: 047 564 1187/207, 531 1191
Email: tourismpsj@wildcoast.co.za
Website: www.portstjohns.org.za/tourism

GARDEN ROUTE

DIEPWALLE STATE FOREST
Between Knysna and Plettenberg Bay, Diepwalle is part of Knysna's remaining forested groves of Outeniqua yellowwood, ironwood and stinkwood. It's a lovely dappled zone of mountain biking routes, walks and a scenic drive. The Elephant Walk through towering indigenous trees leads to the King Edward Tree, a gigantic 600-year-old Outeniqua yellowwood that soars to almost 40m (130ft). Its girth is a healthy 7m (23ft). If it's your lucky day, you could be spoiled by a flash of scarlet wings belonging to the gorgeous emerald Knysna lourie in flight.
Tel: 044 382 5510
Email: knysna.tourism@pixie.co.za
Website: www.knysna-info.co.za

PLETTENBERG BAY
This seaside village's gorgeous position on red sandstone cliffs overlooking great curves of white beach and the lagoon from the Keurbooms and Bietou rivers makes it the place to be for upwardly mobile holidaymakers. Lookout Beach is where the trendy hang out but the long blonde stretch of Robberg Beach comes a close second at holiday time. At one end of Robberg Beach is Plett's most recognisable landmark, the Beacon Isle timeshare resort, cut off from the mainland by water at high tide, while at the other end is the tall, rugged Robberg Peninsula jutting out

BLOUKRANS BRIDGE
Roughly 35km (20 miles) east of Plettenberg Bay and then 2km (1 mile) beyond the Tsitsikamma Forest village, this bridge spans the Bloukrans River. For adrenaline junkies only, the bridge is the highest commercial bungee jump in the world, at 216m (709ft). For a terrifyingly long seven-second descent (it is when you're hurtling through nothingness), you can let out a primal scream before the jerk of the fully paid-out rope has you bouncing briefly skyward again. You get a video for your death-defying efforts.
Tel: 042 281 1458/255
Email: info@faceadrenalin.com

In the 19th century, 400–500 forest elephants lived around Knysna. Ruthless hunting decimated them, and today only a single elephant from the original herd is alive. Two young elephants were introduced from Kruger park, but unfortunately the venture was unsuccessful. The last intensely shy and elusive elephant is very rarely seen.

into restless seas. This nature and marine reserve has a series of walks along sheer-sided clifftops with magnificent views, winding down to deserted secret beaches. The full circular walk takes four hours, or can be broken into a two-hour hike or a half-hour ramble. In winter, dolphins and southern right whales can often be watched frolicking beyond the surf.
Tel: 044 533 4065
Email: info@plettenbergbay.co.za
Website: www.plettenbergbay.co.za

TSITSIKAMMA AND STORMS RIVER

Eternally green and fertile, the thickly forested belt of the Tsitsikamma National Park stretches from Nature's Valley (as pretty as its name) to past the wild, dramatic estuary of Storms River Mouth, a distance of almost 70km (40 miles). At the mouth, you couldn't find a better positioned spot than the restcamp that's sandwiched between hissing white water assaulting wet, black rocks and the soaring tangled cliffs behind. A 1km (half-a-mile) boardwalk from the restaurant leads visitors to a suspension bridge from where they can view the seething waters of the river mouth. Walkers can tackle waymarked coastal trails, swimmers can try out the unspoilt sandy cove nearby.
Tel: 042 281 1607
Email: rassiee@sanparks.org

Storms River Mouth is the starting point of the five-day Otter Trail where hikers, who need to be fully self-sufficient for the duration of the trail, follow the pristine coastline to Nature's Valley. They encounter forested cliffs, wind-worn rocky terrain, river-cut gorges and crashing foaming seas. Dolphins and whales are also not unusual along the way.

ZULULAND, MAPUTALAND & INHACA

HLUHLUWE-UMFOLOZI PARK
Originally two separate reserves established to protect the endangered rhino population, Hluhluwe and Umfolozi were consolidated in 1989. Today the park is South Africa's fourth largest, supporting enormously diverse animals with the Big Five part of the package. The experience is true Africa: rolling hills, acacia woodland, palm-fringed banks and subtropical forest where 'monkey-ropes' are suspended over the rivers. And, yes, samango monkeys live in the treetops. Highlights are stunning views from high spots, guided wilderness trails with knowledgeable rangers, reed-and-thatch restcamps on the banks of the Black Mfolozi, and the absence of fences around the camps!
Tel: 033 845 1000/999
Email: bookings@kznwildlife.com
Website: www.kznwildlife.com

GREATER ST LUCIA WETLAND PARK
So incredibly unspoiled and made up of so many different habitats – mountain, bushveld, palm groves, sand forest, grassland, wetland, coastal forest and coral reef – the Greater St Lucia Wetland Park was declared fit for UNESCO World Heritage status in 1999. It stretches for an impressive 80km (50 miles) from its southern end to Sodwana Bay in the north. Crocodiles and hippos lurk in Lake St Lucia, as do pelicans and flamingos and any number of other waterbird species. Deep-sea fishermen and scuba divers flock to Sodwana Bay for different reasons. For underwater enthusiasts, the hard and soft corals, anemones, coloured tropical fish and larger denizens of the deep off Sodwana are the best in the country.
Tel: 033 845 1000, 035 590 1528
Email: bookings@kznwildlife.com
Website: www.kznwildlife.com

ZULULAND
For historical more than formal reasons, the KwaZulu-Natal region extending northward of the Tugela River is known as Zululand. This was, after all, Zulu territory under the once-powerful King Shaka. Subtropical and beautiful, it is an untamed wilderness of game reserves, fertile interiors cut by rivers and remote pristine shores. The northern corner of this vast region, encompassing the southernmost extreme of the St Lucia wetlands to Kosi Bay near the Mozambican border, is referred to as Maputaland. It rates among South Africa's most isolated areas, reached only by dirt road – a tapestry of wild country, Zulu villages, wetlands and freshwater lakes.
Tel: 031 366 7500/04 7144
Email: tkzn@zulu.org.za
Website: www.zulu.org.za

LOGGERHEADS AND LEATHERBACKS
Between Cape Vidal and Mozambique's Ponta do Ouro, a marine reserve means that loggerhead and leatherback turtles can safely make their nesting sites on the sandy beaches. This they do at night in summer, above the high-tide mark. About 10 weeks later, hatchlings emerge from their nests in the night and scramble furiously to the sea. In an odd twist of fate, only one or two out of 1000 hatchlings will survive to maturity.
Tel: 035 590 1162 Turtle hotline
Email: tkzn@zulu.org.za
Website: www.zulu.org.za

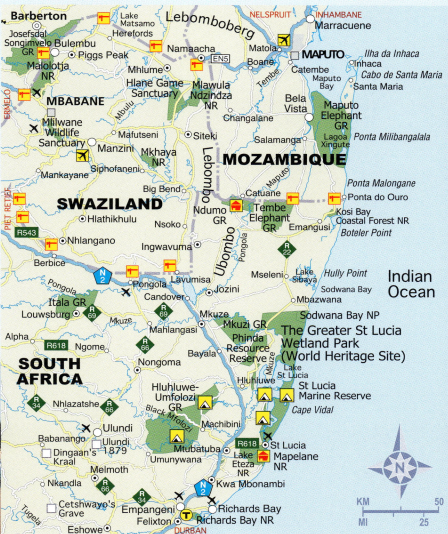

CONSERVING THE RHINO IN HLUHLUWE-UMFOLOZI

The park, founded in 1895 and therefore South Africa's oldest, is recognised worldwide for its commendable role in conserving rhino. It is credited for raising rhino numbers from a scary 20 at the beginning of the 1900s to today's count of almost 2000 beasts. In 1994, the World Conservation Union struck the white rhino off its endangered list – the first species to be removed from this list. White rhinos are so-called not for the shade of their hide but after the early Dutch word 'wijd' which described their flat broad lip – good for grazing. The black rhino has a more pointed, hooked lip that enables it to nibble off leafy branches.
Tel: 021 423 8005, 012 428 9111
Email: reservations@parks-sa.co.za
Website: www.parks-sa.co.za

MAPUTO'S MAPUTALAND

From Swaziland, Maputo is not even 100km (60 miles) distant. Southward, the town lords over Mozambique's own Maputaland which takes in the Maputo Elephant Reserve, Ponta Malongane and Ponta do Ouro – a shore-based haven for increasingly enthusiastic anglers, deep-sea fishermen, snorkellers and scuba divers. Directly opposite the town, across Maputo Bay, Inhaca Island appeals to fishing and birdwatching aficionados. The Maputo Elephant Reserve continues to be threatened by slash-and-burn subsistence farming and poaching. Be warned that roads are pockmarked by potholes, soft sand patches and erosion – a hangover from the war. Best take your 4x4.
Tel: 09258 1 307 320/3
Email: info@futur.org.mz
Website: www.futur.org.mz

PONTA DO OURO & INHACA

Divers and snorkellers submerge themselves in clear tropical waters off Ponta do Ouro and Malongane to enter the brilliant-coloured world of corals, mischievous little fish, inquisitive big fish (potato bass, painted surgeons) and moray eels. Lodges all along the Maputaland coast can arrange dives with leatherback turtles and manta rays, which glide silently through the waters off Inhaca Island. The steel-hearted can try a shark dive off Ponta do Ouro. At the southmost end of Ponta do Ouro's beach, if you walk around the point you can stand with one foot in South Africa and one in Mozambique.
Tel: 011 803 9296/52
Email: travel@mozambiquetourism.co.za
Website: www.mozambiquetourism.co.za

Mana Pools

MAPUTO TO MUTARE

The route from Maputo to the Zimbabwean borderpost heads north up the Mozambican coastline, along the EN1 to the main crossroads of Inchope, where you can re-fuel for the next stage of your journey. Roads from Inchope cut east to Beira, north to Gorongosa National Park, west to Mutare and south to Maputo. If you have a yen to explore a little (but you'll need a 4x4), you could spot the odd elephant and lolling hippos in Gorongosa. Once a top wildlife park famous for its lion, the damage has been done by poaching and the war. Some rehabilitation has established a basic structure, with Chitengo camp and campsites offering accommodation, and the locals can usually point you towards signs of wildlife.

Once across the border, Mutare is your direct link to Zimbabwe's capital, Harare. Mutare has a pretty position in the moist Eastern Highlands, lying at the foot of the Bvumba mountains. Here a mountain gap feeds road and rail to Mozambique. The town is characterised by its palm-fringed main street and loud, lipstick-red flamboyants. You leave Mutare via the high Christmas Pass which at night looks down on a mass of twinkling lights cupped firmly in the valley.
Tel: 09263 20 64711
Email: info@ztazim.co.zw
Website: www.zimbabwetourism.co.zw

MANA POOLS NATIONAL PARK

This wilderness area – one of Zimbabwe's wildest and most special – is a World Heritage Site. It lines the great Zambezi for 50km (30 miles) as the river flows between the headwaters of Mozambique's Cahora Bassa dam (as massive as Lake Kariba) and the eastern edge of Kariba. Hot and humid in summer, it's one of the few areas where you can walk freely among the wildlife, surrounded by mopane, apple-ring acacia, monkey-thorn trees, and greasy-grey baobabs along the great escarpment. Hippos snort in the muddy waters, prehistoric crocodiles drowse lazily on sunny river islands, and elephant, buffalo and waterbuck wander through Mana's pans and pools.

CAMPING AND CANOEING

Mana Pools is hemmed in by a slew of hunting areas, and signs of permanent human habitation only happen at Kanyemba, on Mozambique's border. Canoeing safaris – an absolutely great way to absorb the Zambezi's magic and commune quietly with the wildlife – end at Kanyemba, but are arranged from Kariba. The park is open beginning May to end October, offering by way of accommodation a main campsite at park headquarters, Nyamepi, and many campsites along the river. Otherwise choose between luxury thatched canvas cottages at the park's eastern end or, nearer to Kariba, the elegant Ruckomechi luxury camp under mahogany and winterthorn trees.
Tel: 09263 4 706 077/8, 707 624/9
Email: natparks@africaonline.co.zw
Website: www.zimparks.com

LAKE KARIBA

This is Africa's third-largest dam, created when a massive wall trapped the waters of the powerful Zambezi River to supply the country with hydroelectric power. Kariba's shores are dotted with some of Zimbabwe's finest game lodges, which lure eager visitors to indulge their passion (wildlife aside!) for yachting, fishing and houseboating. Summers on the waters are very, very hot. Temperatures are the highest of all Zimbabwe's wilderness areas, with October to February the hottest. A defining image of Kariba is its drowned trees, ghostly eafless branches rising out of the waters, providing a perfect perch for darters, cormorants, kingfishers and herons. The dam's defining sound is the haunting call of the fish eagle as it prepares to snatch its prey from the waters.

LUSAKA

The A1 highway cutting through Makuti, where travellers turn off to Kariba, continues on to Chirundu before crossing the Otto Beit bridge into Zambia. From here the road heads for the capital city, Lusaka. It's a chaotic town, where high unemployment has bred poverty and corruption. The CBD is completely overrun by street traders and aimless loiterers. The double-lane boulevard named Cairo Road, the main thoroughfare through the CBD, embodied once the lofty dream of Cecil John Rhodes to forge a road from Cape to Cairo.
Tel: 09260 1 229 087/9/90
Email: zntb@zamnet.zm
Website: www.zambiatourism.com

LIVINGSTONE

Zambia's tourist capital Livingstone (see also p77) sprawls on the opposite side of the Victoria Falls, which generally are accessed from the Zimbabwean side. This sleepy town used to be the old colonial capital and is slowly coming out of decades of stagnation and the lack of funds. At safari-style lodges on the Zambezi, the atmosphere is a lot more secluded than the tourist frenzy of Victoria Falls, allowing a different perspective on Mosi-oa-Tunya – the 'smoke that thunders'. The Royal Livingstone, a multimillion-dollar colonial-style complex, is definitely king of the gorge with its supreme spot just upstream of the falls. From here you could choose to do anything from river rafting, canoeing, bungee-jumping and microlighting to sipping sundowners at the riverside.
Tel: 09260 3 321 404
Email: zntblive@zamnet.zm
Website: www.zambiatourism.com

Crimson sunsets here are incomparable, softening into pinks and mauves over the Matusadona mountains. Most fishemen come for the tigerfish, but there are also over 20 species of bream, and carp and black bass. Matusadona National Park on Kariba's southern shores, although 4x4 territory, draws people to its thatched and tented resorts and luxury safari camps, while on adjacent shores Bumi Hills' luxury lodge is for the well-heeled. Sanyati Lodge on the rocky cliffs of Sanyati gorge is the eldorado of Zimbabwean fishermen.
Tel: 09263 61 2328/3213
Email: kpa@mweb.co.zw
Website: www.zimbabwetourism.co.zw

VICTORIA FALLS (ZAMBIA)

The many moods and aspects of these magnificent falls (see also p78) depend entirely on seasons and rainfall. Knife Edge, a thin headland jutting out in front of the escarpment over which the falls pour, has you gazing into the Boiling Pot while water crashes and thunders all around. After high rains, you'll be thoroughly soaked. The spray also stops you from seeing to the foot of the gorge. Slippery surfaces are a hazard and you should take great care wherever you walk. During sparse rainfall years, visitors can actually walk across the river to Livingstone Island, perched right on the escarpment edge, to peer into the heart-stopping abyss.
Tel: 09260 1 229 087/9/90
Email: zntb@zamnet.zm
Website: www.zambiatourism.com

VICTORIA FALLS (ZIMBABWE)

At the confluence of the Zambezi and Chobe rivers is a little town called Kasane and, nearby, Kazungula – the borderpost into Zimbabwe. It's at Kasane that four countries meet – Namibia, Botswana, Zambia and Zimbabwe. Within the latter's boundary, it's also the start of the region enfolding Zimbabwe's star tourist attraction, the majestic Victoria Falls.

VICTORIA FALLS

This World Heritage Site is shared by Zambia, but the views onto the falls are the most all-encompassing from Zimbabwe. From horizon to horizon the roaring curtain is immensely visible as you stand with the rainforest at your back, the spray-filled chasm at your feet. At full flood, the green-white water extends over 1700m (5600ft) and an estimated 500,000m³ surge over every minute. Beyond the falls, the Zambezi River cascades through the mountain-hemmed Batoka gorge for 130km (80 miles) before opening out into Lake Kariba. An Edwardian bridge built in 1905 links Zimbabwe with Zambia.

VIEWING THE FALLS

The river swells to maximum flow at the falls between April and June. At Devil's Cataract, if rains have been good, compressed water pummels through the gap between Cataract Island and the bank you're standing on – an awesome roaring, earth-trembling fury of beauty and power at your feet. In contrast, the dry season exposes a flat platform of black basalt at this spot. A path at the lip of the falls meanders from Devil's Cataract through moist, mist-drenched riverine forest (the 'rainforest') and into rainbowed sunlight. Here, looking onto the main falls, updrafts of spray from the thundering chasm soak you to the skin. But emerging a 'drowned rat' is all part of the sensurround – gotta feel it to experience it! Wander through the various viewpoints to Danger Point overlooking Boiling Pot. Danger's the word! A slippery, moss-covered rocky platform drops sheer to the churning waters below. Once over it, there seriously is no coming back. Of course, another way to expand your visual boundaries is to hop aboard a tiny Piper aircraft for the Flight of Angels over this majestic phenomenon of nature. The 10- to 15-minute flight is named after David Livingstone's overquoted words on seeing Victoria Falls for the first time.

THRILLS ON WATER

Visitors with more courage than grey matter regularly launch themselves off the Zambezi bridge with nothing but a high-tensile rope attached to their ankles. Sheer, blind terror and an adrenaline-fuelled blood rush must do some people good because there's no shortage of takers to be catapulted a nose-breadth from the thrashing Zambezi waters in No 2 gorge. A little safer but providing just as much of a blood rush is whitewater rafting below the thundering falls from July to mid-August. In wet years, the Zambezi is considered the wildest single-day whitewater run in the world. For 22km (14 miles), inflatable rafts steered by expert oarsmen bop, bump and bounce through 19 narrow, high-walled gorges, eliciting spray, spontaneous shrieks and, most times, bobbing waterborne bodies. Lower waters and more exposed rocks make mid-August to December a more testing run suited to the experienced. At the end, video footage of the day's fun gives adventurers plenty to crow about. For a gentler outing, canoeing and kayaking excursions explore the islands in the broad, much calmer Zambezi above the falls. Excitement comes in the shape of manageable mini-rapids. And for the adrenaline-phobic, a sunset river cruise above the falls is intensely beguiling with its sundowners, burnt-orange skies and wildlife taking advantage of the evening air along the riverbanks.

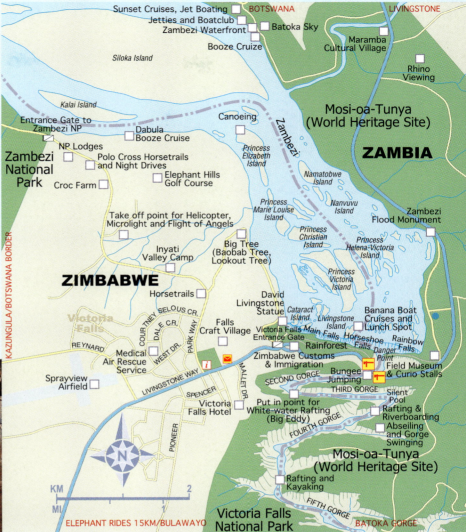

VICTORIA FALLS HOTEL

A visit to the falls would not be complete without a look-in at the Victoria Falls Hotel – the epitome of white-gloved colonial yesteryear. Refurbished many times since it was built in 1904, it is linked to the Edwardian railway station via a shady, treed walk. Distinctive in its orange-tiled roof, colonnades, courtyard and patios, the hotel gardens, set under enormous tree canopies, offer leafy peaks through to the falls and bridge. Dine elegantly to a jazz quartet in the Livingstone Room, let the melodic marimbas tickle your ears on the patio or be absorbed by the elaborate tribal masks of the Makishi dancers.

Tel: 09263 13 44203/5
Email: vicfallshotel@tvfh.zimsun.co.zw
Website: www.victoriafallshotel.com

VICTORIA FALLS VILLAGE

This is simply a conglomeration of hotels, safari operators, curio shops and a craft village peopled by eager rafters, bungee-jumpers and backpackers. The Falls Craft Village sets out to visually depict Zimbabwean lifestyles through its collection of ethnic huts, craftspeople and even an *nganga* – for those intrepid visitors keen to hear what the witchdoctor sees for them in the bones. Ever focused on how best to bait visitors, the craft village leads straight into a giant crafts shop to prise you of your tourist dollars.

ZAMBEZI NATIONAL PARK

Inland areas of this park are characterised by savanna and mopane forest, but a 40km stretch (25 miles) fronts prettily onto the Zambezi River. Visitors can walk on their own between picnic areas 1–25 along the eastern boundary, otherwise horseriding and wildlife walks or drives can be arranged from Victoria Falls village. Overhanging fig, ebony and apple-ring acacia give shade to lion, sable antelope, zebra, waterbuck and warthog, while elephant and hippo are often seen frolicking in the water. Lodges, exclusive camps and camps catering for fishing are perfectly poised on the river-edge.

4 CAPE TOWN TO SWAKOPMUND

Cape Town
Between cosmopolitan Cape Town and the hot, dry surrounds of Kimberley, there are some dramatic contrasts in landscape. Initially, travellers will be distracted by an evolving, changing mountainscape – all part of the sandstone Cape Fold Mountains, which subside and then flatten out to the dessicated dusty Karoo leaving only erosion-resistant kopjes.

Tuli Block
At Botswana's most easterly point, in the Tuli Block, the confluence of the Limpopo and Shashe rivers marks the meeting point of three countries: Botswana, Zimbabwe and South Africa. This is verdant riverine woodland inhabited by plenty of elephant.

Matetsi Safari Area
This zone made up of a mix of mopane groves and teak and mukwa woodland hugs the Zambezi. It is carefully monitored hunting territory, the aim being to sustain the natural habitat by controlling numbers and providing the local communities with an income. Elephant, buffalo, sable and roan are prolific.

Cape Town — 969km — Kimberley — 538km — Gaborone — 443km — Francistown — 496km — Maun — 370km — Victoria Falls — 438km — Bulaway

Kimberley
In this town of diamonds, the carat reigns supreme. In Arabic, *qírát* described the weight of four grains; later dried carob beans were used.

Mafikeng
Tswana writer and activist Sol Plaatjie, among the first black writers who made ripples with their work, lived in Mafikeng for years. His diaries recorded the (unrecognised) impact local Barolong members had in aiding Baden-Powell's defence in the 1990 siege.

Makgadikgadi
The western turning at Phuduhudu crossroads takes you to Baines' Baobabs. The scene at Kudiakam Pan has been immortalised in paintings not only by Thomas Baines but also Prince Charles.

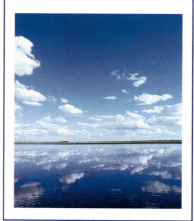

Matobo Hills
Some of the peaks rising amidst these giant bouldered kopjes are still held sacred by the Ndebele. In secret crevices and overhangs are the remains of clay ovens used centuries ago to forge deadly *assegaais*, and if one looks carefully, the rocks form natural receptacles – once used by Lobengula and his warriors to store their grain.

Splash out and spoil yourself at the end of your long trip. Let the buttresses, turrets and stained-glass windows of Hotel Heinitzburg, a renovated early 20th-century castle in Windhoek, lure you in for a night.

Central Kalahari GR
Water is precious in these fossil-rivered thirstlands – the flow ceased 16,000 years ago. Wild animals survive as a result of artificially pumped pans, while humans rely on drinking water offered solely by the Matswere Game Scout Camp.

Gobabis
The second theory for this settlement's name (see also p62) is that, through a misspelling over the years, it was in fact 'goabbis' – 'place of elephant'. This is the more accepted assumption (despite the distinct absence of pachyderms!).

Windhoek
Hotel Heinitzburg has a reputation for serving good cuisine, accompanied by wines stored at optimum temperatures – in the castle dungeon. The fantastic views over Windhoek are also a plus.

Swakopmund
Time to give in to this town's friendly Germanic hospitality and gently unwind in rolling mists and timeless sand dunes.

Francistown — 408km — Central Kalahari GR — 414km — Ghanzi — 306km — Gobabis — 202km — Windhoek — 360km — Swakopmund

Sowa Pan (South)
The route skirts south of Sowa Pan. If you take the 4x4 track to the palm-lined village of Mosu, a viewpoint overlooks the sprawling pan from the edge of a tall escarpment.

Ghanzi
Surviving unbelievably well in this hot, dusty, flat terrain – besides the thorny acacias – are the sleek, well-fed cattle. Deceptively dry in torrid summers, the yellow grasses regenerate as luscious, succulent green shoots after the rains.

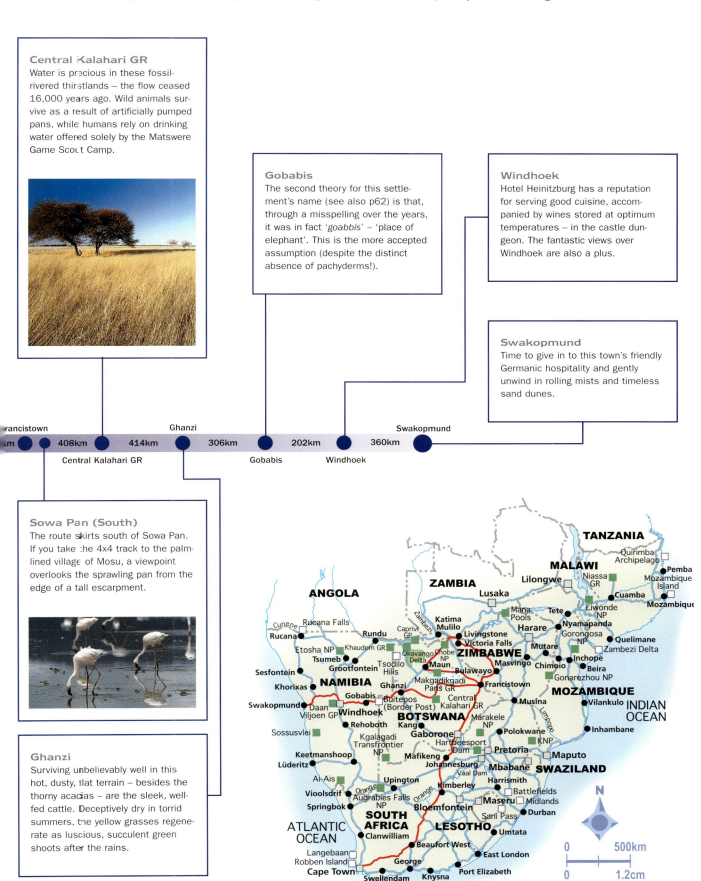

55

Worcester to Gaborone

WORCESTER & HEX RIVER VALLEY

If getting there fast is not your game and you've time to take the slow-train route to Worcester, forego the Huguenot Tunnel (which has lopped 11km/7 miles off the original road) and take rather the Du Toitskloof Pass road. It slowly winds its way through the stony contorted folds of the Du Toits mountains towering so high above you, you have to crane your neck to see where they tear at the skyline. On the other side, a section of the Breede River's long, fertile valley ambles past Worcester, making this town a major table grape and (bulk) wine-producing zone. The only place of interest worth stopping for is the Kleinplasie Living Open Air Museum which, through its replicas of frontier huts and

THE LITTLE KAROO

Together the vast, arid, Little and Great Karoo swallow up almost one-third of South Africa's total area. The classic Karoo landscape is made up of dry biscuit-coloured flatland interrupted by dome-shaped rocky outcrops called kopjes, often capped with an erosion-resistant lid of dolerite. Eons ago volcanic action created the doleritic protrusions which, over time, were whipped and weathered by floods into today's 'rondavel' shapes. Populations in this land are sparse. In place of the San and Khoikhoi who used to roam here are resilient farmers and their woolly sheep.
Tel: 023 449 1000
Email: karootour@internext.co.za
Website: www.centralkaroo.co.za

KAROO NATIONAL PARK

Skip Beaufort West and try this out instead! Just a few kilometres out of Beaufort West, the 600km^2 (235-sq-mile) park is for walkers and lovers of wide open spaces and pure unadulterated silence. Facilities are basic and characterless but a 4x4 trail and a night in a remote mountain hut are what you want to go for. Three trails – an 11km (7-mile) day walk, a fossil trail and a short tree-identification trail – leave from the main restcamp. The park's geology dates back 250 million years and the Karoo's spell as a vast inland sea has yielded fossils of some very strange and fascinating creatures. Despite the Karoo's reputation for featureless sandscapes, there's a surprising outcrop of flat-topped

workshops, recreates the life of the early Dutch pioneers between 1690 and 1900. Here, local people busy themselves with pursuits such as tobacco-twisting, candle-making and *witblits* ('white lightning', a lethal brandy-style potion made from peaches or grapes) distilling. After Worcester, the highway toils on up through the sandstone Hex River mountains, whose highest peaks Matroosberg, and Buffelshoek, are topped in winter with snow-icing. Far, far below like uneven jig-saw puzzle pieces, the vineyards are their most spectacular in the russet, burgundy and gold mantle of autumn.
Tel: 023 356 2041/48 2795
Email: damens@breedevalley.co.za
Website: www.breedevalley.co.za

MATJIESFONTEIN

The nicest way to break the monotonous, unbroken stretch of the N1 is this hotel settlement built in 1900 and offering an unmonotonous respite for the eyes. In 1883 Scotsman James Logan saw an opportunity to create a dining stop along the railway before trains had their own dining coaches. It gained in popularity, and the Lord Milner was touted as a health spa – making a big deal of the dry and clear Karoo air. It opened its white turreted, iron-lace-decorated arms to such esteemed guests as Lord Randolph Churchill, Olive Schreiner and the Sultan of Zanzibar. The two dusty streets of the Victorian-style railway station, post office, tearoom, shop and hotel are, in their entirety, a national monument.
Tel: 023 561 3011
Email: milner2@mweb.co.za
Website: www.matjiesfontein.com

hill-mountains in this park. You could bump into a solitary black rhino, otherwise there are plenty of antelope and gazelle, mountain zebra, bat-eared fox and soaring raptors such as the black eagle. When you continue on your journey, and Beaufort West is behind you, look out for the Three Sisters, the most famous and most distinctive of the Great Karoo's sheer-sided conical hills. They have also given their name to a tiny settlement nearby, where the N12 peels off the N1 and heads up north.
Tel: 023 415 2828
Email: wendyj@parks-sa.co.za
Website: www.parks-sa.co.za

KIMBERLEY BATTLEFIELDS

Although this onetime gold-mining town is better known for its diamonds (see p31), Kimberley has its relics, too, from the 1899–1902 Anglo-Boer War. It was just 30km (19km) south of Kimberley, on the N12, where the Boers took the Brits by surprise after digging themselves into trenches at Magersfontein. Today, a hike along the western face of some hills reveals monuments, memorials and remainders of the trench lines, and a recreation of events in a small site museum puts things in perspective. A military historian keeps war buffs enlightened and amused if they sign up for a one-day battlefields tour. Battle sites Modderrivier, Graspan and Paardeberg are also nearby.
Tel: 053 832 7298
Email: maryanne.snyders@fbdm.co.za
Website: www.northerncape.org.za

GABORONE

It is clear that this city expanded from rural settlement to metropolis on overly swift feet and with a decided lack of foresight in its planning. Sprawling and disjointed, it supported 250,000 people by 1990 instead of the 20,000 planned for by the Department of Public Works. Featureless shopping malls are its focal point.
Tel: 09267 395 3024
Email: botswanatourism@gov.bw
Website: www.botswanatourism.org

MAFIKENG

Together, the twin towns of Mafikeng and Mmabatho make up the capital of North West province. In character, the two halves are poles apart. Mafikeng – dull suburbia – has a colonial heritage resting mainly on the shoulders of British leader Colonel Baden-Powell and his defence against the Boer siege of 1990. Mmabatho's early role as capital of the 'independent' homeland, Bophuthatswana, was a prerequisite for flashy spending – broad boulevards, grand government offices, a gambling haven and a showcase 80,000-seat sports stadium with no shelter against the blinding sun. If museums are your bag, the displays on the Siege of Mafikeng, the San and Tswana peoples and their hunting tricks are good in the Mafikeng Museum.
Tel: 018 381 3155
Email: tidcmf@yebo.co.za
Website: www.tourismnorthwest.co.za

Chief Gaberone of the Batlokwa tribe settled in the area in the 1880s, and gave his name to today's mushrooming city. While it was still a ramshackle settlement, Rhodes planned his Jameson Raid here in 1895, precipitating the Anglo-Boer War.

TULI BLOCK

The privately owned game conservation area of the Northeast Tuli Game Reserve, butting onto the Tuli Block's commercial farmland, is sandwiched between the great Limpopo to the south and the Shashe to the east. Here, the Mashatu and smaller Tuli game reserves fit into the Northeast Tuli conservation area. The elephant herds are legendary, and big cats – lion, leopard and cheetah – love prowling the reserve's rocky kopjes and lolling in the branches of its dappled riverine forests, as do lynx and wild cat. The night drives (unusual in Botswana), enabling visitors to sneak a peak at these nocturnal creatures, are a treat.
Tel: 09267 395 3024
Email: botswanatourism@gov.bw
Website: www.botswanatourism.org

Francistown to Matobo Hills

FRANCISTOWN
This gateway town to northern Botswana can claim to be where the first murmurings of southern Africa's gold rush started. Prospectors arrived in droves from shores as distant as Australia, and their initial zeal is immortalised in the more-or-less defunct mines with names like Jim's Luck and Bonanza. Francistown is Botswana's second largest centre, evident in the shanty towns attached to its outskirts. Francistown's main thoroughfare, Blue Jacket Street, harks back to a denim-jacketed Australian prospector who, so the story goes, crossed Australia's Western Desert on foot, pushing his trusty wheelbarrow.
Tel: 09267 241 6279/395 3024
Email: botswanatourism@gov.bw
Website: www.botswanatourism.org

MAKGADIKGADI & NXAI
The salt pans at Makgadikgadi are distinctive in their shimmering heat and uninterrupted far-flung empty spaces. In the midday heat haze, eyes deceive you as objects on the horizon float on thin ribbons of water, then melt away into the landscape. The barren, salt-encrusted, silver-grey flatness measures (almost) the length and breadth of Portugal, and is proof of a superlake that once covered much of northern Botswana. The seasonal salt pans left so long ago by the receding waters, particularly Sowa Pan, are Africa's largest flamingo breeding site. During breeding season they transform into a 'pink tide' of crimson-accented greater and

lesser flamingos. With the arrival of the rains (December to March), herds of wildebeest, antelope and zebra migrate from their winter territory around Makgadikgadi's Boteti River to Nxai Pan, predators hot in pursuit. At Kudiakam Pan, a stand of seven giant baobabs – the Seven Sisters – is also called Baines' Baobabs. The famous painter Thomas Baines captured them in his inimitable style in 1862. An unusual National Monument comes in the form of Kubu Island, whose ghostly baobabs and bleached rocks stained by fossilised guano leave an indelible impression. An uninhabited area girded by a ruined stone wall has archeologists speculating on initiation and ritual.
Tel: 09267 397 1405/18 0774
Email: dwnp@gov.bw
Website: www.botswanatourism.org

TREACHEROUS PANS
The crusted surface of the pans is highly deceptive – an invisible watertable can lurk just below the dry-cracked salt crust. Drivers need to be fully self-sufficient, with decent navigating skills (and equipment) as there is precious little by way of landmarks to steer by! Wheels sinking into soft surfaces are common but there is a lack of trees or posts to tie winches to. Travellers should arrive armed with a few imaginative backup plans!
Tel: 09267 395 3024
Email: botswanatourism@gov.bw
Website: www.botswanatourism.org

QUADBIKING
Quadbike excursions are handled at Nata Lodge and Gweta Restcamp. Believed to have a limited impact on the Makgadikgadi ecosystem, quadbiking is better done in convoy because of deluding heat mirages and the distinct absence of landmarks. The capricious watertable should make you wary of veering off demarcated tracks. Otherwise it's a whooping, bone-jarring ride of crackly dips and rises.
Tel: 011 768 2040
Email: bushbandits@intekom.co.za
Website: www.bushbandits.co.za

Hwange

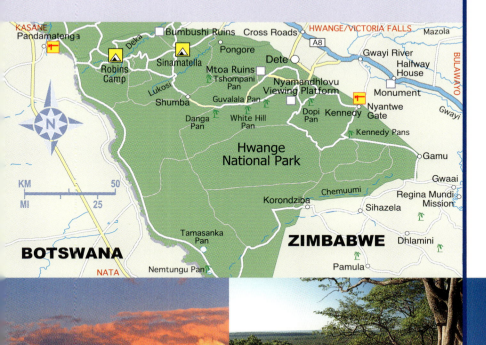

HWANGE NATIONAL PARK

In the 19th century, Ndebele kings used this Zimbabwean tract as a hunting reserve; in 1929 it was turned into a national park to lure Victoria Falls-bound tourists into game-viewing; and by the 1970s, enormous herds of wildlife were assured with 60 pump-driven waterholes. Wildlife, bar poached-out rhino, is still prolific today – large cats inclusive. A series of wildlife-filled short-loop drives near Main Camp keeps most visitors within 10km (6 miles) of here. A highlight is Nyamandhlovu Pan's viewing platform standing high over a waterhole much liked by elephant (Nyamandhlovu can be translated as 'head of the elephant'). The Kennedy Pans are magnificent at dusk when elephants bathe and frolic here.
Tel: 09263 4 706 077/8
Email: natparks@africaonline.co.zw
Website: www.zimparks.com

SINAMATELLA & ROBINS CAMPS

A full morning's drive takes visitors to Sinamatella perched on a 50m (165ft) granite ridge giving on to a stunning panorama. This is a place where, come night-time, lions cough and hyenas let out their deliriously chilling whoop. Robins Camp, for some reason, also draws lion to its terrain. Come daytime, crocodile and hippo lurk in Mandavu dam, while elephant and hippo play and snort in Masuma dam. The graceful, scimitar-horned sable antelope, whose head is the national parks emblem, is also pretty much a guaranteed sight in the park. Look out for rarer specimens too – the pangolin (scaly anteater), aardvark and wild dog.

MATOBO NATIONAL PARK

The Matobo Hills have been inhabited for 40,000 years – first by the San hunter-gatherers, then the Torwa who built Kame, next Changamire and his Rozvi clans, and finally the Zulus, who edged out the Rozvi. It is sacred, a place of power, and the spiritual home and final resting place of Mzilikazi, founder of the Ndebele nation. The Ndebele's sacred rain shrine Mjelele is hidden in a rock cleft in the hills. Also here, within a natural amphitheatre formed by massive balls of stone, is the simple, austere, bronze plaque of Cecil John Rhodes' grave. The Shona Karanga, living here before the Ndebele, called it the 'high place of *midzimu* spirit elders'. Today World's View is also known as Malindidzimu, 'dwelling place of benevolent spirits'. Falling away on all sides is a giant's playground of knuckled hills – ridge after granite ridge to the fiery horizon. The park has its share, too, of cave paintings: a human-crocodile figure at Mjelele; kudu, giraffe and zebra in flight at Nswatugi; 2m-high giraffes, a snake with an antelope's head and fascinating domestic scenes at Silozwane; and rare outline paintings at the White Rhino Shelter. White rhino have been introduced into Whovi Game Park and can be seen ambling among the dramatic pinnacles and boulder stacks.
Tel: 09263 4 706 077/8
Email: natparks@africaonline.co.zw
Website: www.zimparks.com

CHOBE

CHOBE'S HABITAT DIVERSITY

Visitors enter the northern section of Chobe through Kasane, meeting point of four countries. This park of over 11,000km^2 (4300 sq miles) lies to the northeast of the Okavango Delta. The largest numbers of wildlife on the southern African subcontinent roam its incredible diversity of habitats. Four distinct areas in the park are the Chobe River frontage and the floodplain around Serondela campsite; the grassy woodlands of the central Nogatsaa region dotted with pans; the papyrus and reeded swampland of the Linyanti River; and the vast Savuti plain (the 'marsh' is no longer) and Mababe Depression edged by the 20m-high (65ft) Magwikwe sand ridge. Dense riverine forest and swampland tranform into mopane and mixed deciduous forest, which in turn opens out to grassy plains, rising into rocky kopje outcrops at Savuti.

SAVUTI CHANNEL

Records of early explorers show that the Savuti Marsh was fed constantly by the Savuti Channel from 1850 to 1880 but, abruptly, the flow stopped for 80 years. Water flowed in the channel again from 1957 to 1982 (with intermittent breaks), but in recent decades this again appears to be inexplicably ceasing. After much study, geologists have surmised that underground faults are still in motion, with the crust buckling and heaving periodically and thus affecting river flow.

Huge colonies of painted carmine bee-eaters claw to the vertical riverbanks in which they nest. In summer, they engage in colourful acrobatics over the river as they snare fleeing insects in mid-air. Look out, too, for the iridescent shimmer of the malachite kingfisher.

CHOBE RIVERFRONT

Drawn like pins to a magnet, animals of every hue, size and shape home in on the riverbanks to slake their thirst in the hot, dry summer. Only rhino is absent from the endless parade; this is made up for by rarer, seldom seen species such as the small puku antelope and oribi, the world's smallest grazing antelope. Lion and leopard love hanging out on the long arched branches of the riverine woolly caper bushes. Not to be missed is a three-hour afternoon cruise navigating the romping hippos in the Chobe and watching an incomparable African sunset.

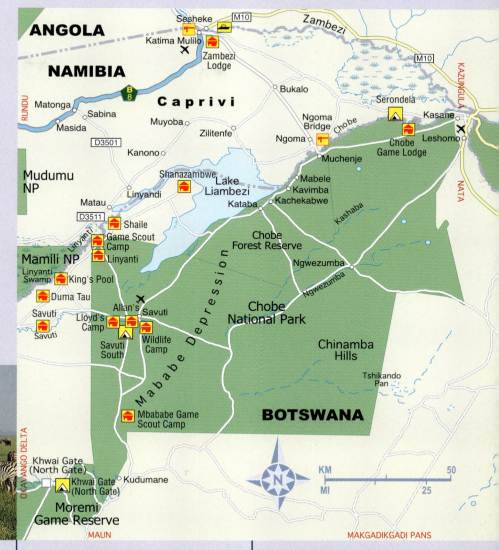
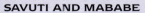

SAVUTI AND MABABE

Massive herds of elephant and buffalo cross these expansive flat plains, which also happen to be the favoured territory of prowling lion. Arriving in late November for their foaling season, a sea of black-and-white striped rumps undulates between Linyanti and Savuti, heralding the start of the zebra migration. Heavily in tow are the predators – leopard, cheetah and hyena. Not uncommon here, too, is wild dog. If the animals are not sufficient to catch your attention, there is 4000-year-old (but badly faded) rock art at Gobabis Hill.

LINYANTI MARSHES

Great, dark herds of buffalo and water-loving elephant often drink and splash about in the broad swathe of flooded plain expanding out from the Linyanti River. Once the zebra populations have finished with their foaling in Savuti, they head out on the road again, arriving at Linyanti in their masses between February and April. This migratory pattern could very well change, however, with the present drying of the Savuti Marsh. So watch it while you still can. . .

SLEEPING IN CHOBE

For visitors to Chobe the options are endless. They come in the form of lodges, luxury camps, tented and bush camps, and campsites with running water and ablution facilities. With the prolific presence of water, most are either perched on riverbanks or look across lovely waterscapes.

Bulawayo to Swakopmund

CENTRAL KALAHARI GAME RESERVE

Travellers enter through the Matswere gate in the northeastern corner of the reserve. Plonked dead-centre of Botswana, this is also the heart of the Kalahari. It is more than 16,000 years ago that rivers ceased to flow here. But on closer inspection the featureless, flat, shimmering sea of baked sand hides the signs of strangely adapted plant and animal life: devil's claw – a spiky weed pod containing natural aspirin – dung beetles, and the ubiquitous tall-horned gemsbok, picking its solitary way through the hot sand. The reserve takes up almost 53,000km^2 (20,600 sq miles) and the barren spaces within it are the last domain of the nomadic Kalahari San.
Tel: 09267 397 1405
Email: dwnp@gov.bw
Website: www.botswanatourism.org

THE GHANZI LANDSCAPE

On the long, long road to Ghanzi and then to Buitepos, Botswana's border with Namibia, don't expect the Kalahari landscape to change for a while. Stretch after stretch of sandveld in various shades of ochre and red from the quartz in the sand are broken only by patches of yellowed grassland (this does turn a delicious green after the rains) and clumps of hardy, twisted acacias. At least these come with descriptive names like camelthorn, candle-pod and *mhahu*. Luckily cattle and ostrich find the seeded grasses and the thorn and scrub bush nutritious – the Ghanzi area is a very successful animal farming zone.
Tel: 09267 395 3024
Email: botswanatourism@gov.bw
Website: www.botswanatourism.org

Two water-based plants the Kalahari desertlands manage to produce (putting a new spin on the San-derived name, 'thirst-land') are the tsamma melon and the gemsbok cucumber. Both the San people and all animals of the desert get moisture and sustenance from these two hardy 'vegetable-fruits'.

BUITEPOS TO GOBABIS

Consisting of little more than a customs and immigration post and petrol station, there's not too much to crow about where Buitepos is concerned. The tarred, dull and straight Trans-Kalahari highway forges its way to Gobabis before the final stretch to Windhoek. There are two speculatory origins for Gobabis's name (see p55). The most colourful is 'place of quarrels' in the Khoikhoi language. During its earliest beginnings in 1856, a missionary tried (unsuccessfully) to steer squabbles between the Damara and the Khoikhoi into a peace agreement. Unappreciated, he was sent packing some 10 years later. Hostile relations then crescendoed, instigating, in 1895, an onslaught of German troops to the settlement.
Tel: 09264 62 562 428
Email: info@namibiatourism.com.na
Website: www.namibiatourism.com.na

WINDHOEK

It's a relief to eventually approach the range of low hills on which Windhoek (see also p88) has settled. Although, in its staid orderliness, not the most exciting of towns, during the week there is an interesting miscellany of cultures – Owambo, Kavango, Herero, Damara and Khoikhoi – mingling on the streets. If you pass Namibia's yellow and white double-storeyed parliament building, consider its name, the Tintenpalast – meaning 'ink palace' and representing, it's said, all the ink that goes into government's excessive paperwork! Windhoek's oldest surviving building is the Alte Feste ('old fort'), built in 1889 to house the first German protectionary troops.

Tel: 09264 61 290 6000
Email: info@namibiatourism.com.na
Website: www.namibiatourism.com.na

SWAKOPMUND

This seaside town is marked by its cavalcade of tall dunes retreating from the sea to the flat gravel plains of the interior – punctuated now and then by lonely *inselbergs* and squat, interlocking hill ranges. It's also marked by the sea mists that regularly roll in, sometimes penetrating 50km (30 miles) inland. There's a sense of *gemütlichheit* in the strong Germanic influence – evident in the spoken language, architectural features and food. A paved and landscaped walkway threads for over 1km (half a mile) along the seafront to the red-and-white lighthouse and an iron jetty runs out to sea with benches for sitting and contemplating life.

Tel: 09264 64 404 827/3 129
Email: namibi@iway.na
Website: www.namibi.org.na

Check out Post Street, in the heart of Windhoek. Along this pedestrian mall is a fountain at which stands a sculpture of steel columns capped by 33 of the original 77 Gibeon meteorites. They were discovered near Gibeon in southern Namibia and are speculated to have been part of the largest meteor shower in the world – dated to some 600 million years ago.

SPITZKOPPE

Situated northeast of Swakopmund, the Spitzkoppe rises some 1700m (5500ft) above the dusty plains of the southern fringes of Damaraland. A day drive takes visitors through the desert terrain of this region, which evolves from Skeleton Coast dunes to desert mountain to the scrub-covered inland plateaus. The granite *inselberg* of Spitzkoppe – remnant of an ancient volcano – is honed to a sharp peak at its highest point and is loved by rock climbers. Elsewhere on this outcrop are rhino rock paintings. On the Pondoks nearby, curious visitors can climb along a wire cable to Bushman's Paradise where, contrary to the name, shellac paint has ruined the rhino paintings.

Tel: 09264 61 255 977/0 558
Email: office.nacobta@iway.na
Website: www.nacobta.com.na

ACTION IN SWAKOPMUND

Adventure tourism is being milked for what it's worth in Swakopmund's dune playground. Speedsters can tear up and down the slopes, spraying sand trails as they go astride dune buggies, quadbikes or sand boards. Skydivers get to see rippled dune-fields from a different perspective. On terra firma (or is it aqua?), ducks, cormorants, pelicans, flamingos (in season) and waders congregate at Swakop River mouth. When you're tired-out by all this activity, The Tug restaurant, a beached tugboat once called *Dame Hugo*, has a wonderful pub and good seafood – particularly when experienced from the glassed-in table overlooking the seething seas below.

Tel: 09264 64 404 827
Email: namibi@iway.na
Website: www.namibi.org.na

Henties Bay & Skeleton Coast

The icy Benguela current pushing up the Namib coast from the Antarctic sucks in and traps the humid air that normally would cross the shores and move inland. For this reason, the Namib desert remains among the driest in the world.

HENTIES BAY
Eighty kilometres (50 miles) north of Swakopmund, along the coastal salt road, the Omaruru flows into the Atlantic. In 1929 a fishing enthusiast, Major Hentie van der Merwe, began fishing here, and before he knew it, a little fishing resort had sprung up in the bay. It's said that in summer, the settlement's population swells to 10,000. Despite the windy, sand-blasted coastline, anglers from all over southern Africa descend in bakkies bristling with fishing rods, burly sunburnt fishermen at the wheel. Word has it that the oddly shaped pool tables in the Spitzkoppe beer garden are worth a raised eyebrow. As the most northerly settlement on the Namibian Atlantic coast, travellers can refuel and stock up on supplies here.
Tel: 09264 64 501 143
Email: info@hentiesbay.com
Website: www.hentiesbay.com

SKELETON COAST
Early Portuguese explorers called it 'as areias do inferno' – the sands of hell! This treacherous, fog-blanketed coast has lured too many unsuspecting ships to its shores but, disappointingly, there is little trace other than scattered rusty remains. Travellers require a permit to explore this inhospitable, waterless expanse and are reminded of it by the skull and crossbones adorning the entry gates! Terrace and Torra bays have campsites, the latter amid soaring, crescent barchan dunes. The fishing is good, as is the birdlife – many waders migrate here from the Northern Hemisphere. You could also spot a black-backed jackal or brown hyena on its way to stalk a seal.
Tel: 09264 67 304 716
Email: ulrika@namibiareservations.com
Website: www.namibiareservations.com

NAMIB-NAUKLUFT PARK
Formed from a conglomeration of several parks and geographical areas, the Namib-Naukluft covers over 23,000km^2 (8900 sq miles) of desert and semi-desert. It encompasses the wondrous Sossusvlei dune sea, the birdlife at Sandwich Harbour and even the Welwitschia Drive outside Swakopmund. The park's ever-changing shadowed dunescape originating in Sossusvlei ends suddenly at Kuiseb River, just south of Walvis Bay, giving way to gravel plains interrupted by isolated kopjes in different shades of brown. A protrusion of parkland in the east rises up to the high-sided granite-based Naukluft plateau, its cliffs cut by streams and narrow ravines through overlying porous limestone bands.
Tel: 09264 61 236 975/85 7000
Email: reservations@nwr.co.na
Website: www.nwr.com.na

Sossusvlei

SANDWICH HARBOUR & KUISEB

Still in the Namib-Naukluft, some 50km (30 miles) south of Walvis Bay, wave and silt action are changing the face of Sandwich Harbour, whose protected – and less saline – lagoon (because of freshwater springs flowing into it) used to attract both fresh- and saltwater birds in their thousands. Nevertheless, waterbirds and flamingos still congregate here. Almost directly east of the coast, straight across the park to its easternmost reaches, is the broad, sandy and mostly dry Kuiseb riverbed. Visitors can camp out at a site near the river bridge, but only when the river's not flowing. At the main Canyon, dramatic walls rising sheer from the sand enfold a veritable maze of narrow gorges.

Tel: 09264 61 255 977/0 558
Email: office.nacobta@iway.na
Website: www.nacobta.com.na

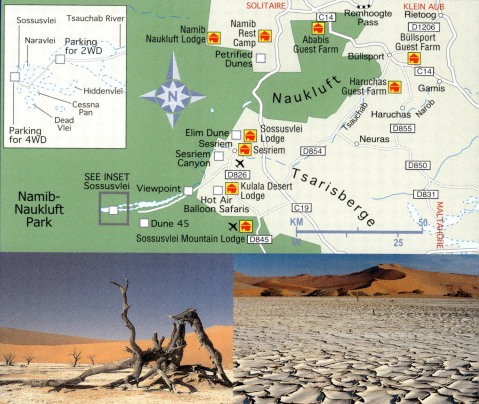

SESRIEM CANYON

The Tsauchab River's slow, inexorable, erosive action through 15 million-year-old bands of sand and gravel conglomerate produced this kilometre-long (half a mile) canyon. Visitors can amble between its 30m-high (110ft) walls of multilayered rock and marvel at nature's relentless power. 'Sesriem' is derived from the Afrikaans words for the 'six thongs' that needed to be tied together to lower a bucket into the water at the foot of the gorge. There are still pools in the gorge today. Sesriem is the headquarters for trips into Sossusvlei – permits are required.

Tel: 09264 61 290 6000
Email: info@namibiatourism.com.na
Website: www.namibiatourism.com.na

THE DRIVE

If visitors want to capture this most photographed spectacle of nature in the gentle light of sunrise, they need to overnight at or around Sesriem (plenty of official campsites) to catch the opening of the gates. There is still quite a drive along a sand-and-gravel road to the 2WD carpark (only 4x4s can make the last 4km/2 miles into the pan, but open jeeps do ferry visitors in). Most people will stop along the way to click-click at Dune 45 – which rears into the sky at exactly 45km (28 miles) from Sesriem and has a couple of perfectly placed trees silhouetted against its base.

THE SPECTACLE

A sight that begs to be seen – this multitude of gigantic coppery-red parabolic dunes are said to be the highest and oldest in the world. They march (motionlessly) across 32,000km^2 (12,500 sq miles) of western Namibia – because of changing wind directions they don't move, their stability making them the most vegetated of all dunes. Some touch the sky at 200m (656ft) and the ever-changing light produces, at times, a knife-edged spine splitting two halves into high-contrast light and shade, at others an undulating sea of soft ochre-orange curves. You can climb the dunes or simply watch the procession of tiny ant-people winding along the ridgetops.

CENTRAL KALAHARI GAME RESERVE

RESERVE FACILITIES
The summer months from November to March are a blistering 40°C (104°F) and over, so better you stay away. April to May or September to October present a milder, more bearable alternative. Camping grounds are basic and it's crucial to note that Matswere Game Scout Camp near the northeastern entry gate is the only source of drinkable water. If you're looking for scenic surrounds at your campsite, you get this in the form of thorny acacias at Deception Pan and the 'ghost' trees of Piper Pans.

KALAHARI SAN
The initial focus of the Central Kalahari reserve was to create a traditional hunting and gathering sanctuary for the last groups of the Bushman population, the Kalahari San. Here they lived a nomadic existence, searching for sources of water, wildlife, and edible and water-based plants. They were relocated, however, for wildlife conservation and tourism, and presently live in small village communities on the fringes of the reserve.

DESOLATE TERRAIN
The lost Missionaries' Road, which once carved its way across the inhospitable interior carrying the early pioneers, is identifiable today only by a rusty trail of broken, sun-ravaged wagons. The only thing that grows along the ancient Deception Valley are isolated groves of umbrella thorn and buffalo thorn acacias, whose roots are sometimes buried 50m (165ft) deep in the sand to tap into underground water. Lion are sometimes spotted dozing under the acacias, and once the sun sets, brown hyena skulk across the sands. At the pans, water is artificially pumped from subterranean sources to sustain the wildlife.

KHUTSE GAME RESERVE
Khutse tags onto the bottom of the Central Kalahari reserve like the rudder of a boat. This reserve's closeness to Gaborone attracts lots of weekend visitors to its dry grassland plains dotted with acacias. Its prolific pans – relics of the ancient superlake once covering northern Botswana – make sure the wildlife doesn't go thirsty, and the special treat here is the wild cats. Lion, leopard and cheetah all call Khutse home. Cheetah, in particular, are partial to the stretches of open plain for their 120kph (75mph) sprints as they high-tackle their prey.

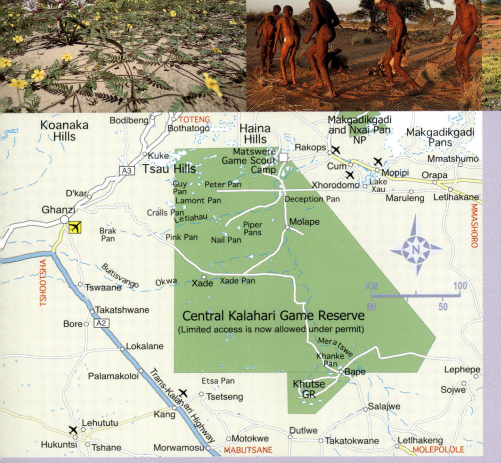

SWAKOPMUND SURROUNDS

CAPE CROSS SEALS
If seals are your bag (and you don't mind the smell!), the Cape Cross Seal Reserve, north of Henties Bay, is a noisy breeding ground for Cape fur seals. Estimates vary from 80,000 right up to 250,000 during breeding season around November/December! On another tack, the crosses giving the cape its name make an interesting story. Portuguese explorer Diego Cão planted a 2m-high (6ft) cross here in 1485

WELWITSCHIA DRIVE
A round trip of up to four hours, this drive runs east of Swakopmund and remains within the confines of the Namib-Naukluft Park. As you cruise through the gravel plains of the Namib, the almost prehistoric, dusty welwitschias (*Welwitschia mirabilis*) crop up singly, looking positively wilted and dishevelled. You'd never believe that they start out with only two long, leathery leaves – by the time the wind has finished playing its games, they've been torn into multiple frayed strips. Most medium-sized plants are 1000 years old (the older ones are believed to have existed for 2000 years!) and they survive on condensation from the coastal fogs.

MOUNTAINS OF THE MOON
Further east of the Welwitschia Drive is a great roving expanse of tightly packed dips and hills, like scoured knuckles in shades of black, brown and grey. Sometimes you're driving in among them, at other times you're on an escarpment looking down on them as they disappear into the hazy horizon. Carved out of the landscape by the Swakop River, they do resemble a surreal moonscape – or at least, how one imagines the moon to be.

to honour his king. It was removed in 1893 by a German sailor, after which it found its way into the Oceanographical Museum in Berlin. The following year, Kaiser Wilhelm I insisted that a replica (with the original inscription and an added one in German) be re-placed at Cape Cross. It stands there today, together with a dolerite cross which actually occupies the original spot.

5 SWAKOPMUND TO VICTORIA FALLS (ZAMBIA)

National West Coast Recreation Area
If you're not in a hurry and you're prepared to stop and smell the roses (in this case, actually, it's the not-so-sweet-smelling seals), stop off at the Cape Cross Seal Reserve on the coast directly north of Swakopmund. The eared Cape fur seals are in fact not a true seal species; they belong to the sea lion family.

Daan Viljoen Game Park
If, after having spent so much time in true wilderness, you can't face the civilisation of Windhoek, turn the wheel towards Daan Viljoen (see also p17) for your night stop. Share Augeigas dam with the waterbirds and revel in the rolling hills and thorn trees while you watch the sinking sun.

Swakopmund — 756km — Cunene/Kunene — 893km — Windhoek — 452km — Grootfontein — 250

Kaokoland and Kunene
In the Herero language, *kaoko* is 'left-hand side' (of the river) while *kunene* is 'right-hand side', hence Kaokoland describes the land to the south of the river and Kunene implies any land to the north (that is, Angola).

Grootfontein
If you haven't already seen it, the Hoba meteorite (see also p22) is worth a detour on the C42 to Tsumeb. Turn off on the D2859, which has a trail of signposts. Roughly 3x3m (10x10ft) in size, it's the largest known single meteorite on earth. It's speculated that other fragments could exist undiscovered – all of them part of a once much larger meteorite.

The local Leya people of Zambia make offerings each February to the ancestral spirits they believe still dwell in the Zambezi's Batoka gorge. The Zimbabwean Tonga people are protected by their serpent-cum-fish rivergod, Nyaminyami.

Rundu
Between Rundu and the Caprivi Strip, travellers will notice roadside stalls selling local Kavango handicrafts and carvings. The Kavango ingenuity is expressed in the form of stools, walking sticks, masks and wild animals, all fashioned out of wild teak.

Livingstone Island
Having been taken to the island now named after him, David Livingstone wrote in his diary: '[They] brought me to an island in the middle of the river, on the edge of the lip over which the water rolls. Creeping with awe to the verge, I peered down into a large rent which had been made from bank to bank.'

Zambezi Bridge
Constructed of steel in the early 1900s, this single-arch, cantilevered bridge spanning the Zambezi River was designed by Sir Douglas Fox.

Rundu — 516km — Katima Mulilo — 193km — Via Zambia — Livingstone — 10km — Victoria Falls

Caprivi Strip
Dense woodland, tangled and glossy greenery, and an untouched wildness to the unruly vegetation – the Caprivi lodges aim to make the most of this stage-setting along this expanse of fertile floodplain, and most have striking riverbank locations.

69

Swakopmund to Sesfontein

BRANDBERG NATURE RESERVE

From the B2 heading out of Swakopmund, the route peels off north towards Damaraland – major 4x4 territory. You're now in flat scrub country, so when the tall imposing Brandberg massif makes itself apparent on the horizon, it comes as a surprise to the senses. Why it's called 'brandberg' (burning mountain) is not at first evident, as it's sometimes streaked grey-white, sometimes has reddish-hued potential (with a little imagination), and is sometimes pockmarked with tenacious trees. It's likely that at times the rock takes on a glow as it stands reflected in the dying sun. Famous for its White Lady painting, Brandberg divulges a great many

THE WHITE LADY

You need to want to see this ancient painting, especially when it's a searing 40°C (104°F), as it demands an energy expending walk together with a guide, which could take up to an hour if agility is not at the high end of your fitness scale. It's protected by a railing but stands about 40cm (16in) tall. Speculation puts it at 16,000 years old! At first believed to be a lady because of the figure's long, straight, light-tinted hair – this fact also confused early experts who professed her to follow the Cretan or Egyptian artwork style – it's now possible that it's a male decorated with painted clay in a shamanic situation.
Tel: 09264 61 255 977/85 7000
Email: reservations@nwr.com.na
Website: www.nwr.com.na

TWYFELFONTEIN & BURNT MOUNTAIN

The long, sandy road to Twyfelfontein is worth the drive alone through the narrow Aba-Huab valley lined with mind-boggling rock terrain. All around, an ever-changing mountainscape dominates larger than life: at times pebbled and stony, at others, boulder-strewn or baring a shattered cliff-face, at yet others, covered with scrub and tenacious, tortured trees. Then there are the 2500 or so petroglyphs – rock engravings – and paintings that combine to create Twyfelfontein's intensely special art gallery. The mountain itself, a gorgeous orange-red at the end of the day, has an aura of mystique with its bizarre, eroded shapes, while the more unusual engravings – a lion with an erect tail, a seal (so

more to tenacious hikers. Best experienced on a multiple-day excursion, a local guide can help you track down the more elusive sites. Numas ravine cuts into the western face and will reveal rock art depicting a snake, giraffe and an antelope, with more paintings further along, near a spring. On the eastern face, the shelters and overhangs of Tsisab ravine (White Lady territory) feature many more paintings – but not before some strenuous clambering over massive boulders. Hikers can camp at unofficial sites in both ravines but be aware there's no water; otherwise, there's the Brandberg campsite.
Tel: 09264 61 285 7200/000
Email: reservations@nwr.com.na
Website: www.nwr.com.na

DAMARALAND

Because of its remoteness, this vast wilderness extending east of the Skeleton Coast Park and northward to Kaokoland can only be explored properly in a 4x4. None of the roads are tarred, sizable towns do not exist and western civilisation is present only in the form of lodges and, in many cases, community-run campsites for travellers. The Damara people subsist with their livestock in this unforgiving terrain. As you progress north, the dryness manifests in fleshy, thorny euphorbias, umbrella'd canopies of camelthorn acacias and the shepherd's tree which, most times, doesn't appear to offer too much shade to shepherds overcome by the heat.
Tel: 09264 61 290 6000
Email: info@namibiatourism.com.na
Website: www.namibiatourism.com.na

far from the sea!) and two tiny handprints – reflect the experiences of ancient peoples living here from around 300BC. Nearby, Burnt Mountain (Verbrandeberg) rises at the foot of a 12km (7-mile) volcanic ridge. Contrary to reports that it glows at sunset, it has a desolate, brown, stony face covered in black streaks reminiscent of a furnace, as if it really has been burnt. Across the road from it, at a cleared parking area, visitors can descend a steep path to the Organ Pipes, a 100m (109yd) row of thin, fluted columns where cooling dolerite has split into vertical lengths.
Tel: 09264 61 255 977/0 558
Email: office.nacobta@iway.na
Website: www.nacobta.com.na

PETRIFIED FOREST

Closest of the sites in the vicinity of Khorixas is the Petrified Forest to the west – not exactly a 'forest', rather a hillside of scattered broken fossilised logs, the longest measuring 30m (98ft) with a circumference of 6m (20ft). A local guide takes you on a 500m (550yd) amble, explaining how the logs were thought to have been carried here by floodwaters from melting ice some 260 million years ago. The logs, soaked through with water rich in silica (a form of quartz) over time were preserved in perfect form – take a close look at the bark and concentric rings in cross-section.
Tel: 09264 61 250 558
Email: office.nacobta@iway.na
Website: www.nacobta.com.na

SOUTH OF ETOSHA

As you nose your dust trail ever north across Damaraland, it's your overnight stops that break the monotony of the flat scrub landscape. The following, off the C35, are worth a look-see. Huab Lodge's luxurious thatched bungalows sit on the banks of the Huab River (most times, dry), amid the granite kopjes of a private game reserve. Here, hot springs could lure you in place of the pool or you could be persuaded to stay awhile for a game drive, guided hike or horse outride to rock paintings. Further north, Kavita Lion Lodge, bordering the southwest corner of Etosha, has bungalows and a pool, but its appeal lies more in the guided walks and excursions into Etosha as well as Kaokoland. You will also come face to face with the rogue or injured lions that are nurtured here. Further west, near Etosha's border, Hobatere Lodge's thatched bungalows, pool and waterhole are on the Otjovasandu River. The desert landscape of escarpment and valley has inspired some writers to compare it with the Great Rift Valley. Judge for yourself. Wildlife walks and drives explore the lodge's own ranchlands, with forays into Etosha's western expanses.
Tel: 09264 61 285 7200
Email: reservations@nwr.com.na
Website: www.nwr.com.na

VINGERKLIP

Not to be confused with the Finger of God south of Mariental that toppled off its perch in 1988! This giant chalky Vingerklip, the limestone remnant of erosive action in the Ugab River floodplain over many millions of years, stands 75km (47 miles) east of Khorixas. It's spotted miles before you get to its massive base and a human figure beside its gigantic girth is reduced to an inconsequential speck as it rears to 35m (115m). Its most fingerlike feature is the 'thumb' protruding at its crown. Views from here over the heavily scarped valley are stupendous – descriptions of it as the Arizona of Namibia are totally apt.
Tel: 09264 61 256 580
Email: norelle@namibian.org
Website: www.namibian.org

SESFONTEIN

For travellers, this town is Damaraland's most northerly remnant of civilisation, set in shale and limestone hills. It heralds the even wilder Kaokoland. Its landmark is the German fort, built four years after a military post was set up here in 1896 following the rinderpest outbreak. The intention was to monitor cattle disease, with the added headache of curbing poaching and arms smuggling. It (of course) fell into disrepair before it was salvaged as a lodge. Those looking for a little extra to their stop here can join a day tour to a Himba or Damara village, or visit rock paintings.
Tel: 09264 61 285 7200, 65 275 534
Email: reservations@nwr.com.na
Website: www.nwr.com.na

Kaokoland to Khomas Hochland

THE DORSLAND TREKKERS
Northeast of Sesfontein, between Ombombo and Otjondeka, is the first of the monuments to the tough, weather-beaten Dorsland trekkers. They were an intensely religious group living in the Transvaal who packed their wagons and headed into the sunset after Reverend Thomas Burgers, whose teachings they weren't quite in synch with, was elected the new president in 1872. Dubbed the *doppers* (meaning 'dampers' after their propensity for blocking all efforts at progressive reform), their idealistic zeal had them trekking across the Kalahari *dorsland* ('thirstland') to find their land of Beulah – the Old Testament's Land of Israel, earmarked for 'God's chosen people'.
Tel: 021 850 0010
Email: janjoubertsafaris@absamail.co.za
Website: www.namibiatourism.com.na

RUACANA FALLS
Before the Calueque dam was constructed 20km (12 miles) upstream of the Cunene River, the Ruacana falls used to put on a far more dramatic display. Today, the pumping volumes of water are diverted through the underground turbines of the hydro-electric power station. The little town of Ruacana, 15km (9 miles) from the falls, itself grew from a camp established for the workers. After decent summer rains, water still tumbles and pummels spectacularly over the rocks – March to April are usually good months to see this. The Cunene's waters first separate into rocky channels before hightailing it over the tall escarpment and coursing through a 2km-long (1-mile) gorge.
Tel: 09264 61 256 580
Email: norelle@namibian.org
Website: www.namibian.org

EPUPA FALLS
The best thing about this area is its remoteness and absence of visitors. Tenacity gets you here, and if it's wildness you're after, that's exactly what you get. The falls are contained within channels, water cascading in a series of drops and disappearing into a dark, narrow cleft. Epupa ('falling waters' in Herero) is ascribed to the most elongated watery ribbon, something over 30m (100ft). It's said that at low waters, visitors should try wallowing in the pools above the falls; the eddies and rapids are manageable if you hold on tight (no drifting towards the lip!) – but just a little too hectic for the crocodiles.
Tel: 09264 61 255 977/32 740
Email: epupa@mweb.com.na
Website: www.epupa.com.na

DORSLAND MONUMENTS
Heading northwest after the monument near Otjondeka to Kaoko Otavi, you'll come across the ruins of a church (a heap of rubble, despite its status as a National Monument, proclaimed in 1951!) in the Joubert mountains. Thereafter, via the D3705, D3700 and D3701, Swartbooisdrift on the border with Angola marks the spot where these hardy pioneers crossed the Kunene – spelled Cunene in Angola – to create the foundations of their new home. Despite their idealism, heat and exhaustion, fever and dysentery claimed the lives of many. Over time, the disillusioned group dispersed, some back to the Transvaal, others to Grootfontein east of Etosha.
Tel: 021 850 0010
Email: janjoubertsafaris@absamail.co.za
Website: www.namibiatourism.com.na

RAFTING ON THE KUNENE
Half- to five-day whitewater rafting trips are the highlight of activities run by the Kunene River Lodge. Starting upstream of Swartbooisdrift at the Ondarusu rapids, trained guides manoeuvre rafts over frothing turbulence that can culminate in testing grade IV waters, eventually finishing downstream at Epupa falls. If names like the Crusher, Smash and Dead Man's Grave don't get the adrenaline coursing through your veins, nothing will. For more sedate thrills, there's quadbiking (maybe not so sedate), birdwatching and a more liquid form of entertainment, booze cruises on the river.
Tel: 09264 65 274 300/56 580
Email: info@kuneneriverlodge.com
Website: www.namibian.org

OWAMBOLAND
The Owambo country north of Etosha comes as a shock after the unpopulated Kaokoveld. Over half of Namibia's population lives in this dusty, overgrazed zone of hot, debilitating winds – the dust haze sometimes so pervasive it's necessary to use headlights, creating a bizarre dust-embalmed time capsule. January–February rains transform this into a system of shallow watercourses and vleis called *oshanas*, precious to the communities for their subsistence farming. If you're looking for diversion, at Uutapi (Ombalantu) is a gigantic baobab – the locals call it *Omukwa* – that has been in its time a safe haven for cattle against invaders, a chapel, and an interrogation chamber for prisoners of war.
Tel: 09264 61 255 977
Email: office.nacobta@iway.com.na
Website: www.nacobta.com.na

Kaokoland

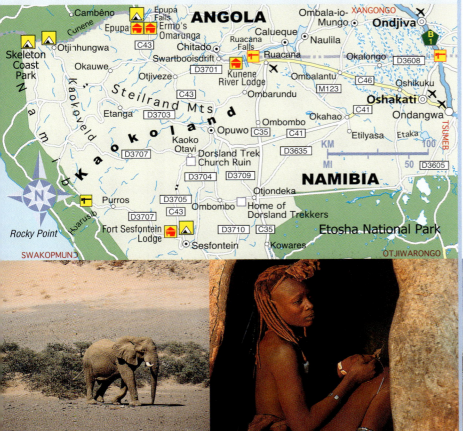

KHOMAS HOCHLAND
Erosive forces over hundreds of millions of years have abraded and sculpted this upland into ridges, valleys and hills marching across the landscape. Its heights modulating between 1750m and 2000m (5740–6560ft), the Khomas Hochland bridges Namibia's inland central plateau and the dramatic flatland of the Namib plains. Three dizzying passes cutting through the Hochland, Bosua, Ushoogte and Gamsberg, connect the coastal strip with Windhoek.
Tel: 09264 61 290 6000
Email: info@namibiatourism.com.na
Website: www.namibiatourism.com.na

CROSSING THE DESERT
Also referred to as the Kaokoveld, this primeval part of Africa demands that any traveller crossing its expanse be 100% self-sufficient – food, water, medical supplies, fuel and vehicle spare parts – as there are no towns, very few lodges, and a lack of fresh water. Roads are gravel tracks and you'll find you often average only 50kph (30mph) – Opuwo to Epupa falls is a full day's travel, for example. A convoy of two or more vehicles almost goes without saying. The stark, rugged desert peaks of the northwest are the most remote, with the vertiginous Van Zyl's Pass bridging the transition between flat, barren wasteland and upland plateau.
Tel: 09264 65 220 805, 61 290 6000
Email: info@namibiatourism.com.na
Website: www.namibiatourism.com.na

THE HIMBA
The only signs of habitation are the scattered beehive huts belonging to semi-nomadic pastoralists, the Himba, descended from the earliest Herero tribes. A very beautiful people, the Himba can be seen following their hardy cattle and goats in search of grazing, distinctive in the fat and ochre body paint that enhances their features and colours their hair. They share their land with the last of the desert elephant (little more than 40) who've adapted so well that they can go four or five days without water, their legs carrying them across 70km (40 miles) in a day to slake their thirst.
Tel: 09264 61 290 6000
Email: info@namibiatourism.com.na
Website: www.namibiatourism.com.na

VON FRANÇOIS FORT
This fort along the C28 (some 55km/34 miles from Windhoek) was named after Major Curt von François who was responsible for establishing military headquarters in Windhoek. The outpost initially protected the route between Swakopmund and today's capital but ended its life as a 'drying out' station for over-imbibing German soldiers. Forty kilometres (25 miles) from Windhoek, the abandoned double-storey Liebig House belonged to Dr R Hartig, head of a farming concern. Built in the early 20th century, the building's wonderful views and derelict fountain in a room downstairs hint at definitely more opulent times.
Tel: 09264 61 290 6000
Email: info@namibiatourism.co.na
Website: www.namibiatourism.com.na

ETOSHA PAN

ETOSHA'S GEOLOGY
The shimmering white salt pan that stretches as far as the eye can see has earned Etosha its name: 'great white place'. Of the park's vast 20,000km^2 (7800 sq miles), the flat saline desert takes up 5000km^2 (1950 sq miles), luring wild animals of all shapes and sizes to benefit from its mineral content. Twelve million years ago, this existed as an immense shallow depression watered by the Kunene River, but climatic changes and tectonic upheaval caused water levels to subside. For only a few days a year, rains fill the dips and channels, with yellow-billed pelicans and pink flamingos massing on the waters.

ETOSHA'S CAMPS
The three camps are distanced about 70km (40 miles) from one another and you don't do the park full justice unless you spend three or so days in at least a couple of them. Perhaps the most historical is Fort Namutoni, with its tower and ramparts (see p22). Habituated warthogs ferreting outside your door and little mongooses darting actively underfoot come with the permit. Visitors love the makalani-palm-fringed pool. The floodlit waterhole is great for vociferous frogs but funnily enough not wildlife – leave that to the game drives. Halali's basic bungalows squat at the foot of dolomite outcrops. The camp crest is a horn, symbolising the old German tradition of blowing it at the end

WHAT YOU NEED TO KNOW
Independent travellers can only explore Etosha's eastern two-thirds; the remaining third in the western extreme is the sole domain of tour operators. Visitors have a selection of three restcamps all with shop, restaurant, fuel and braai sites, and each differing nicely in character. Prebooking and permits are a necessity. Ordinary vehicles can navigate Etosha's gravel roads but a 4x4 allows more freedom in exploring the more difficult tracks and, of course, a better vantage point. Vehicles may not cross the pan but a track does make an inroad to the Etosha lookout, where you are surrounded by the immense dry, cracked, saline crust.

of a hunt. A short walk from the camp winds up to a bouldered kopje where benches in strategic spots look down onto a floodlit waterhole. All manner of wild animals sidle up to drink, rhino included. Okaukuejo's waterhole is legendary for its rhino visitations – and true to form, I once witnessed a snorting, passive-aggressive face-off between three males here. Otherwise, a constant parade of zebra, wildebeest, gemsbok and antelope picks its way up and down to the water. Elephants come to play when the park is dry. Okaukuejo's bungalows are spacious with great outdoor braai spaces.
Tel: 09264 67 229 300 Namutoni
Tel: 09264 67 229 800 Okaukuejo

Amazing strides in technology have enabled permanently placed 24-hour webcams at each of Etosha's camp waterholes. These record the minute-by-minute rank and file of wild animals coming to freshen up. People anywhere in the world can log on to experience the vibe of Africa.

NOAH'S ANIMALS

Etosha's enduring appeal is perhaps the staggering variety – and numbers – of its wildlife. A bit like Noah's Ark which had all the animals, two by two, you're likely to see all of the Big Five (except for buffalo), most of the antelope species (including the rarer sable and roan), blue wildebeest, Burchell's zebra, giraffe, and then a whole lot of the smaller creatures. Two unusual gazelles to look out for are the shy Damara dik-dik and black-faced impala, not often seen elsewhere. Even the perky, wide-eyed curiosity of the diminutive ground squirrel is totally endearing.

Visitors won't fail to miss the ubiquitous – and quite gorgeous – pale chanting goshawk with its salmon-pink legs and beak or the powerfully-winged bateleur, both often poised on high perches. Lappet-faced and white-backed vultures also congregate in the wooded savanna.

ETOSHA'S HIGHLIGHTS

What marks Etosha's environment is how the terrain transforms from dense thickets of mopane woodland to open yellow grasslands, and from thorny acacia scrub to vast flat salt pan. Quite astonishing is that you encounter animals in midday's searing sun as equally as the cooling late afternoon hours. Zebra, giraffe and gemsbok are eternally chewing in the grasslands. Namutoni's reputation for leopard and lion will find you often catching a female lion stalking an animal in the long grasses or snoozing lazily under a tree alongside the road. Olifantsbad near Okaukuejo is elephant paradise, with enormous herds marching in single file over the hill, ears flapping, eager to trumpet and spray and splash in their mudbath.

Khaudom to Victoria Falls (Zambia)

KHAUDOM GAME RESERVE
Even by Namibian standards, this is true wilderness, reinforced by the remoteness of these extreme eastern reaches. Little visited and offering no facilities whatsoever, travellers venture into Khaudom to test their wildlife-tracking skills, as animals are skittish and unused to car engines. Edging onto Botswana's Kalahari, the park's patches of solitary baobabs and dry woodland survive on sandy soils that become impassable during the rains in late November to March. Fossil riverbeds, known as *omuramba*, are lined with reedbeds which rejuvenate in the wet season, luring animals crossing their traditional east–west migratory path.
Tel: 09264 61 285 7000/4 2111
Email: reservations@nwr.com.na
Website: www.nwr.com.na

MAHANGO GAME RESERVE
This reserve (no facilities) sticks out like a thumb off the western end of the Caprivi Strip and in fact is part of the newly created Bwabwata National Park. Its eastern extent butts onto the Okavango River with, as a result, a luxuriant profusion of riverine woodland hiding colourful twittering life of the bird kind. Birding fanatics will be overwhelmed by how many different species they can train their lenses on in the space of a couple of hours' quiet time at the river – look out for the Meyer's and Cape parrots daubed with wild red, green, blue and yellow. Great herds of migrant elephant pass through, too.
Tel: 09264 61 285 7000/200
Email: reservations@nwr.com.na
Website: www.nwr.com.na

MUDUMU NATIONAL PARK
Again, the lie of the land in this park – fringing the Kwando at its western extent – has fostered a beautiful tall-treed setting of green foliage and dappled light. Best in winter (June to October) because wildlife is drawn inexorably to the river's perennial waters, the park is regaining lost ground from its destructive years as a hunting concession. Also passing through, besides the water-loving hippos, crocs and antelope species, are elephant and buffalo. The phrase 'birds for Africa' is most apt here too. If you've had your fill of roughing it (there are no facilities), treat yourself to Lianshulu Lodge's luxurious reed-and-thatch A-frames outside the park.
Tel: 09264 61 285 7000/200
Email: reservations@nwr.com.na
Website: www.nwr.com.na

To spot the wildlife (antelope species including gemsbok and roan, plains game, the large cats, and even wild dog), visitors need to brush up on their knowledge of animal habits – when they stalk their prey, feed, drink, and rest.

CAPRIVI & COMMUNITY
With the formation of Bwabwata, the remaining sectors of the previous Caprivi Game Park have been handed over to rural communities, who engage in subsistence farming in the wetlands and along the river systems. South of Kongola, the Lizauli Traditional Village sets out to inform and entertain visitors with demonstrations of daily life and traditions, from farming and tool-making to music and games. Training and education see individuals recruited as game scouts for the nearby national parks.
Tel: 09264 66 686 802, 61 290 6000
Email: bruno@iway.na
Website: www.namibiatourism.com.na

MAMILI NATIONAL PARK
Much resembling the Okavango Delta, Mamili is Namibia's only conserved swampland. Its land nestles in the crook of a river boundary formed by the Kwando on one side and the Linyanti on the other. When rains are good, the park is flooded between May and August, transforming into channelled wetlands, wooded islands and papyrus marshes. Naturally, semi-aquatic wildlife thrives in this environment, opening up your chances of catching a glimpse of the shy sitatunga, puku, red lechwe and even otters. If you love solitariness, you are quite likely to be the only visitors in this park at any one time.
Tel: 09264 61 236 975/85 7000
Email: nwr@iafrica.com.na
Website: www.nwr.com.na

KATIMA MULILO
Sealing off the eastern end of the Caprivi Strip is regional capital Katima Mulilo, a not-so pretty town redeemed by its extremely pretty wooded surrounds on the Zambezi. The vivid hues of tropical birds and chattering monkeys in the shady trees flanking the river will distract you entirely from the humdrum town. Of course, the fishing is good; doing battle with a razor-toothed tiger fish or the less feisty bream is another worthy distraction. Otherwise, tune-up, refuel and replenish supplies, then quench your thirst at the floating pontoon bar moored at the Zambezi Hotel (do note, though: limited opening hours).
Tel: 09264 66 253 027/5 403
Email: info@namibiatourism.com.na
Website: www.namibiatourism.com.na

LIVINGSTONE
Zambia's old, colonial-style capital (see also p51) is slowly, sleepily reviving itself, but the action very definitely focuses on adventure activities making best use of the Zambezi River's mutable waters. Do stay away in hot and horrid October (38°C; 100°F), made worse by its 90% humidity; and know that the winter months of June to September are dry and dusty. What Livingstone does well is its plethora of secluded, atmospheric lodges along the river. If you're more into white-gloved hospitality, the multimillion-dollar Royal Livingstone, with its green lawns and riverside sundowner deck, harks back to old colonial gentility.
Tel: 09260 3 321 404
Email: zntblive@zamnet.zm
Website: www.zambiatourism.com

ZAMBIAN FALLS VIEWS
The views onto the Main Falls may not be as spectacular but the sensation of being in closer contact with the frothing waters and drenching mist-spray is mesmerising. A dramatic (slippery!) footbridge carries awestruck visitors to Knife Edge Point for views of the Eastern Cataract).Then there are views downstream to the Zambezi Bridge, along the first zigzagging arm of the deep-cut Batoka gorge, and if you walk down to the riverbank itself, you peer into the bubbles of the Boiling Pot.
Tel: 09260 1 229 087/90
Email: zntb@zamnet.zm
Website: www.zambiatourism.com

In an upliftment initiative, local craftspeople at the Caprivi Art Centre have received specialised training in various crafting skills to bring in money that benefits the community. Visitors can make original finds among wood and soapstone carvings, earthenware pots, woven baskets and traditional weapons.

MOSI-OA-TUNYA NATIONAL PARK
This tiny reserve, Zambia's smallest, is made up of the Victoria Falls section and the game park. In the wildlife sector, visitors can take their own vehicle in, join a game drive (arranged in Livingstone) or sign up for a guided walking tour at the park gates. In spite of the pint-sized territory, visitors still see zebra, giraffe and a handful of antelope. Best of all, you fall just short of a guarantee that you'll end up nose to snout with Zambia's only surviving (and carefully guarded!) white rhinos.
Tel: 09260 1 229 087/90, 278 129
Email: zawaorg@zamnet.zm
Website: www.zambiatourism.com

LIVINGSTONE ISLAND PICNIC
During the dry season (June to October), when the river is low, a boat ferries up to 10 eager diners to Livingstone Island for a meal of their choice – brunch, lunch or afternoon tea. Seated around a linen-bedecked table and sipping on sparkling wine, they are discreetly served by uniformed staff a breath-holding step away from the lip of the abyss.
Tel: 09260 3 321 404
Email: zntblive@zamnet.zm
Website: www.zambiatourism.com

ZAMBEZI RIVER (ZAMBIA)

TAKE A FLIP
If you'd prefer to match the fish eagle's view of the Great Zambezi, fold yourself into a little plane to better understand the river's geological progression (if the river is low) where it has sliced seven zigzags across the 1.7km (1-mile) basalt lip over which the falls thunder. The tumultuous flow is eroding an eighth line at Devil's Cataract, on the extreme western end. You also get great views of the lazy river-flow above the falls as the Zambezi meanders around green islands before it disappears into mist-enshrouded depths, then reemerges at the foot of the sharply cut gorges which snake sharply off into the distance.

In Zimbabwe, rafts 'put in' at Big Eddy. In Zambia, the put-in is at Boiling Pot – this is the closest you get to the Victoria Falls in a raft. Rapid 9 is called Commercial Suicide by the operators – they all portage around it!

THE WHITEWATER RAPIDS
High-water runs – usually tamer because of fewer obstacles – take place around beginning July to mid-August. Low-water runs – wilder because of exposed rocks – happen from roughly mid-August to late December. Rafts bounce and slide for a winding 22km (14 miles) from rapid 4 to 18 (sometimes to 23 – request this upfront) on the Zimbabwean side, and from rapid 1 to 18 (or 23) on the Zambian side.

ALL-DAY SPLASH-OUT
Rafting company Safari Par Excellence has dreamed up the Big Day Out, aimed at maniacs for whom one adrenaline rush doesn't quite cut it. The day begins with whitewater rafting, progresses to river boarding and jet-boating, moves on to a helicopter trip up the Zambezi gorge and culminates in a lung-expanding-yell of a bungee jump. Expect to shell out the bucks! If this is not quite for you, you could try abseiling a dry gorge, swing across the gorge via a high-level cable or, akin to a bridge jump, launch yourself into the centre of the gorge on a giant swing.

THE ZAMBEZI BRIDGE
Constructed in 1905, the graceful 152m (500ft) main arch span of this bridge is suspended above the Zambezi as it courses through the Batoka gorge. Linking the Zambian and Zimbabwean banks, it embodied at the time another step in Cecil John Rhodes' dream to forge a Cape-to-Cairo road and rail link. Both road and railway line still operate today. Visitors must pass through immigration and customs to get onto the bridge – a worthwhile excursion as the views are stupendous and you can watch zealots lunging toward the river 110m (360ft) below.

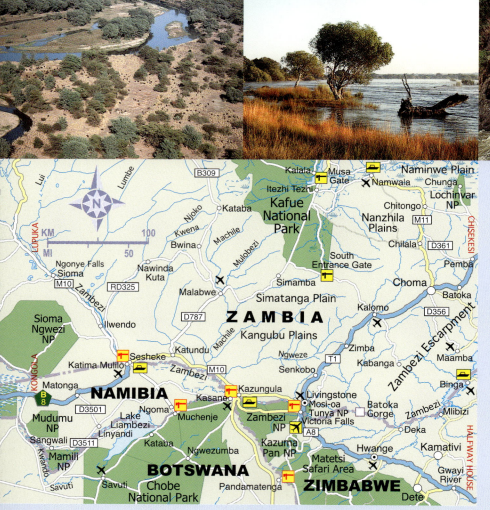

CAPRIVI STRIP

LAND OF CONTENTION
Sometime in the early 1960s right through to 1990, the Caprivi Strip was the centre of strife and contention. And even in the late 1990s, conflict bubbled over. Historically, this 500km-long (300-mile) strip was the domain of the Barotse; in time it became a British protectorate, later passed into the hands of Germany, and then fell under South Africa's wing until Namibia gained her independence. The Strip also failed to evade spillover from the Angolan civil war. More peaceful today, there are moves to involve the local farming communities in conservation efforts along the Caprivi and in reaping revenues for their own benefit.
Tel: 09264 66 686 802
Email: bruno@iway.na

BWABWATA NATIONAL PARK
Formed from remnants of the now dismantled Caprivi Game Park (see also p23), Bwabwata occupies a western and an eastern tract within the Caprivi Strip, on the Okavango River to the west and on the Kwando River to the east. Protracted conflicts here during the struggle for independence have undoubtedly taken their toll with burning and clearing of vegetation, and the hunting out of wildlife. On the plus side, the natural migration route runs through here, and the verdant aquatic vegetation can't fail to tempt the passing animal parade back to its turf. For now, elephant, hippo, crocodile and feline prowlers, lion and leopard, inhabit the recovering terrain.

CROSSING THE GOLDEN HIGHWAY
Travellers to the Caprivi should know that, between Divundu in the west to Kongola on the Kwando River, there are no facilities along the 'Golden Highway' (B8) crossing the Strip end to end. Until recently it was necessary to tackle this stretch by joining the official convoy that crossed twice daily, but latest requirements are to check beforehand with the local authorities. Overriding advice, however, is: safety in numbers. The Caprivi's flat landscape is characterised by fertile floodplains interspersed with groves of mopane and woodland forest – although remnants of parallel dunes throughout are reminders of drier times.

POPA FALLS
At the Caprivi's westernmost extent, near Bagani, the Okavango River disperses into a broad series of rapids that cascade over the rocks, creating water channels and splashing around islands. The Popa falls don't exactly live up to their name but you can spend some idle moments negotiating the walkway into the middle of the river to clamber over the rocks. You might see the ears and nostrils of a hippo protruding from the water or startle a prehistoric crocodile soporifically sunning itself. In actual fact, a pair of nostrils breaking the surface could just as easily be a croc eyeing you out. . .

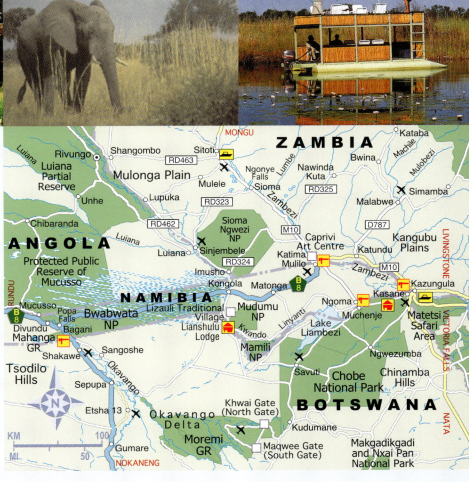

6 DURBAN TO MAPUTO/ WINDHOEK

Temple of Understanding
As you head out of Durban towards Pietermaritzburg on the N3, a detour onto the N2 south to Chatsworth takes you to the gorgeously opulent Hare Krishna Temple of Understanding. The giant domed gilt-and-marble temple-room is awe-inspiring, the moat and lotus-shaped garden deeply calming.

Spioenkop Battlefield
At Spioenkop (see p86), just 35km (20 miles) west of Ladysmith, 1700 British soldiers knuckled down behind shallow trenches on a hill in thick mist. When it lifted, they faced 500 Boers who used snipe tactics, trapping them in a day of debilitating heat. About 600 Britons died, and lie buried where they fell, in the Acre of Massacre.

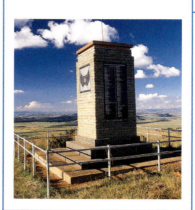

Jozi Mall Deluxe
Visitors can't leave Johannesburg without visiting its newest, most innovative mall, Clearwater, in Strubens Valley, corner of Hendrik Potgieter and Christiaan de Wet. It rises in the rocky northwestern hills, all smoky glass, stainless steel, wood and polished porcelain. In fine weather its massive glassed roof slides back to let in the sunshine. You'll find coffee, Italian fountains and Nina Roche.

Durban — 95km — Midlands (Howick) — 211km — Battlefields (Dundee) — 425km — Johannesburg

Valley of 1000 Hills
For the most picturesque drive ever between Durban and Pietermaritzburg, take the turning to Hillcrest on the R103 to witness an eternally green sea of hills and valleys carved by the curving Umgeni River. The hills are dotted with Zulu beehive huts, and hotels, coffee and curio shops make the most of spectacular views.

Nelspruit
A growing, bustling commercial centre of complexes and shopping malls, Nelspruit, Mpumalanga's capital, is a gateway for Swaziland to the south, Kruger Park's southern extent to the east, and Maputo on the Mozambican coastline. It's also a launch-point northwards to the dramatic Blyde River escarpment.

A total treat is drifting silently (except for the intermittent roar of the burners!) over the Lost City and quietly grazing animals in the Pilanesberg, with you suspended beneath a gorgeous primary-coloured, giant hot-air balloon.

Sun City & Lost City
After many hours cooped up in a car, your muscles are cramped, circulation is sluggish, and the mind dulled from deciphering too many number plates. Time to spoil yourself and hit the bright lights: one night in the fairytale Palace of the Lost City and a show extravaganza at Sun City next door...

Windhoek
The origin of Windhoek's name is a bit of a mystery. It was known to the Nama as Ai-gams ('steam-water') and to the Herero as Otjomuise ('place of smoke'), after hot springs to the east of the city which drew nomadic people to its waters. In the 1840s, Nama leader Jan Jonker Afrikaner in a letter referred to Wind Hoock – the name that's stuck.

Pretoria — 58km
1425km — Via Trans-Kalahari Highway — Windhoek
Maputo — 545km

Maputo
Maputo is the pivot of Mozambique's lagoon coastal stretch, starting at Ponta do Ouro on the border with South Africa and ending at Inhambane way up north. Think tropical fish and game-fish, manta and eagle rays, and even whale sharks in season. But do note: August/September is very windy, so no good for diving.

81

Durban to KZN Midlands

DURBAN
What strikes visitors most about Durban is its humidity, which takes some getting used to. Summers are intensely hot and clammy, often building up to dramatically thunderous electrical storms. The other fact that strikes travellers is the predominance of Durban's Indian culture – it has, apparently, the largest Indian community outside Asia. Of the million-plus people of Asian descent, 68% are Hindu with the remainder Muslim – which explains the presence in Durban of South Africa's largest mosque. The city was named after Cape Colony governor Benjamin D'Urban, who oversaw the small town and mission station established in 1835 after chief, Shaka Zulu, conceded land to the British.
Tel: 031 366 7500/04 7144
Email: tkzn@zulu.org.za
Website: www.zulu.org.za

SALT, SURF AND SAND
A necklace of long, sandy beaches pounded by breaking rollers and foaming surf make Durban the country's surf capital – sun-bleached hair, baggy shorts, surfboards and all. Some of the world's great surfers were fostered on these waves. Shark nets protect the 6km-long (4-mile) Golden Mile between the Umgeni River mouth south to Addington, on the Point, and beach-goers can look out for the flagged sections which are patrolled by lifesavers. Besides the bobbing surfboards, canoes also patrol the waters in prolific profusion – paddlers can hire (or buy) anything from slalom, whitewater or polo canoes to sea kayaks.
Tel: 031 304 4934/32 2595
Email: funinsun@iafrica.com
Website: www.durbanexperience.co.za

uSHAKA MARINE WORLD
Latest and greatest (in family entertainment) is Durban's giant uShaka Marine World, incorporating elements of the former aquarium and dolphinarium but dishing up much, much more. Dolphins, seals, penguins and the aquarium vie with the Snorkel Lagoon where waterbabies can watch rock lobsters, eel and octopus being fed, before snorkelling over an ancient cannon, through a 'shipwrecked' cargo vessel, then facing up to deep-sea predators through a wall of glass. Or kids can head off to the Wet 'n Wild World of speed chutes, super tubes and a rollercoaster tunnel ride, then replenish spent calories in the Phantom Ship restaurant with its window onto the shark tank.
Tel: 031 328 8000/1
Email: znobandla@ushakamarine.co.za
Website: www.ushakamarineworld.co.za

At the beachfront are the last of Durban's colourfully festooned rickshas. A major means of transport in the 1900s, these open carriages are embellished with beads, tinsel and streamers and pulled by Zulus in traditional regalia crowned by a staggeringly elaborate, tall headdress – all a curious meshing of Indian and Zulu influences.

BE ENTERTAINED
The gigantic Ferris wheel turning above the street marks the spot for The Wheel, an enormous eating and shopping zone, while kids needing some entertaining can climb all over the two tugboats and minesweeper SAS *Durban* at the Natal Maritime Museum, along the Victoria Embankment. For a little culture, the BAT arts centre next door is crammed with visual-art studios running workshops and tempting shoppers with original and unusual craft souvenirs.
Tel: 031 366 7500/04 7144
Email: tkzn@zulu.org.za
Website: www.zulu.org.za

PIETERMARITZBURG
This has been described as the 'best preserved Victorian city in South Africa' and is certainly characterised by its columns, pediments, tall City Hall clocktower and elegant red-brick architecture. A stroll through the narrow, labyrinthine alleys of The Lanes, one of the oldest quarters, gives you a good taste of the city. As a seat of learning with its respected university, the student population makes this a lively place. The statue of Mohandas Gandhi on Church Street reminds us of the time this fledgling lawyer was instructed in 1893 to leave his first-class train compartment at the Pietermaritzburg station because of his skin colour.
Tel: 033 345 1348/9/451
Email: info@pmbtourism.co.za
Website: www.pmbtourism.co.za

Midlands Meander

HOWICK

Lying some 18km (11 miles) north of Pietermaritzburg, this little town's reputation depends mainly on its beautiful high falls. The perfect setting of the restaurant looking directly onto the Howick falls reaps the benefits with its viewing platform. Nearby are the Albert falls (at 7m/23ft high not too impressive) and a lake with rondavels to stay in, sitting in a scenic setting. Rambling, birdwatching and picnicking are the name of the game here.
Tel: 033 330 5305
Email: nr@futurenet.co.za
Website: www.howick.org.za

Howick's other claim to fame is that it was here Nelson Mandela was arrested in August 1962 – the start of his 27-year internment. A memorial, unveiled by Mandela, marks the spot on the R103, outside Howick. At his arrest he'd been, as usual, travelling in disguise – a trick that had earned him the name Black Pimpernel.

FARMING COUNTRY

KwaZulu-Natal's Midlands occupy the green, fertile land northwest of Pietermaritzburg to Estcourt – start of battlefields territory. This is mainly farming country, intensely picturesque with its undulating hills, forested tracts, horse studs and cattle ruminating in rolling pastures. The Midlands' early settlers were mainly English farmers and their influence is patent in the quaint and charming country inns, tearooms and craft shops.

A SLOW MEANDER

Artists and craftspeople have found a tranquil and scenic retreat in the beauty of the Midlands and have craftily devised a series of meandering routes that link the towns of Hilton, Nottingham Road and Mooi River. Dispersed along the length of these routes are galleries and studios displaying everything from pottery, leather, woven cloth and stained glass to herbs, cheese and wine.
Tel: 033 330 8195
Email: info@midlandsmeander.co.za
Website: www.midlandsmeander.co.za

Dundee to Soweto

DUNDEE
Between Ladysmith and Dundee, the country panning to the east is the heart of the Battlefields route (see p86) where, during the 19th century, fierce and bloody battles were waged first between Zulu and Boer, then between Zulu and British forces, and finally between Boer and Brit. Give Dundee a miss, but its superb Talana Museum is conveniently on the R33 to Vryheid. The Battle of Talana Hill was the fiery salvo in the 1899 Anglo-Boer War and 10 historic buildings still survive from that time. Fascinating photographs, uniforms and weapons in the museum imbue both Anglo-Zulu and Anglo-Boer conflicts with the bravery, fear and pain of war.
Tel: 034 212 2121 ext 2262
Email: tourism@dundeekzn.co.za
Website: www.tourdundee.co.za

HARRISMITH
Quiet and rural though this town is, proactive individuals keen on promoting tourism have worked hard to put Harrismith and its surrounds on the map. Everything from a 150 million-year-old petrified tree outside the town hall to the British blockhouse to the Botanic Gardens 5km (3 miles) south of the town (featuring Drakensberg-specific plant species) is proudly touted. And the Platberg ('flat mountain') has a great story attached to it. The seed was planted for the cross-country Berg marathon staged here annually when a major involved in the

BASOTHO CULTURAL VILLAGE
To the west of Harrismith and to the east of Golden Gate National Park, visitors can embark on a tour of this village to gain some insight into the traditions of the Basotho people. First up are the gorgeously decorated, tin-roofed circular and square huts. The mud-plastered walls are painted by the women, who frame the doors and windows with graphic repeat motifs in daring colour combinations – lime and lilac, buttercup-yellow and indigo. Individuals are decked out in traditional dress and visitors can listen to local musicians, try out the beer or watch a healer scattering his predictive bones.
Tel: 058 721 0300
Email: basotho@dorea.co.za
Website: www.dorea.co.za/ecotourism

VRYHEID
Beyond main battlefield country, Vryheid sits in the Zulu heartland, a totally unspoilt, undeveloped region of rolling grasslands, green shadowed hills and thornveld. Meaning 'freedom', the town was founded by the Boers as the capital of their (short-lived) New Republic and the Nieuwe Republiek Museum in the Old Raadsaal building focuses on this brief Boer stronghold. This lovely part of the country is visited mainly as part of a Battlefields tour.
Tel: 034 2133 ext 2229
Email: information@vhd.dorea.co.za
Website: www.vryheid.co.za

Anglo-Boer War once commented on 'that little hill of yours' to a local inhabitant. He took exception and challenged Major Belcher to summit the Platberg in under an hour. The major did so with ease, but graciously donated a floating trophy for the first person to reach the top in a race to be held every year. Today, the tough course follows several peaks across the top of the mountain.
Tel: 058 672 1044
Email: Montrose@telkomsa.net
Website: www.zulu.org.za

GOLDEN GATE HIGHLANDS
Nature has excelled herself in dramatically sculpted sandstone ridges, peaks, cliffs, caves and weird formations. Shape and form, though, are not the only feature. Colour – the product of sandstone and iron oxides – emerges in variations of rust-red and copper to amber and bronze. Massive, strikingly banded cliff faces are named Sentinel and – of course, Golden Gate. They are the domain of powerfully winged raptors – black eagle, jackal buzzard and the rare lammergeier (bearded vulture). At ground level, one-hour rambles to a two-day trail will find you sharing the wilderness with small and large antelope, jackal and Burchell's zebra.
Tel: 058 255 0075/12
Email: names@sanparks.org
Website: www.sanparks.org

Soweto

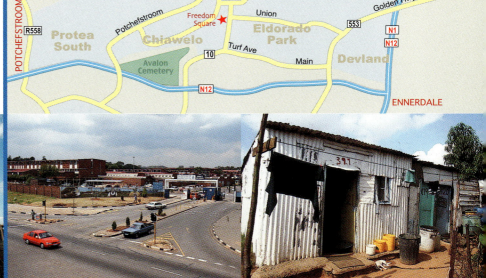

The Vaal Dam is the central storage reservoir for the mighty Vaal River. The area supplied by this river system produces over 50% of the country's gross domestic product, generates over 80% of its electricity, and permeates an area containing some of the world's largest gold, platinum and coal mines.

VAAL DAM
The catchment area of this giant body of water lies mainly in the Free State but also extends into North West, Gauteng and Mpumalanga. In size the dam covers 300km^2 (117 sq miles) and supplies water to the industrial powerhouse of South Africa, centering on Gauteng. Its wall has twice been raised to increase the dam's supply capacity, and today it stands at just over 63m (207ft). To Gautengers generally, the Vaal is their splash pool for all manner of watersports, especially boating and water-skiing. Holiday and retirement homes line its extensive shores.
Tel: 011 327 2000, 016 450 0000
Email: tourism@gauteng.net
Website: www.gauteng.net

THE RESISTANCE YEARS
Soweto, its name created from the acronym South West Townships, has made its mark on the pysche of the New South Africa. It played a crucial historical role in the early days of resistance when the ANC took a more vocal and visible stand against apartheid. Soweto rose to meet the challenge, embracing a more political, dynamic and also violent attitude (witness the famous June 16 riots in 1976). It was also in Soweto that the Freedom Charter was sealed, at the Congress of the People in 1955. Hugh Masekela, Miriam Makeba and Bishop Desmond Tutu are all prodigies of Soweto. Today it is a muddled mix of poor and wealthy – a sprawl of shanties, mass-produced shoebox houses and more solid, middleclass homes.

SOWETO TOURS
A tour through Soweto, home to between three and four million people today, has become one of the most necessary items on the itineraries of visitors to Jozi. It is the best way for people to get a feel for black urban culture, and also to experience the sharp contrasts in status and wealth – the shanties of Nelson Mandela Freedom Squatter Camp stand cheek by jowl with Diepkloof Extension, a wealthy suburb of brick double-storey homes. Another upmarket suburb, Orlando West, is locally dubbed 'Beverly Hills'. Tours usually take in a squatter camp, migrant hostels, Freedom Square, Winnie Mandela's former home, a *shebeen* – but these can also be tailored to specific requests.
Tel: 011 886 1822, 327 2000
Email: richard@soweto.co.za
Website: www.soweto.co.za

BATTLEFIELDS & CENTRAL DRAKENSBERG

SIEGE OF LADYSMITH

The greatest concentration of battlesites spreads out east of Ladysmith and northward to Vryheid. To best recreate the atmosphere of these often bloody battles, an informed guide is highly recommended. A good place to start is the Ladysmith Siege Museum, firstly for its location and secondly for the story that unfolds through words and photographs of the 118-day siege by Boers against the British in the Anglo-Boer War (1899–1902). West of Ladysmith at Spioenkop, now a nature reserve, more British soldiers fell to the Boers (in 1900) than at any other battle due to the Afrikaaners' revolutionary guerilla-style tactics.

High-profile individuals who became embroiled in the Zulu, Boer and British wars were France's Prince Imperial, last of the Bonaparte line and killed in 1879 in a Zulu ambush; Sir Winston Churchill, who made a daring escape after being captured near Estcourt; and Mohandas Gandhi, who in 1899 helped establish a medical unit.

ISANDLWANA & RORKE'S DRIFT

At Isandlwana, east of Dundee, some 25,000 Zulu warriors under King Cetshwayo gathered in 1879 below Isandlwana Hill, unbeknownst to the British camped on the other side. Waiting quietly for the perfect moment to attack, the Zulus surprised a soldier peering over the ridge. They launched into their famous crescent-shaped *impi* formation and swarmed over the hill, the two 'horns' surrounding the 1200 unsuspecting soldiers and totally annihilating them. Thereafter, between 3000 and 4000 triumphant Zulus attacked around 100 British soldiers – many of them ill – at a field hospital at Rorke's Drift further west. Fighting for 12 hours, the British successfully defended themselves, earning eleven Victoria Crosses among them.

BLOOD RIVER

North of Dundee is the Talana Museum (see p84) commemorating among others the Battle of Talana Hill between Brits and Boers in 1899. Search the photographs carefully for Mohandas Gandhi, who helped carry wounded soldiers from the Spioenkop and Colenso battlefields. Sixty years earlier, a time of conflict between Zulu and Boer, the Battle of Blood River was waged to the northeast in 1838. The bronze *laager* here is a monument to behold – 64 life-sized wagons encircle the battlesite to keep the memory alive of how the Boers emerged from the mountains to defeat 12,000 Zulus, inflicting 3000 casualties among the warriors. A public holiday, Day of the Vow, was celebrated by Afrikaaners to honour a supposed pact made with God to revere the day if He assured their victory. It has since become the Day of Reconciliation.
Tel: 034 212 2654 Talana Museum

BARRIER OF SPEARS

The massive mountain chain that is the Drakensberg (the Dutch-Afrikaans name could be roughly translated as 'mountain of the dragons') was the creation of earth tremors that deposited basalt lava onto the sandstone plains. To the Sotho it was Quathlamba – 'barrier of spears' – and today, as a World Heritage Site, it is officially named the uKhahlamba-Drakensberg Park. Since it extends over such a vast area, its size is made more digestible by a loose division into northern, central and southern Drakensberg. The soaring buttresses, sheer cliffs and dragon-tooth ridges defy description; instead, they open the gates of paradise to multitudes of walkers and hikers.

NATAL DRAKENSBERG PARK

Running in a great swathe at the foot of the dramatic southern and central escarpment right up to Cathedral Peak is the Natal Drakensberg Park. It encompasses icy trout-fishing rivers and pastoral rolling hills rising up to the dominating heights of solid rockface. All across the park's slopes, catering to travellers with different aims and different budgets, are hotels and resorts, restcamps and campsites, mountain huts and caves. Winter brings lashings of snow and icy clawing winds but summer comes with blanketing mists, unexpected thunderstorms, and the risk of flooding rivers. Most of the hikes require a permit.

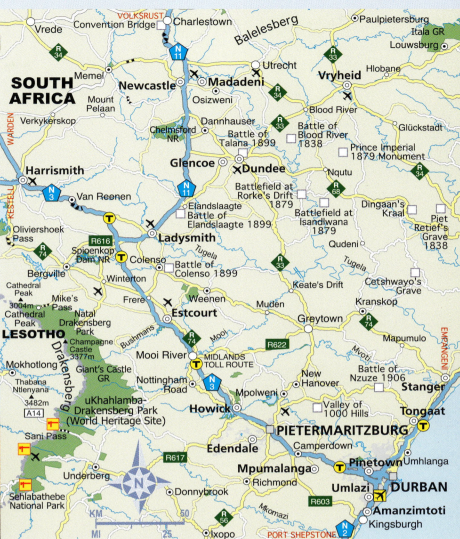

GIANT'S CASTLE

The Giant's Castle Game Reserve, looked on by the great, brooding mass of stone of the same name, was first created to offer sanctuary to the eland – which successfully number around 1500 today. The reserve's main camp at Bushman's River allows trailists to explore the surrounding beauty and walk to a cave harbouring 500 San Bushman paintings. A special hide lets birding fanatics unobtrusively observe the mountain raptors gliding on the high thermals.

CHAMPAGNE CASTLE

Quite in contrast to champagne air and fairy princesses, the story goes that in Victorian times, two British officers set off to climb this peak, a bottle of bubbly firmly ensconced in their rucksack. When they paused to rest, however, the bottle was already half-empty. With requisite British politeness and reserve – both of the officers loath to lay any blame on the other – it was agreed that the mountain instead should be held responsible for the liquid slippage! The peak itself, second highest in South Africa (3377m; 10,975ft), rises pinnacle-like between two escarpment edges.
Tel: 036 468 1063
Email: champagnecastle@futurenet.co.za
Website: www.champagnecastle.co.za

CATHEDRAL PEAK

An interrupted skyline of freestanding rocky pinnacles marks the range that includes Cathedral Peak. With names like the Organ Pipes, Cleft Peak, the Pyramid and the Bell, mountaineers love this zone, which also has the best hiking in the entire Drakensberg range. From the high end of the spectrum to the low: Mike's Pass ascends 500m (1640ft) in 5km (3 miles) while down in the valley, Ndedema gorge features San Bushman art and the largest forest of the Drakensberg. Well-known Cathedral Peak Hotel nestles closer to the basalt mountain ridges than any other.
Tel: 036 488 1888
Email: reservations@cathedralpeak.co.za
Website: www.cathedralpeak.co.za

87

Windhoek to Maputo

WINDHOEK
Any traveller to Windhoek (see also p63) won't miss the steeple of the high-standing (in more ways than one) Christuskirche, the German Lutheran church, which stands on a traffic island at the top of Peter Müller Street. Featured on every tourist brochure for Windhoek, the sandstone church displays part neo-Gothic, part Art Nouveau decorative aspects. Most recognisable is the front façade's stained-glass windows, financed by Kaiser Wilhelm II. The church reportedly was built by German rulers to celebrate so-called peace between themselves and the Owambo, Herero and Nama peoples.
Tel: 09264 61 290 6000
Email: info@namibiatourism.com.na
Website: www.namibiatourism.com.na

Like a lone (but persistent) strand of spaghetti that simply has no end, the Trans-Kalahari Highway endures for 595km (370 miles). Completed in April 1998, it runs from Walvis Bay in Namibia to Lobatse in Botswana, linking Windhoek with Gaborone.

TROPIC OF CAPRICORN
The highway crosses the open-ended space of the Central Kalahari which, unlike the Namib, is not classified as real desert (believe it or not, its minimal rainfall decides this). In the vistas of grasses, scrub and thornveld, expect an artist's palette of sepia tones. Kang is a place to break your journey – its only redeeming factor is the relatively new Ultra-Stop and the service station facilities that come with it. On the way, you cross the Tropic of Capricorn, the imaginary line at latitude 23.5° south of the Equator; it is here that the sun is directly overhead at noon on the summer solstice, 22 December.
Tel: 09267 395 3024
Email: botswanatourism@gov.bw
Website: www.botswanatourism.org

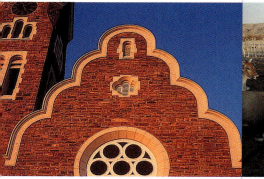

WINDHOEK'S 'CASTLES'
If what you're looking for is reassuring, solid, Germanic character, cruise up to the top of Robert Mugabe Avenue to have an exterior peek at Windhoek's three privately-owned castles. Architect Willi Sander designed all three, the last one for himself – Sanderburg, built in 1917 on – good guess, Kastell Street. The first one, Schwerinsburg, constructed in 1913 on a street of the same name, was commissioned by Count von Schwerin and was later graced by the Italian ambassador. In 1914 the count had Heinitzburg built for his fiancée Margarethe von Heinitz (also on a street of the same name). Today the white-battlemented fort-like structure is a very fine hotel.
Tel: 09264 61 290 6000
Email: info@namibiatourism.com.na
Website: www.namibiatourism.com.na

WINDHOEK TO BUITEPOS
You're going to have to find your own entertainment on the long stretch between Windhoek and Botswana's borderpost, as this is major cattle ranchland territory with cows your only diversion. You could, of course, try to identify the quite considerable range of pure breeds the Omaheke region is well known for. Make a start with Brown Swiss, Simmenthaler, Brahman, Santa Gertrudis and Red Poll! A stop at Gobabis will break the journey.
Tel: 09264 62 560 419 (Buitepos)
Email: info@namibiatourism.com.na
Website: www.namibiatourism.com.na

Jwaneng, 130km (80 miles) from the Lobatse borderpost, is Botswana's richest diamond mine and one of the largest in the world. Globally, Botswana is the single leading producer of gem-quality diamonds, yielding over 30 million carats annually. Diamonds make up 83% of the country's export earnings.

The Trans-Kalahari Highway is crossed mainly by travellers to and from Namibia. Essentially, it reduces the distance between Windhoek and Pretoria by some 400km (250 miles).

Oom Schalk Lourens, one of Herman Charles Bosman's characters, described karee-berry mampoer as: 'white and soft to look at, and the smoke that comes from it when you pull the cork out of the bottle is pale and rises up in slow curves. . .'

GROOT MARICO
Life in this tiny Afrikaans town on the Marico River came under the wry, ironical microscope of early 20th-century writer Herman Charles Bosman. Revered by South Africans for his wit – sharp as a switchblade – and his eccentric portrayal of the characters that peopled this dorpie, his stories grew out of his experiences as a teacher here. Another product of Groot Marico is *mampoer*, a fiery, breath-reducing distilled spirit of peaches, apricots or even karee-tree berries.
Tel: 014 503 0085
Email: info@marico.co.za
Website: www.marico.co.za

PRETORIA
The heart of Pretoria beats in Church Square. Looked on by the Raadsaal (Parliament) and Palace of Justice (the Transvaal Supreme Court), it was here that the Voortrekkers gathered with their ox-wagons in 1857 to dedicate the first building, a thatched church. The next day they unfurled the first flag of the South African Republic. A century later, Nelson Mandela and seven other ANC members were sentenced to life imprisonment in the Rivonia Trial held in the Palace of Justice. Next door stands the Herbert Baker-designed Reserve Bank building. Also here is a grim and forbidding Paul Kruger, sculpted by Anton von Wouw.
Tel: (012) 337 4430
Email: andrewm2@tshwane.gov.za
Website: www.tshwane.gov.za

MADIKWE GAME RESERVE
Despite its size (third only to Kgalagadi and Kruger), this South African reserve doesn't receive the attention it merits – although it was only established 15 years or so ago. Created out of reclaimed farmland, the massive Operation Phoenix assured the presence today of the Big Five, cheetah, spotted hyena and the endangered wild dog among many others. Visitors are cosseted by a handful of elite private lodges and escorted on game drives that deliver a real sense of wilderness – simply because of its remoteness and exclusivity in terms of visitor numbers. You can even elect to fly in by light aircraft.
Tel: 018 3672 ask 2411
Email: madikweadmin@wol.co.za
Website: www.parksnorthwest.co.za

ON THE ROAD TO PRETORIA
As travellers head towards Rustenburg, the surrounding bushveld rises to an upland range of hills that's continuous to the Hartbeespoort dam. This is the Magaliesberg range, scenically pretty in its stoniness, dry wooded hillsides and its sometimes precipitous rocky angles. Depending on the season, aloes crowned with orange-red flowers extend their candelabra-like arms, striking in their starkness. You might also see a rare black eagle or Cape vulture eyeing its prey as it circles on high. Lines of craft stalls start appearing, too, manned by local indigenous artists who work in wood, stone, leather or beadwork. If you're not in a hurry, stop off to visit the cheetahs at De Wildt (see also p35).
Tel: 012 337 4430
Email: andrewm2@tshwane.gov.za
Website: www.tshwane.gov.za

MAPUTO
Civil strife in this Portuguese city only ended just over 10 years ago so the impact on its once-beautiful buildings is still being felt today (see also p45). There is no lack of decorative features and, coupled with interesting architecture, they speak of an earlier grandness and opulence. Feast your eyes on elaborate Portuguese Gothic influences in the Natural History Museum, and the late 19th- and early 20th-century Art Deco houses. The copper dome gracing the train station, dating from 1910, was designed by the Eiffel Tower's famous designer, Gustave Eiffel. A museum worth visiting for its revolution photographs is the Museu da Revolucão.
Tel: 09258 1 307 320/3
Email: info@futur.org.mz
Website: www.futur.org.mz

SUN CITY, PILANESBERG & CRADLE OF HUMANKIND

SUN CITY
This glittering gambling mecca rose like a phoenix from the barren veld in the days when gambling was illegal in South Africa and this tract of land belonged to the quasi-independent 'republic' of Bophutatswana. Sun City's most elaborate feature is the Palace of the Lost City, an extravagantly imaginative hotel playground whose fantastical architecture and fun features are weaved round a recreated legend. Artificially generated waves in the Valley of Waves, a vertical waterslide at the Temple of Courage and the vibrating Bridge of Time keep day visitors mightily entertained. You could also chip and putt at the 18-hole Gary Player championship course.
Tel: 014 557 1000
Email: sctyres@sunint.co.za
Website: www.suninternational.co.za

PILANESBERG NATIONAL PARK
The Pilanesberg park, entirely raised above the plain, centres on the Mankwe Dam which is encircled by three rings of little hills. The site is an extinct volcanic crater. During eruptions 1300 million years ago, underground pressure from hot molten lava cracked the surrounding earth into concentric circles. The hills are cooled lava which forced its way through these cracks. Thanks to the ambitious Operation Genesis, 6000 mammals of 19 different species were relocated here from other parks. Truly fulfilling wildlife excursions could have you spotting any of the Big Five, giraffe, hippo, leopard and cheetah, and more recently, wild dog.
Tel: 014 555 5351
Email: Pilanesberg@telkom.net.za
Website: www.goldenleopard.co.za

CRADLE OF HUMANKIND, MAGALIESBERG
The Kromdraai Conservancy, better known today as the Cradle of Humankind, covers an area of around 47,000ha (116,000 acres), and is one of South Africa's few World Heritage Sites. Its most famous feature is Sterkfontein, in the dolomitic caves of the Magaliesberg mountains (also see p35). Among the other sites (but not too much relation to hominid fossils!) are Kromdraai Wonder Cave and the Rhino and Lion Nature Reserve. Sterkfontein, comparable in palaeontological importance to Tanzania's Olduvai gorge, is where in 1936

the first fossils of an 'ape man' skull – believed to be 2.6 to 3 million years old – were found. In 1947 the nearly complete skull of a woman, dubbed 'Mrs Ples', was found by Dr Robert Broom, and in 1995 ankle and toe joint bones were unearthed. Named 'Little Foot', they were proof that over 3 million years ago our ancestors walked upright. In 1998, the oldest complete skeleton of hominid *Australopithecus* was discovered, dated 3.3 million years ago. The caves themselves are no big deal; it's their finds that are. There are short guided cave tours; also a specialist palaeontologist-run tour on request.
Tel: 011 355 1208
Email: cradleofhumankind@gpg.gov.za
Website: www.cradleofhumankind.co.za

KRUGER (SOUTH) & BLYDE CANYON

KRUGER NATIONAL PARK
This park cuts a great wild and tangled swathe along South Africa's eastern boundary. Between the Limpopo River (north) and the Crocodile (south), it swallows up 20,000km² (7800 sq miles) of hot, lush Lowveld. According to park information, Kruger harbours the biggest variety of animals of any park in Africa – and attracts hordes of self-driving, self-catering visitors across 2600km (1615 miles) of tar and gravel highways and byways. With its easy accessibility, developed road network and 14 thatched-rondavel restcamps (huts and safari tents too), Kruger doesn't offer the true wilderness experience – but see plenty of wild animals you most certainly will.
Tel: 013 735 4000
Email: reservations@parks-sa.co.za
Website: www.parks-sa.co.za

BLYDE CANYON LIP
The not-to-be missed cut and sculpted beauty of the Blyde River Canyon is easily accessed from Kruger, via the Orpen or Paul Kruger gates. If you exit through Orpen, you start at the northern extent of the canyon, via the winding Abel Erasmus pass. A leisurely half-day's drive takes you along the dramatic canyon edge with astounding viewpoints. The canyon walls, weathered out of banded layers of red-rock sandstone, plunge for almost a kilometre (half a mile). Left exposed in the valley-centre are giant rondavel-shaped buttresses (catch the views at Three Rondavels). At Bourke's Luck Potholes, water-swirled pebbles have sculpted a fantasia of scooped-out rock hollows.
Tel: 013 761 6004/19

WATERFALLS & PILGRIMS REST
To the south, a 15km (9-mile) loop fringes the canyon for yet more expansive, breath-holding views. Get a perspective generally reserved for the Supreme Being at God's Window; then gaze onto the massive quartzite Pinnacle rearing dramatically out of the luxuriant gorge. Nearby, you could absorb the serenity of the fistful of tall, plumed falls christened Lisbon, Berlin, Mac-Mac and Bridal Veil (not without paying a nominal fee at a couple, though!) before venturing into the one-horse mining town of Pilgrims Rest. You'll have to fight with the tourist buses to see this perfectly preserved and authentically furnished collection of red-roofed, corrugated-iron Victorian buildings.

SOUTHERN KRUGER
Much of Kruger's wildlife is concentrated in the park's well-watered, fertile southern section extending southward of the Olifants River. Along its western edge is a phalanx of highly reputed private game reserves (think Mala Mala, Londolozi and Timbavati). Tangled, wooded belts merging with treed grasslands assure large herds of zebra, wildebeest, giraffe and antelope, which in turn tease out the three large, predatory cats. Test out your viewing abilities on the scenically gorgeous drive north between Lower Sabie and Olifants camps. For closer encounters to get the blood coursing, visitors can also embark on a bushwalk accompanied by armed rangers.

7 HARARE TO GORONGOSA

Harare
Don't leave the city without a beautiful memento of Shona stone sculpture from the National Gallery or the Chapungu cultural village. *Chapungu* is Shona for the bateleur eagle, the spirit messenger of the high savanna, alluding to Harare's siting on a high plateau.

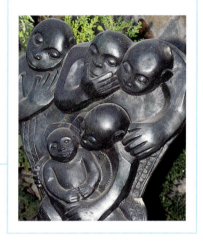

Lake Malawi
The hundreds of iridescent, patterned or peacock-coloured cichlid species, many of them endemic to Lake Malawi, have evolved over millennia from a single common species. Just under 400 cichlids are officially recorded, but many more are being discovered daily. Some estimates go as high as 800, but the estimates vary greatly.

Harare — 371km — Tete — 220km — Blantyre — 177km — Lake Malawi — 714km — Mozambique Island — 399km — Pemba — 388km — Quirimba Archipelago

Tete Corridor
The road between the Zimbabwean borderpost, Nyamapanda, and Tete has been rehabilitated since the war (but don't expect too much!). This route, continuing to Blantyre, is the Tete corridor linking Zimbabwe with Malawi. Fuel and repair facilities in Mozambique remain scarce, but there is a service station in Tete.

Tete
You don't want to hit Tete in midsummer – the mercury can stop just short of 50°C (122°F)! Your only respite is to gaze across the Zambezi's waters to the super-long suspension bridge with its string of curved spans and pylons. Tete's riverside restaurant will sort out your thirst and hunger pangs.

Northern Mozambique
Mozambique Island's character is spiced with a fascinating ethnic mix of ancient Arab, Persian, Hindu, Portuguese and African influences; Pemba's remote bands of sandy beach lie thick with palms; and Quirimba's many islands feature silent mossy ruins, coconut plantations, tiny fishing settlements and once-grand Portuguese plantation homes.

Before the cease-fire agreement of 1992 ending the civil war, Zimbabwean soldiers protected the Tete corridor as best they could. This didn't stop bandits, however – truckers and travellers prepared to risk a 'pot shot' occasionally ran the gauntlet along here.

Gorongosa
If it's wildlife you'd like and your wallet is feeling healthy, go for a flip in a small plane over the Zambezi Delta – the surprise factor to the animals and the views are unsurpassed; otherwise, Gorongosa could yield a few surprises as it finds its feet after the war.

Southern Mozambique
Try the Bazaruto Archipelago for seabirds, turtles, dugongs, and tropical fish; Inhambane for dhows, coconut palms (nearly two million of them!) and cashews; and the coastline down to Maputo for dunes, lagoons and estuaries. So much crammed into one coastline. . .

Chimoio
If you're looking for interest breaks on your long journey, some 5km (3 miles) northeast of Chimoio town, be sure to look out for Cabeça do Velho. This great rock naturally sculpted to resemble an old man's face can be climbed in about 10 minutes to give you views of the surrounding countryside.

| Tete | 437km | Chimoio | | Inchope | 407km | Bazaruto Archipelago | 320km | Inhambane | 474km | Maputo |

Gorongosa 71km

Beira 132km

Beira Corridor
The Beira corridor (referring to the EN6 and the railway line) connected holidaying Zimbabweans with Beira and the sea in the days before the civil war. But though Beira was a prized playground for Zimbabwe, central Mozambique is not nearly as developed as the southern parts.

93

Harare to Niassa Reserve

HARARE
The high-rise buildings and handful of international hotels in the heart of Harare (see also p40) give Zimbabwe's capital a definite colonial-European edge (although the persistent economic crisis, with its fuel and basic food shortages, is effectively doing great damage). The two grids on which the city layout is based make it logical to get around, with the shopping core and glam hotels centralised. An enduring part of Harare's character is Meikles Hotel, sitting on an entire block and hard to miss by the bronze lions ushering visitors into its marble lobby. Word has it that the décor, culinary flavours and scenic surrounds of both Victoria 22 and Amanzi offer the best city dining.
Tel: 09263 4 705 085/6, 758 730/4
Email: info@ztazim.co.zw
Website: www.zimbabwetourism.co.zw

LAND OF OPHIR
The A2 cuts across Mashonaland East to the Nyamapanda borderpost. As you progress northeast along this route, the mountain known today as Mt Darwin lies to the north. In the mid-1500s it was called Fura by the local indigenous people. When early Portuguese explorers penetrated in and, they eagerly surmised *fura* to be the local lingo's version of the biblical land Ophir – repository of buried gold and precious stones once lorded over by King Solomon. The region's wealthy Mutapa dynasty, who ruled at Great Zimbabwe, were believed to be Ophir's modern guardians (*munhumutapa* – or Monomotapa, as the empire came to be known – means 'master pillager').
Tel: 09236 39 62643
Email: ngpa@webmail.co.za
Website: www.zimbabwetourism.co.zw

LIWONDE NATIONAL PARK
The route to Cuamba in Mozambique skirts the southern reaches of this well-managed reserve – one of Malawi's best. The Shire River, flowing out of Lake Malawi and via Lake Malombe into Liwonde, hugs the entire western border and keeps hordes of sneaky crocodiles and yawning hippos submerged and wet. Boat rides on the river are an absolute treat. Elephants are very much in evidence, as is a small herd of rhino within a protected sanctuary. A restocking programme has reintroduced quite a number of animal species, so it can only get better. Riverine forest, mopane woodland and grassland – interspersed with tall ilala palms and fat baobabs – make sure the birds are prolific too.
Tel: 09265 1 620 902
Email: tourism@malawi.net
Website: www.tourismmalawi.com

SHONA SCULPTURE
Zimbabwe's Shona stone sculptors have earned themselves high praise for their skilled and imaginatively conceived art forms. Harare's National Gallery features an African sculptors' workshop (and outdoor sculpture garden), which takes its proud place among the collections of European art and cultural works by artists from the entire African continent. East of the city, the reconstructed 19th-century Shona village Chupungu takes art appreciators on a half-hour guided tour of the country's best sculptures, executed in jasper, verdite and granite. There is a sculpture garden here, too, and African dancing on weekends to stir the soul.
Tel: 09263 4 758 730/34, 705 085/6
Email: info@ztazim.co.zw
Website: www.zimbabwetourism.co.zw

NYAMAPANDA TO TETE
Zimbabwe's northeastern landscape, shoehorned as it is between the attractions of Mana Pools-Lake Kariba to the north and the verdant misty Eastern Highlands to the east, doesn't receive too many overexcited travellers. So don't expect to be entertained by sights along the way. The iconic bouldered kopjes and an abundance of trees add some prettiness to the busy Nyamapanda borderpost, though. On entering Mozambique and wending your way to Tete, avoid travelling once night has descended – vehicles parked on the side of the road without reflectors and stray animals on their own little journey constantly present hazards.
Tel: 09263 9 60867/72969
Email: bpa@netconnect.co.zw
Website: www.arachid.co.zw/Bulawayo

LAKE MALAWI
Being just a hop, skip and a jump away from this virtual inland sea, it's mighty tempting to make a pitstop here on the way to Mozambique. Over 600m (2000ft) deep and stretching almost the length of Malawi, this freshwater lake takes up one-fifth of its territory and nourishes the nation with its abundance of fish. Dugouts trailing nets are a part of the scenery. The lake is famous for its hundreds of species of jewel-like cichlids – accounting for the snorkellers and divers drawn to its depths. Kayaking, island-hopping on catamarans and sunset cruises happily occupy the balance of visitors.
Tel: 09265 1 620 902
Email: tourism@malawi.net
Website: www.tourismmalawi.com

Northern Mozambique

CUAMBA TO NIASSA

The road from Cuamba north across Niassa province traverses remote, wildly rugged country where even the towns have little infrastructure. The powerful currents of the Zambezi River forging its route from Lake Cahora Eassa southeastward to the mouth at Chinde still create a formidable barrier between north and south of the country. Downstream of Tete there is no decent accessible road bridge across the river; the Dona Ana railway bridge (the longest in Africa) connecting Villa de Sena and Mutarara has poor tracks on both sides, and roads to the ferry at Caia are often impassable after heavy rains (January to March).
Tel: 09258 1 307 320/3
Email: info@futur.org.mz
Website: www.futur.org.mz

NIASSA RESERVE

This enormous protected area sprawling across 42,000km² (16,300 sq miles) is pretty undeveloped, reinforced by a lack of roads and official accommodation (although the situation is changing as we speak). Wildlife such as elephant, buffalo, giraffe and zebra is present but in low population densities. The prime option, therefore, is to play the spying game from the elevated advantage of a charter plane – reserved for those with money in their wallets. For photographers, the untamed mountainous and forested landscape is quite beautiful.
Tel: 09258 1 409 937
Email: anarodmoz@hotmail.com
Website: www.niassa.com

MOZAMBIQUE ISLAND

A 3km (2-mile) road bridge connects this tiny isle with the mainland. Ideally located for the trade-wind-dependent dhows, ancient Persian, Indian and Arab traders plied its azure waters before Vasco da Gama made his landfall and the Portuguese built their fort – the crumbling granite walls of Fortaleza São Sebastião still guard the island-shores. Despite the dilapidated air of the many historic buildings concentrated at the island's northern end (the church dates from 1503), the columns, pediments, arches and decorative flourishes speak of the grandeur and charm of earlier days. The south of the island is densely populated with few facilities, so it is badly polluted.
Tel: 011 803 9296/52
Email: travel@mozambiquetourism.co.za
Website: www.mozambiquetourism.co.za

PEMBA & QUIRIMBA

To the north, Pemba's little port sits on a headland protecting a turquoise-watered bay. Papayas, palms and icing-sugar beaches give some idea of what paradise could look like. The remote and unspoiled chain of 27 coral islands belonging to the Quirimba Archipelago, between Pemba and Rovuma Bay in the north, was already a significant Arab trading post by the time 15th-century Portuguese explorers anchored along its shores. Today, the most visited island is Ibo, a major slave-trading post during the late 18th century. Many of the islands are linked by dense mangrove swamps, fed by marked tidal flows. Visitors explore the islands in synchrony with the tides, but there is no fresh water.
Tel: 011 447 6422
Email: quilaleaisland@iafrica.com
Website: www.quilalea.com

Maputo to Beira

A PRISTINE COASTLINE
Not only has Mozambique had to contend with its 20 years or so of civil conflicts; it has also been beaten and battered by tropical cyclones and devastating coastal floods. With the recent influx from the south of 4x4 holidaymakers from South Africa, tourism is bringing much needed money into the country, helping it to slowly and surely rebuild its once lustrous reputation. Despite its difficulties, Mozambique's beautiful long sandy beaches fringed with swaying palms and turquoise-azure seas define the laid-back tropical island life. It is perhaps the country's recent inaccessibility that has protected its natural beauty, keeping it pristine and untrampled by the hordes.
Tel: 09258 1 307 320/3
Email: info@futur.org.mz
Website: www.futur.org.mz

TIME FOR BREEDING...
Mozambique's southern coastline is witness to an endless parade of marine creatures instinctively tuning into their biological clocks to assure future generations. Generally seeking warmer waters in which to calve or feed, humpback whales follow their migratory route along these shores between June and September, dolphins frolic in the waves from June to October and whale sharks pass by between November and January. On firmer territory, giant leatherback and loggerhead turtles nest in the sand dunes from October to March. Many coastal resorts and camps use this as a lure to attract visitors to their sandy portals.
Tel: 011 803 9296/52
Email: travel@mozambiquetourism.co.za
Website: www.mozambiquetourism.co.za

Fishing offered up and down the Mozambican coast can include rock, surf, deep-sea and even fly-fishing.

VILANKULO
Hot, humid and tropical, Vilankulo is the mainland gateway to the idyllic Bazaruto Archipelago. It fulfils its role as a centre offering all the necessary services for travellers – banking, service stations, stores for provisions and, of course, tourist lodges and hotels. It was before the civil war, and still is today, a hugely popular tourist destination, especially among South Africans during the holidays.
Tel: 09258 23 82031/2
Email: information@vilanculos.org
Website: www.vilanculos.org

BILENE & XAI-XAI
Roads heading north up the coast from Maputo are notoriously bad with potholes the norm, so any transport other than 4x4 is unthinkable. Bilene lagoon, protected from the waves by an elongated sandy spit, positively hums on weekends with Maputo locals thronging to its calm waters accompanied by blaring radios and ski-boats. Travellers might prefer its quieter weekday shores. After the November–April rains have washed open the lagoon mouth, it's the turn of the deep-sea fishermen to crowd out Bilene. Further north, Xai-Xai's unspoilt windswept shoreline – Praia do Xai-Xai – is favoured by campers who come for marlin and other deep-sea catches. It's shared with windsurfers, kayakers and paddle-skiers.
Tel: 09258 1 307 320/3
Email: info@futur.org.mz
Website: www.futur.org.mz

INHAMBANE
Settled along the tip of a peninsula, Ponta de Barra, this coconut-palmed port was the southernmost anchorage for Persian and Arab dhows originating in the Arabian seas, which traded in slaves until 1860. The port's location outside the cyclone belt offered a peaceful and calm haven to these ancient lateen-sailed craft which are still being built according to tradition in coastal villages. According to one travel writer, 'dhows are as synonymous with Inhambane as yellow cabs are with New York City'. Visitors can experience the wind filling the triangular cloth sails by catching a dhow ferry from Maxixe across Inhambane Bay.
Tel: 09258 23 20616
Email: turismo.inhambane@teledata.mz
Website: www.mocambiqueturismo.co.mz

BAZARUTO ARCHIPELAGO
Pure nirvana. Bazaruto's five main islands, Santa Carolina (or Paradise Island), Bazaruto, Benguerra, Magaruque and tiny Bangué are spaces of white sand, rising and receding tides of limpid turquoise water, deep azure channels, and occasional willowy palms etched into the sky. This is where African sunsets don't get any better, where a hot-red sun loses its shape and melds with the sea, leaving behind a crimson sky. People come here to fish, submerge themselves in among the coral reefs, or simply hang in a hammock with a book on their nose.
Tel: 011 803 9296/52
Email: travel@mozambiquetourism.co.za
Website: www.mozambiquetourism.co.za

Gorongosa National Park

NORTH OF BAZARUTO TO INCHOPE & BEIRA

After the EN1 crosses the Save River, take time to relish the wild and tangled vegetation to either side of the route as it cuts north. Known as miombo woodland, it is an unruly mixture of *Brachystegia* tree species, among them towering msasa and mufuti. Birds twitter, preen and flit in the leafy tops – you definitely won't miss the ubiquitous (and gorgeous) blue and pink plumage of the lilac-breasted rollers.
Tel: 09258 1 307 320/3
Email: info@futur.org.mz
Website: www.futur.org.mz

BEIRA

Once a popular tourist resort, Beira's crown is a little tarnished today, although the neoclassical and colonial-era architecture of some of its buildings is still reminiscent of Portugal. The Praça do Municipio has coffee shops at its edges, tables out on the pavement under big trees. An espresso washed down with a sweet, sticky pastry will bring back a hint of earlier times. The rusty wreck still lies beached on white sands below the red-and-white candy-striped Macutí lighthouse.
Tel: 09258 3 27282, 1 307 320/3
Email: info@futur.org.mz
Website: www.futur.org.mz

A REHABILITATED RESERVE

Strange use for a wildlife reserve but it's a fact: Gorongosa became the base for the opposition Renamo movement in Mozambique's civil war from 1980 to 1986. Naturally the soldiers survived by shooting the wild animals and today there is little sign of, in particular, the lion for which Gorongosa was once so famous. Elephant and buffalo have since been reintroduced, hippos wallow in the lakes and delicate impala pronk mischievously through the grasslands. Chitengo Camp, overlooking a waterhole, has been upgraded, although facilities are still pretty basic. This is wilderness and you should be fully self-sufficient!
Tel: 011 803 9296/52
Email: travel@mozambiquetourism.co.za
Website: www.mozambiquetourism.co.za

DEFINITELY FOR THE BIRDS

Backed by a rugged – and very photogenic – mountainscape, Gorongosa's tangled, tropical vegetation is its most attractive feature. From grassland lining Lake Urema and the pallid, pale-yellow fever trees edging the park's seasonal pans to the leafy woodland and dense palm belts, this is territory that breeds a wonderful array of birds – and many species here are endemic. Visitors can train their binoculars on the rare palm-nut vulture, martial eagle or silvery-cheeked hornbill with its clown curved beak – or the smaller species like collared palmthrush or racket-tailed roller.

MOZAMBIQUE COASTLINE

INHAMBANE
South of Inhambane town, on the outer edge of the peninsula, Praia de Jangamo has a stunning inland reef that's protected from the onslaught of waves by a sandbar and at high tide is just a few metres deep. So perfect visibility wins the day here, and at times this can penetrate to 40m (130ft). Further south at Pandane, snorkellers will catch brilliant corals and delicate reef fish on one side of the reef, burly game fish on the other side. For the scuba divers, manta rays hover at three cleaning stations around Manta Reef to be nibbled and picked at by little cleaner fish.

BAZARUTO ARCHIPELAGO
For land-based nature lovers, the island beaches of the archipelago are nesting grounds (October to March) for four of the five turtle species here. Aquanauts can play at 12 dive sites around Bazaruto Island – 22 in all around the archipelago – among coral reefs that have managed to stay pristine. A pretty fairy world of sea anemones, sponges, sea urchins and starfish vies with clown-painted parrotfish, translucent jellyfish, clams and oysters, shrimps and crabs. For the nicest place to stay, the wooden-floored, open-sided rooms on stilts at Benguerra Lodge will seduce you with their brass and filigree fittings, billowing cloths and gauzy mosquito nets.

ZAMBEZI DELTA
From the great Zambezi River mouth northwards, travel is limited to the superadventurous as the country becomes more remote with very little, if any, visitor infrastructure – and certainly no help in the event of a breakdown. Savanna, belts of mangroves with their multiple 'air' roots pushing up through the swamps, and shifting sand islands characterise the delta itself. Once over 200km (125 miles) broad, it is steadily shrinking – the casualty of the Kariba and Cahora Bassa hydro-electric projects. Quelimane to the north punts a flip in a small charter airplane as the best way to take in the web of islands and channels.

HEAD FOR THE BEACH
Most people head for the beaches at Tofo and Barra on Inhambane, but Jangamo and Baia dos Cocos – a melange of tall coconut groves, rolling sand dunes and breakers – are a good bet too. Shell collectors will spend hours trawling the waterline for exquisite shells that are still washed up with the surf.

OF DUGONGS AND TURTLES
The archipelago supports five marine turtle species – leatherback, loggerhead, green, hawksbill and Ridley. The largest remaining population of dugongs, lumbering seagrass eaters that are most closely related to the elephant, also survives in Bazaruto's archipelago. Sailors talked of them as 'strange saltwater hippos'.

THE DELTA'S WILDLIFE
The Zambezi Delta's wetlands – a combination of coastal mangrove, seasonal floodplain and miombo woodland – were before the civil war the roaming grounds of great herds of buffalo, elephant, black rhino and waterbuck. Today, Cape buffalo are protected within the Marromeu Buffalo Reserve to the south of the river mouth and number in their thousands, sharing the wetlands with migrating herds of Lichtenstein's hartebeest, wildebeest, sable antelope, eland, and oribi. Elephant and rhino are notable in their scarcity and are suspected to be extinct now in the delta area. Wetland birdlife is, not surprisingly, superb – expect to see white pelicans and openbill, saddlebill and yellow-billed storks.

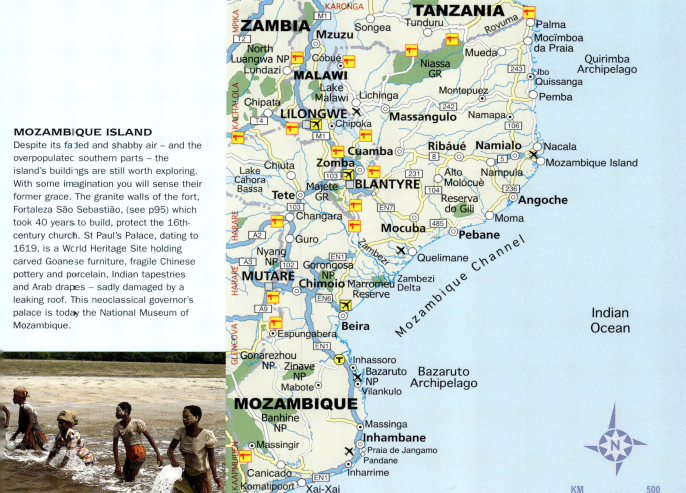

MOZAMBIQUE ISLAND

Despite its faded and shabby air – and the overpopulated southern parts – the island's buildings are still worth exploring. With some imagination you will sense their former grace. The granite walls of the fort, Fortaleza São Sebastião, (see p95) which took 40 years to build, protect the 16th-century church. St Paul's Palace, dating to 1619, is a World Heritage Site holding carved Goanese furniture, fragile Chinese pottery and porcelain, Indian tapestries and Arab drapes – sadly damaged by a leaking roof. This neoclassical governor's palace is today the National Museum of Mozambique.

White-faced women are a common sight on Ilha de Moçambique. Their protective masks are a paste made of root extract derived from the nciro tree, which acts as a moisturiser and offers sun protection.

PEMBA

Because of its isolation, Pemba's gorgeous sands with long lines of palms standing sentinel aren't exactly overrun by visitors – which means there is plenty of potential for development. There are stirrings... Wimbe is the beach most people are drawn to (5km/3 miles east of the village), but don't limit yourself, there are plenty of others. Divers and snorkellers fin round the reef lying 300m (330yd) offshore, leaving others to indulge in sail-boarding, wind-surfing, jet-skiing or big-game fishing. On the village outskirts are *bairros* – the most characterful is Paquite Quete – where villagers, traders and craftsmen congregate to test out your negotiating skills. Be sure to check out the black ebony Makonde carvings.

QUIRIMBA ARCHIPELAGO

The coral island of Ibo is mentioned in Arab writings of the eighth century. Arabs settled here as it enabled effective defence against Madagascan marauders. Today's ruins, though, reflect its Portuguese heritage, especially in the star-shaped fort, São João Baptista, dating to the early 1770s. The disintegrating architecture of the once magnificent – now roofless – mansions and villas of Portuguese officials lend a surreal air to the place, palpable with the ghosts of yesteryear. Today, skilled craftsmen on the island work in silver and have earned respect for their craft. Quirimba's other islands feature fishing settlements, coconut plantations and Portuguese plantation houses.

ORIENTATION – STREETPLANS

HOW TO USE THIS MAP

This page can be used to locate any streetplan. Each entry on the map has a number which corresponds with a page number in the book.

LEGEND FOR STREETPLANS

Symbol	Description	Symbol	Description
	Major road	L	Library
	Main road	P	Parking
	Minor road	i	Information
	Pedestrian mall	✝	Church
M6 R101 N4	Route number	G	Mosque
→	One-way road	✡	Synagogue
HARTBEESPOORT ↑	Directional	+	Hospital
Sunnyside	Area/suburb name	✈	Airport
★ Museum	Point of interest		Park
✉	Post Office		Lake/dam
•	Police station	Apies	Perennial river
L University of Botswana	University		Non-perennial river

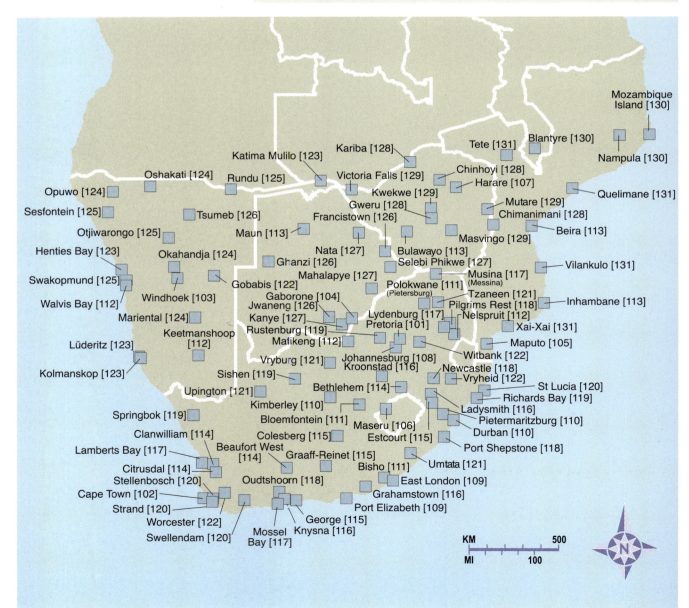

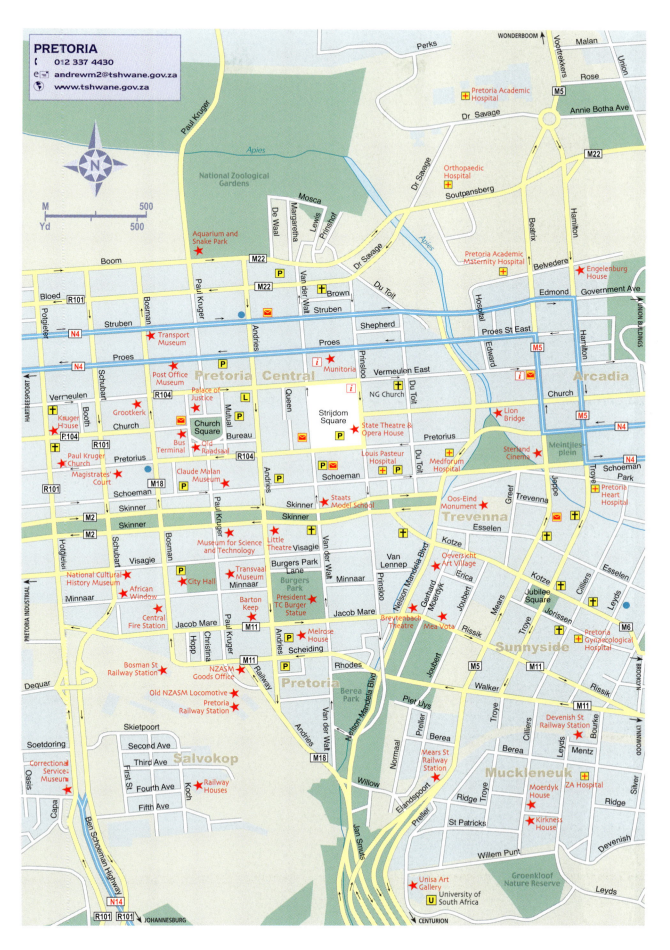

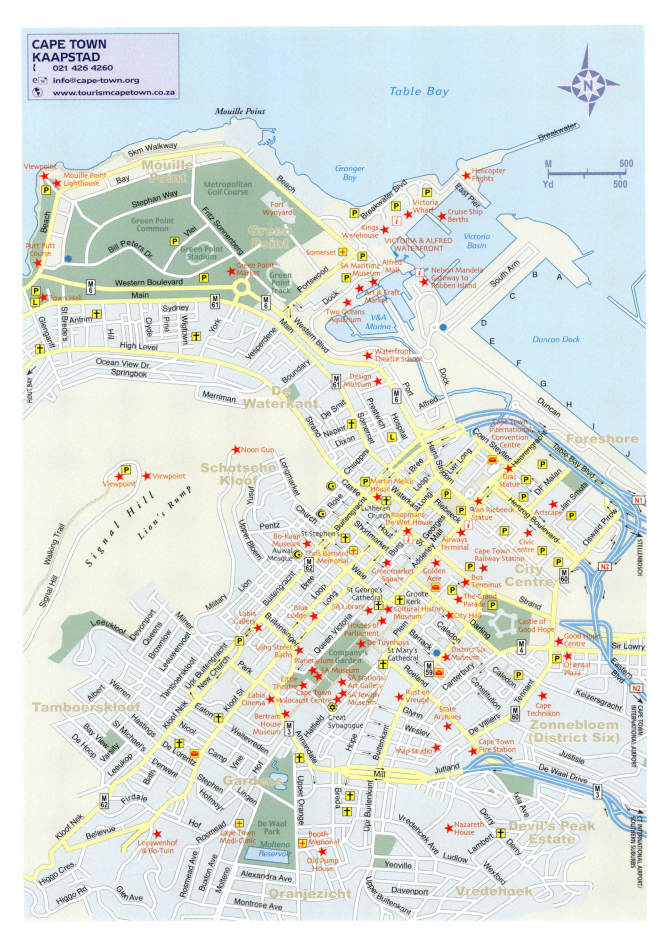

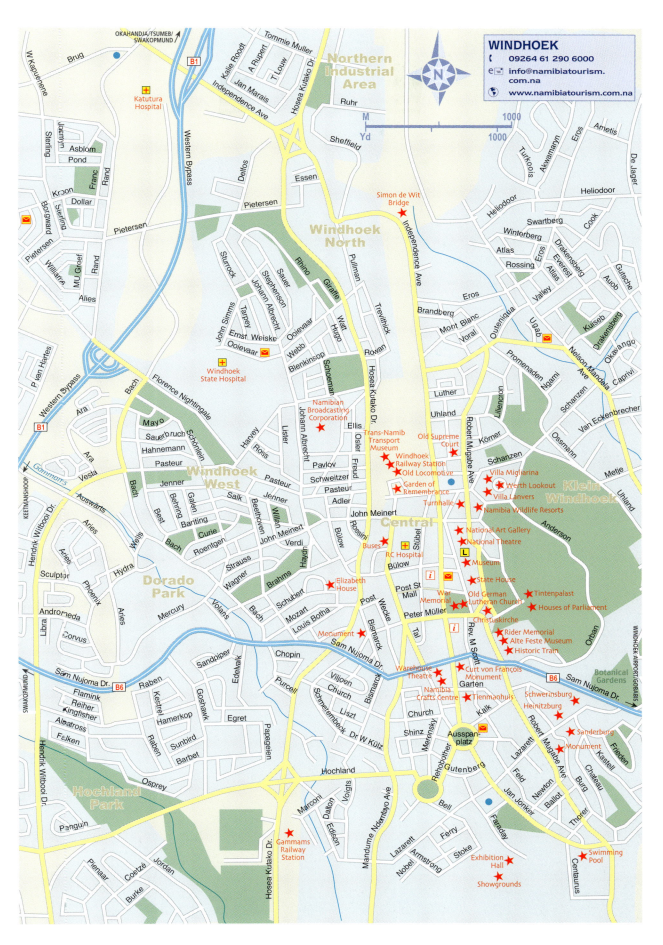

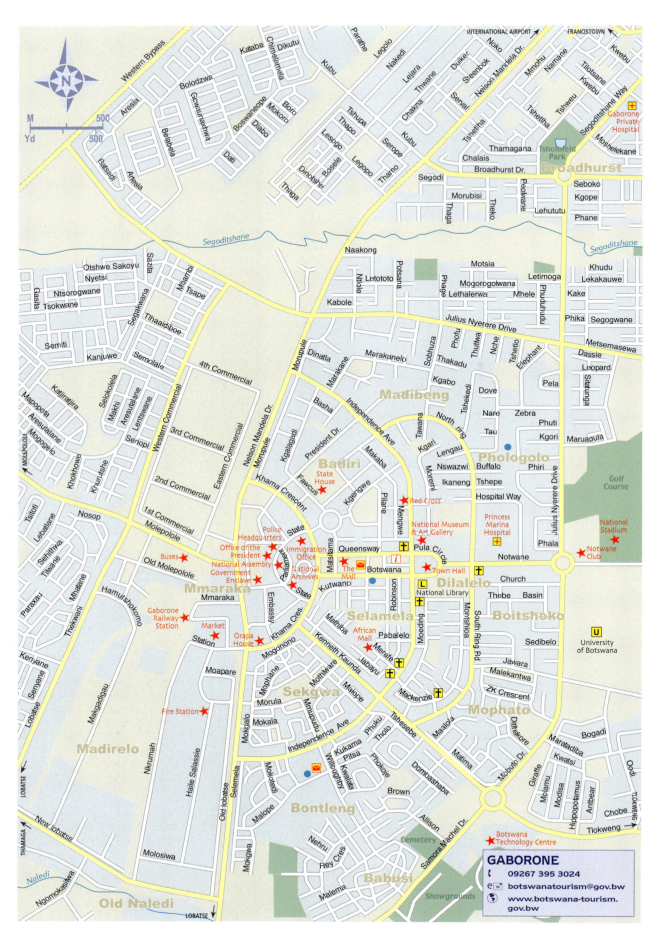

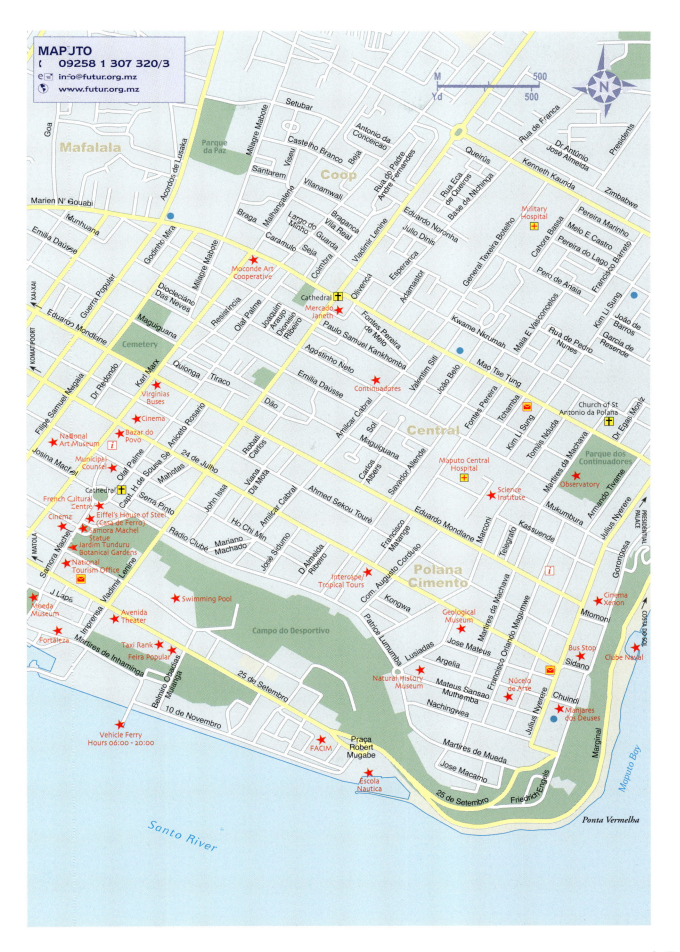

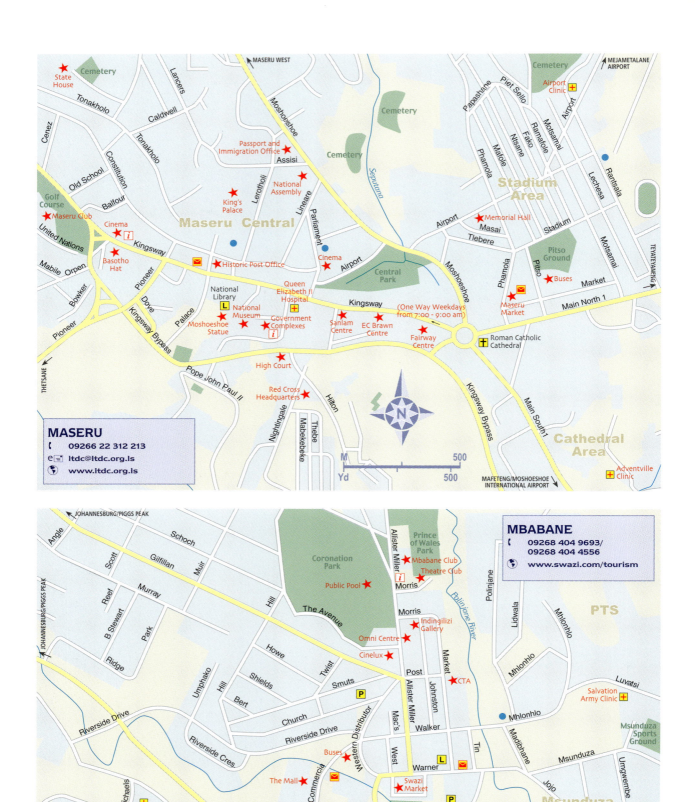

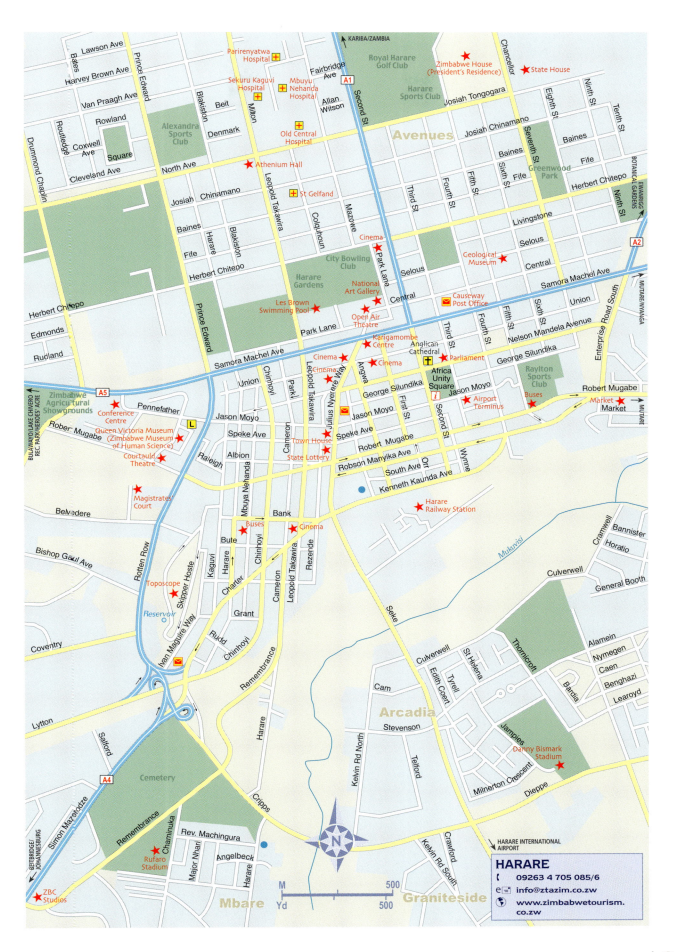

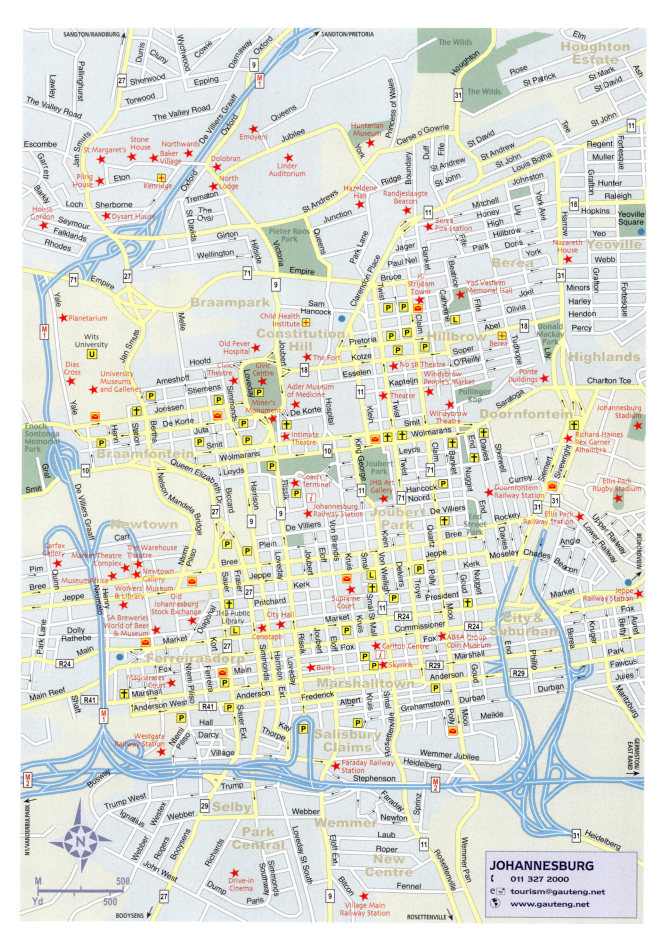

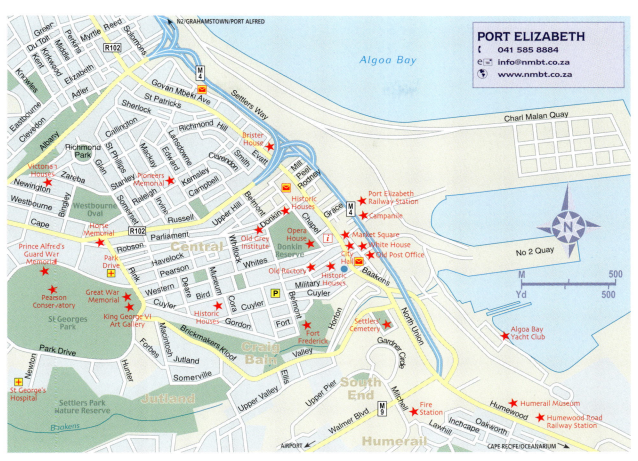
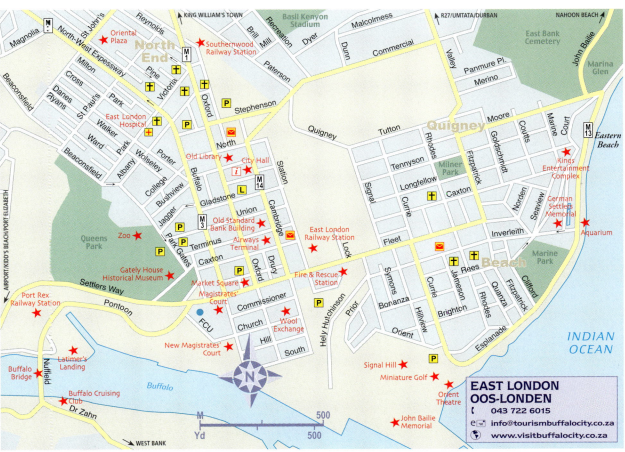

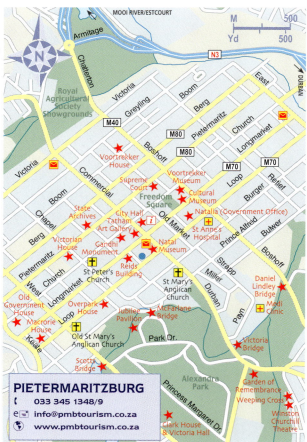

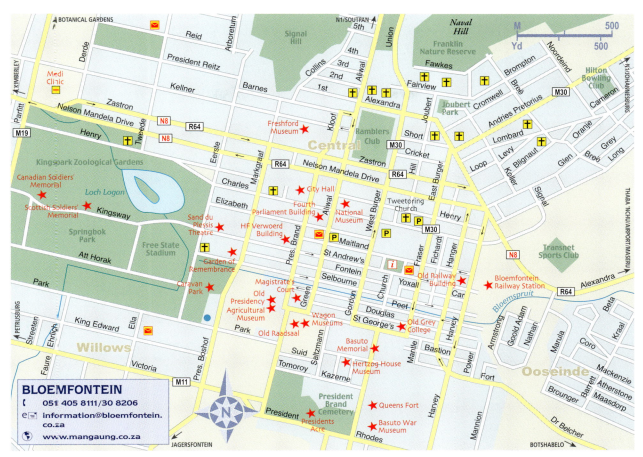
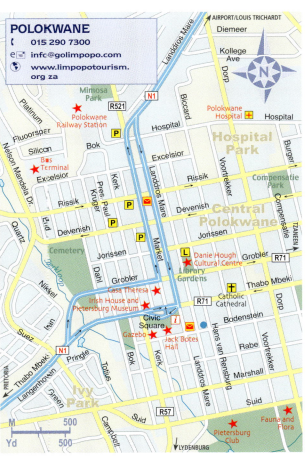
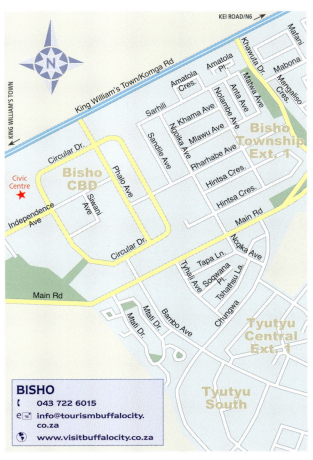

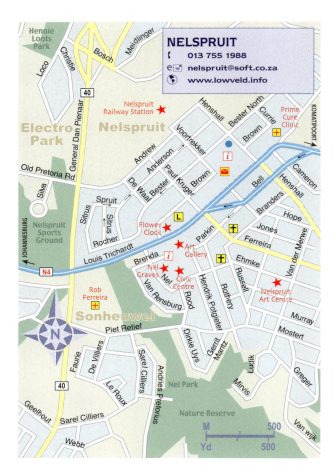
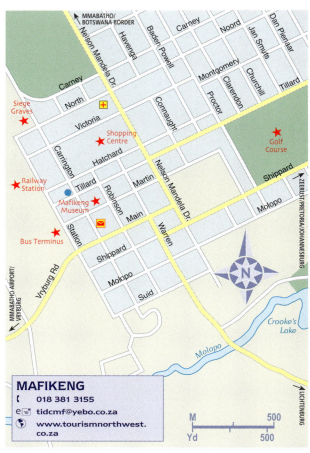
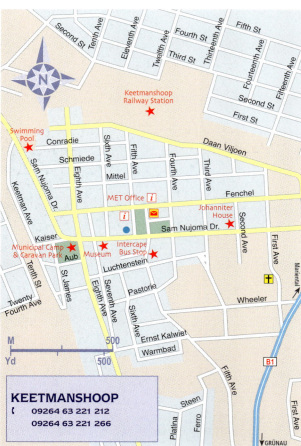
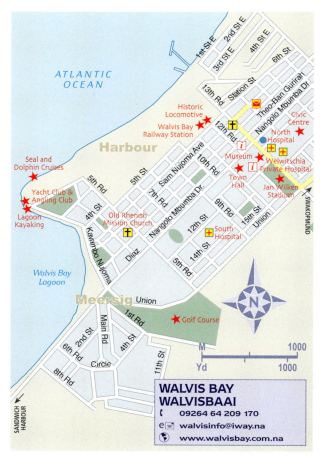

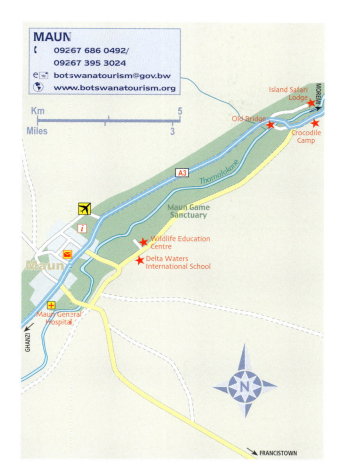

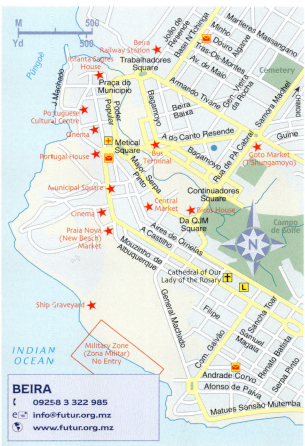

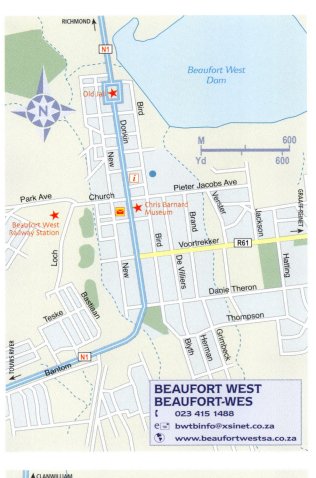
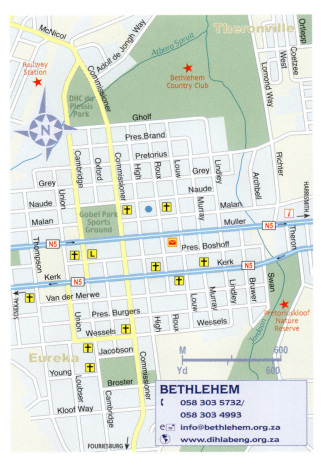
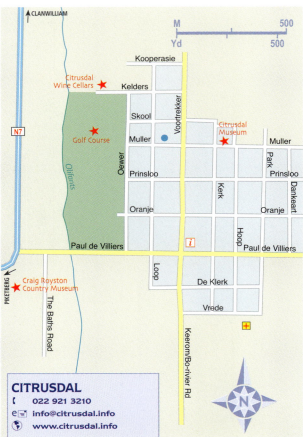
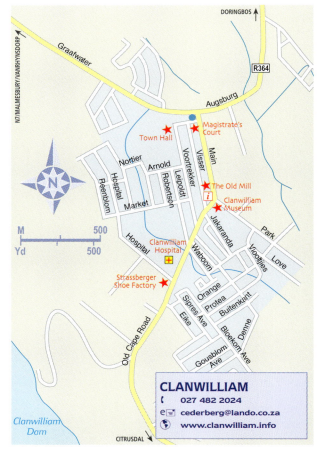

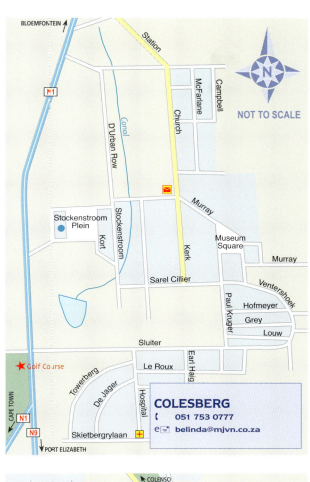
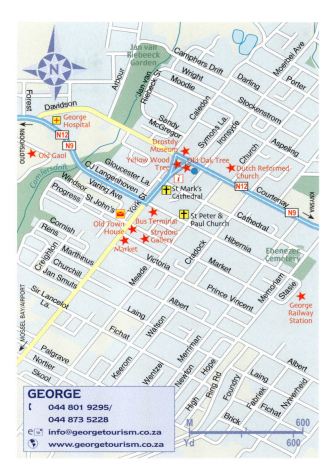

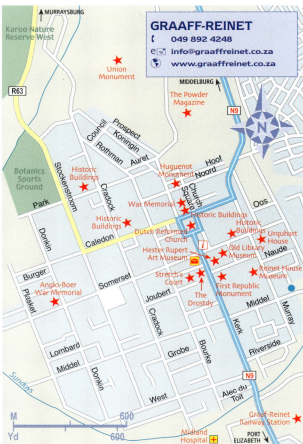

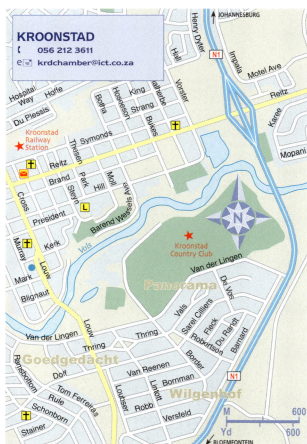
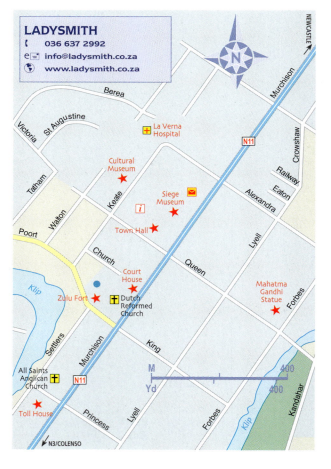

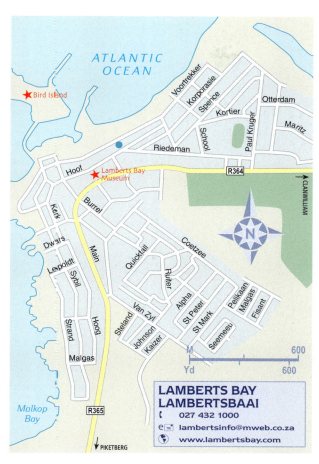

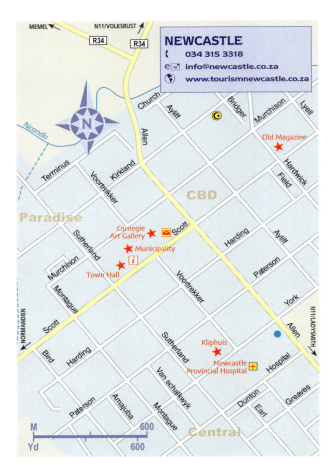
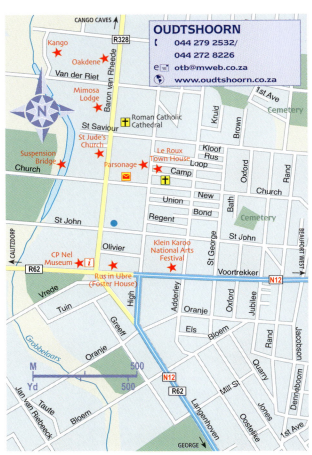
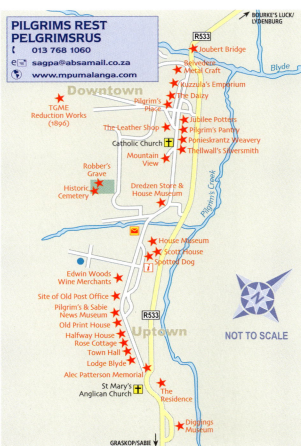
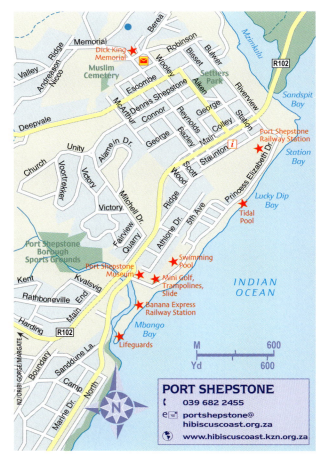

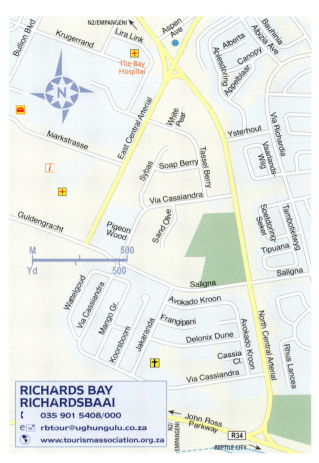
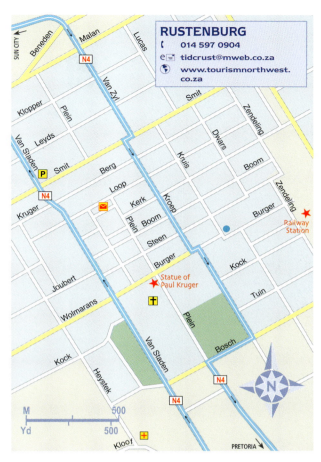

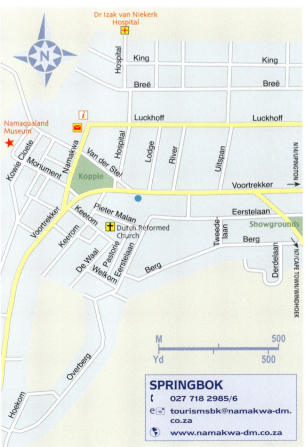

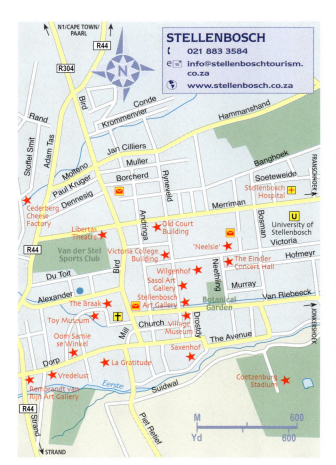

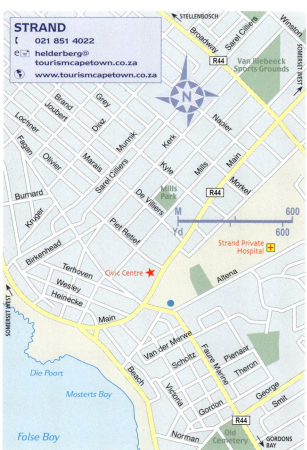
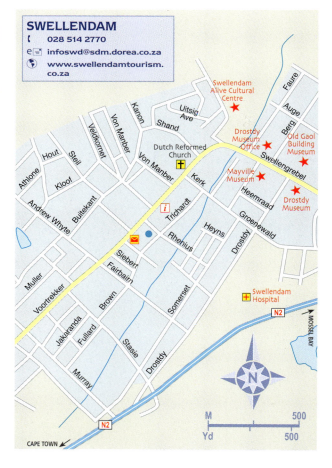

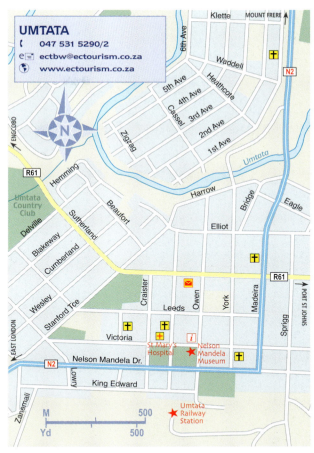
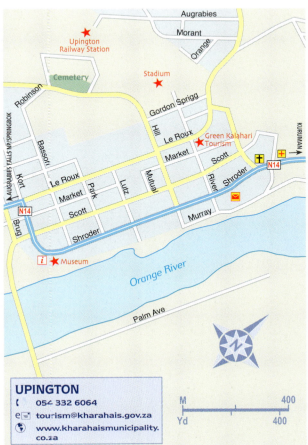
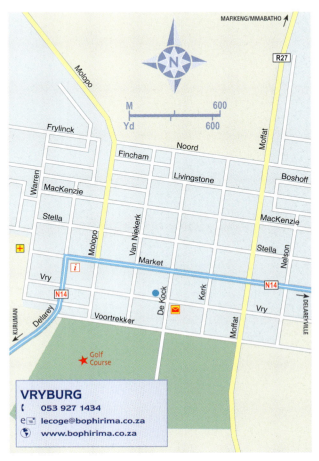

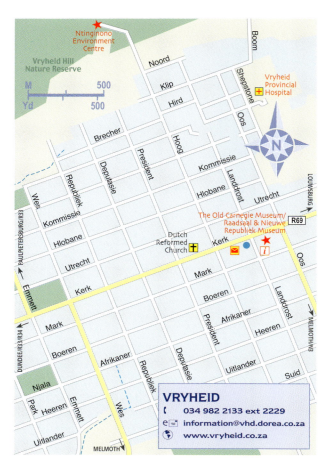

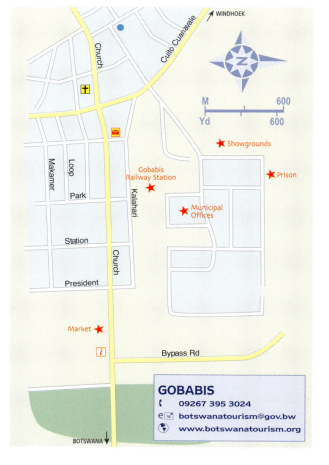

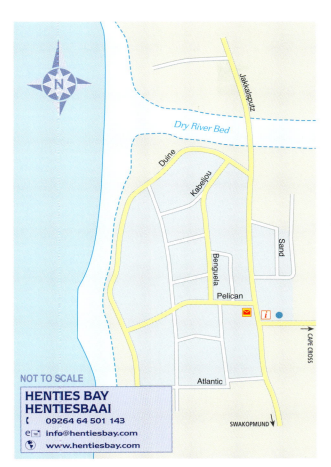
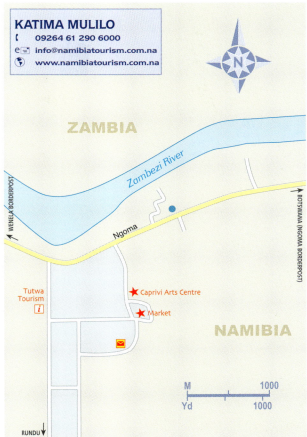
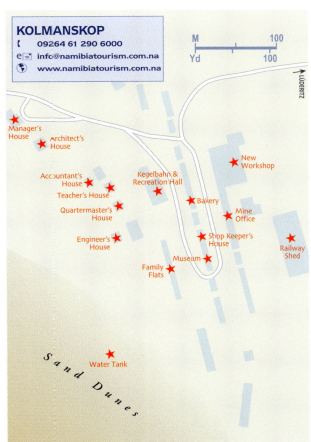
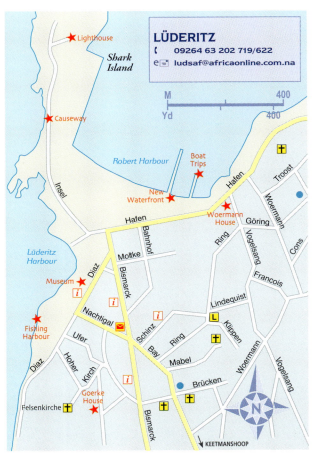

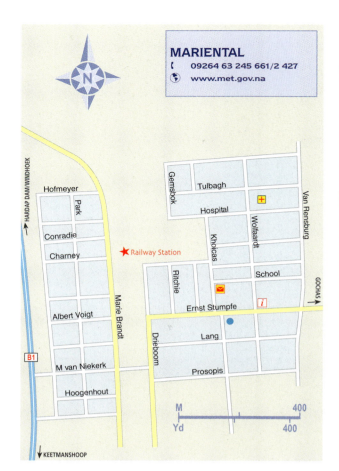
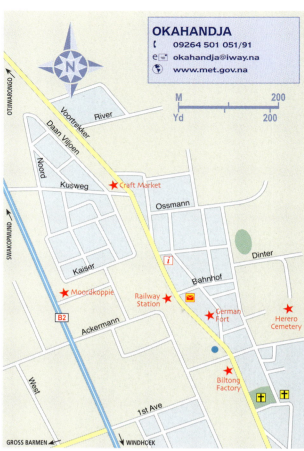

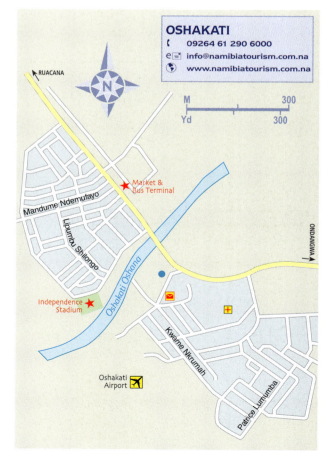

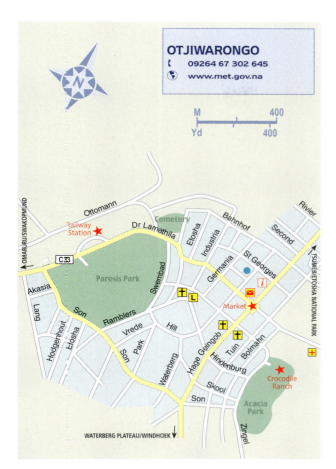
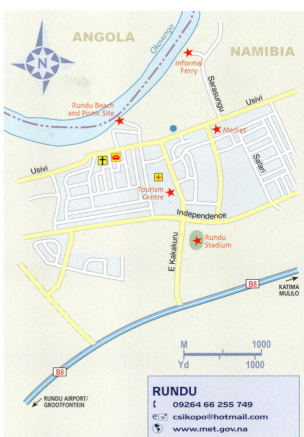

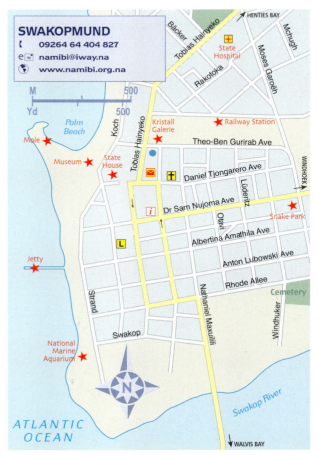

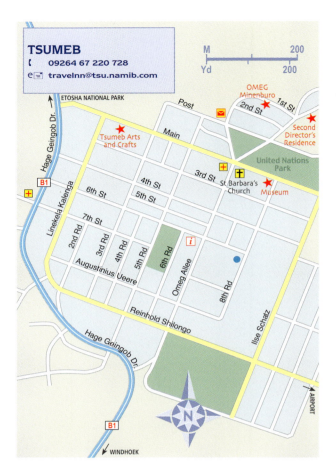

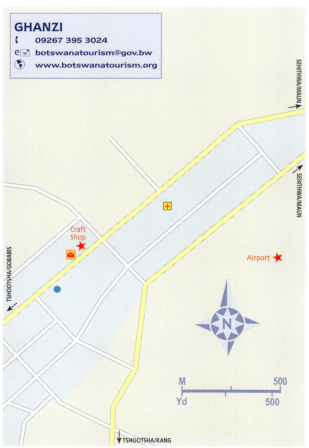

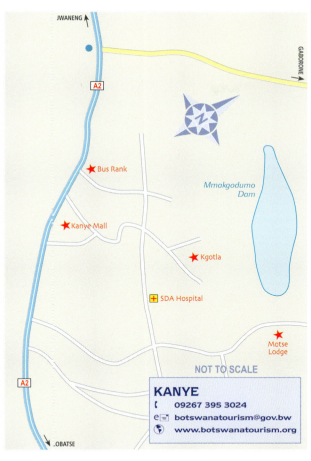
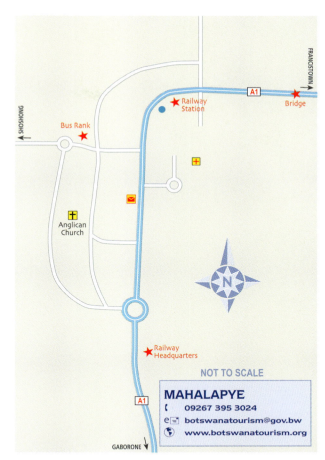
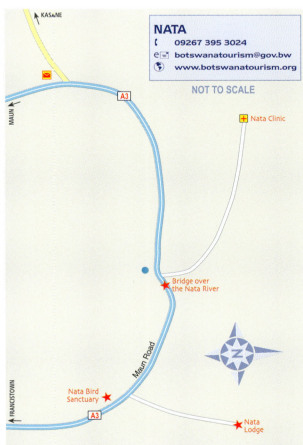
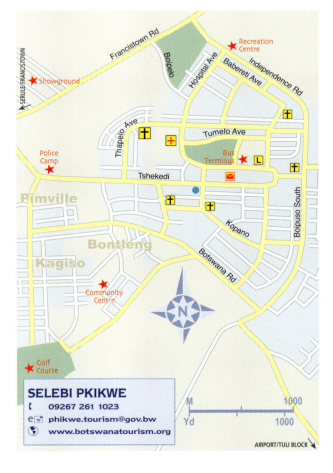

CHIMANIMANI
09263 4 706 077/8
09263 4 707 624/9
natparks@africaonline.co.zw
www.zimparks.com

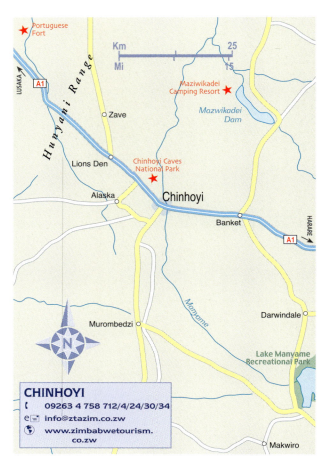

CHINHOYI
09263 4 758 712/4/24/30/34
info@ztazim.co.zw
www.zimbabwetourism.co.zw

GWERU
09263 54 224 071
09263 54 224 230

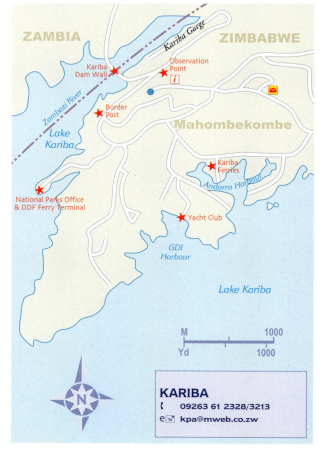

KARIBA
09263 61 2328/3213
kpa@mweb.co.zw

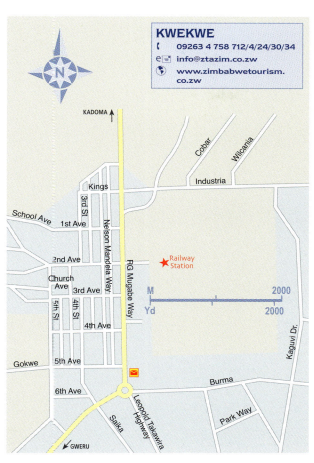
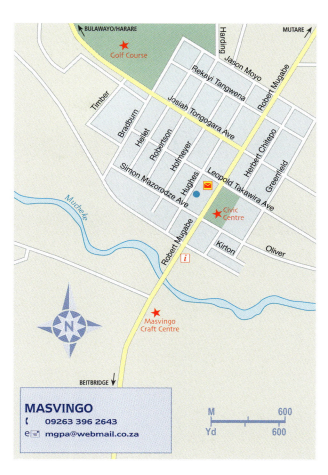
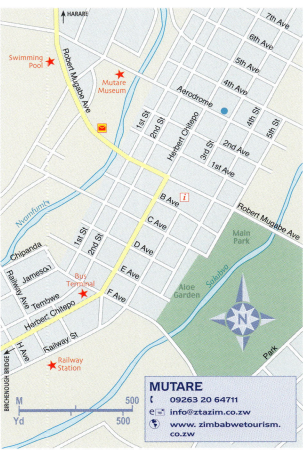

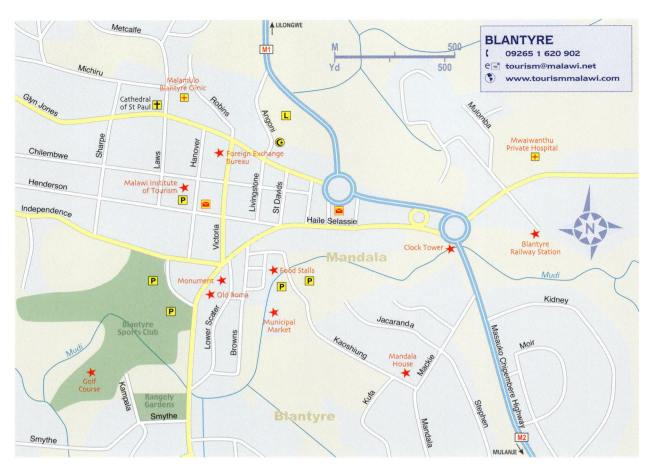

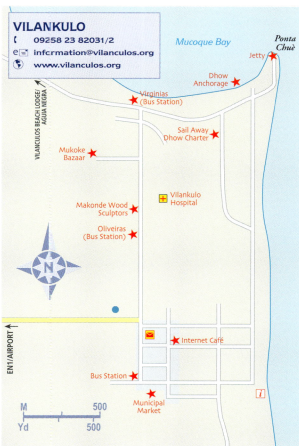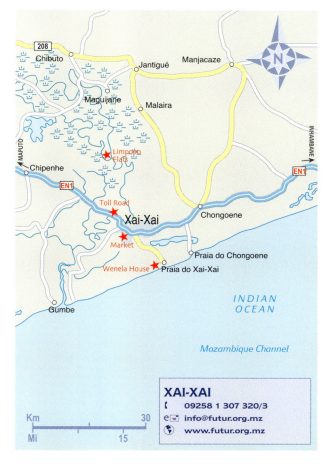

ORIENTATION – MAIN TOURING MAPS

HOW TO USE THIS MAP

This map can be used to locate streetplans or any main touring map page. Each frame on the map has a number which corresponds with a page number.

Locate main and capital cities within these pages, using the quick reference page numbers below:

CITIES & TOWNS (Alphabetical)
Pg – 134 Cape Town – South Africa
Pg – 175 Beira – Mozambique
Pg – 144 Bloemfontein – S Africa
Pg – 172 Bulawayo – Zimbabwe
Pg – 146 Durban – South Africa
Pg – 172 Francistown – Botswana
Pg – 161 Gaborone – Botswana
Pg – 184 Harare – Zimbabwe
Pg – 153 Johannesburg – S Africa
Pg – 149 Keetmanshoop – Namibia
Pg – 155 Maputo – Mozambique
Pg – 145 Maseru – Lesotho
Pg – 170 Maun – Botswana
Pg – 137 Port Elizabeth – S Africa
Pg – 162 Pretoria – South Africa
Pg – 181 Victoria Falls – Zimbabwe
Pg – 156 Walvis Bay – Namibia
Pg – 157 Windhoek – Namibia

LEGEND FOR PAGES 134 - 197

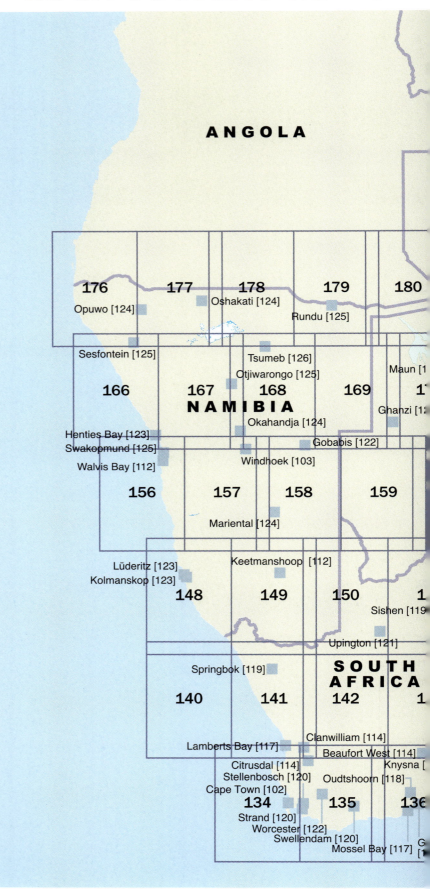

Atlantic Ocean

Indian Ocean

Atlantic Ocean

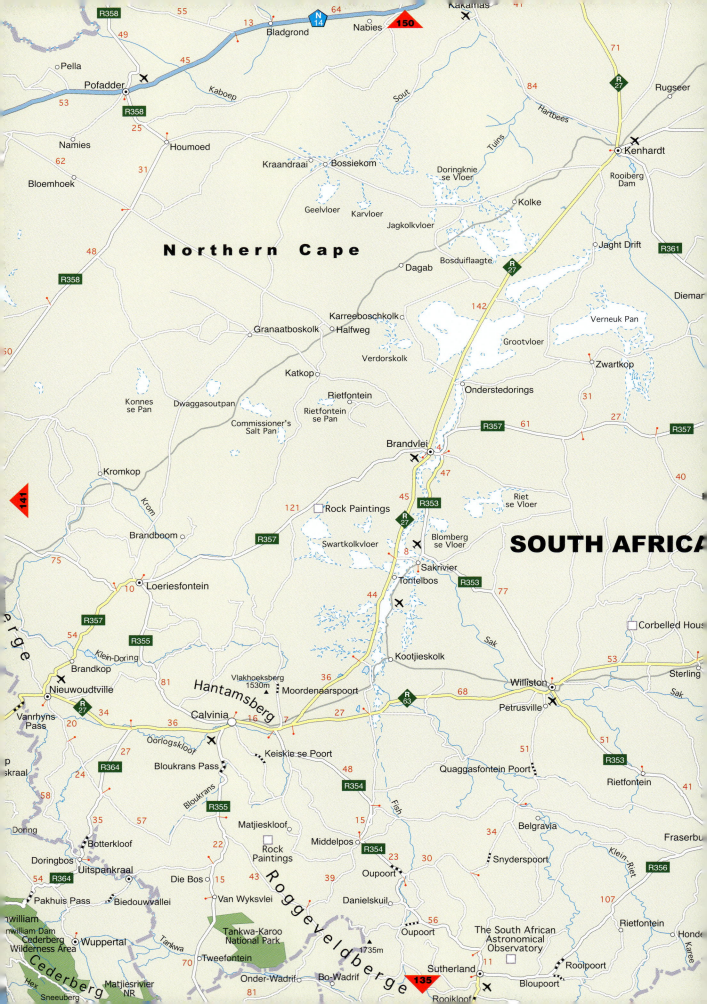

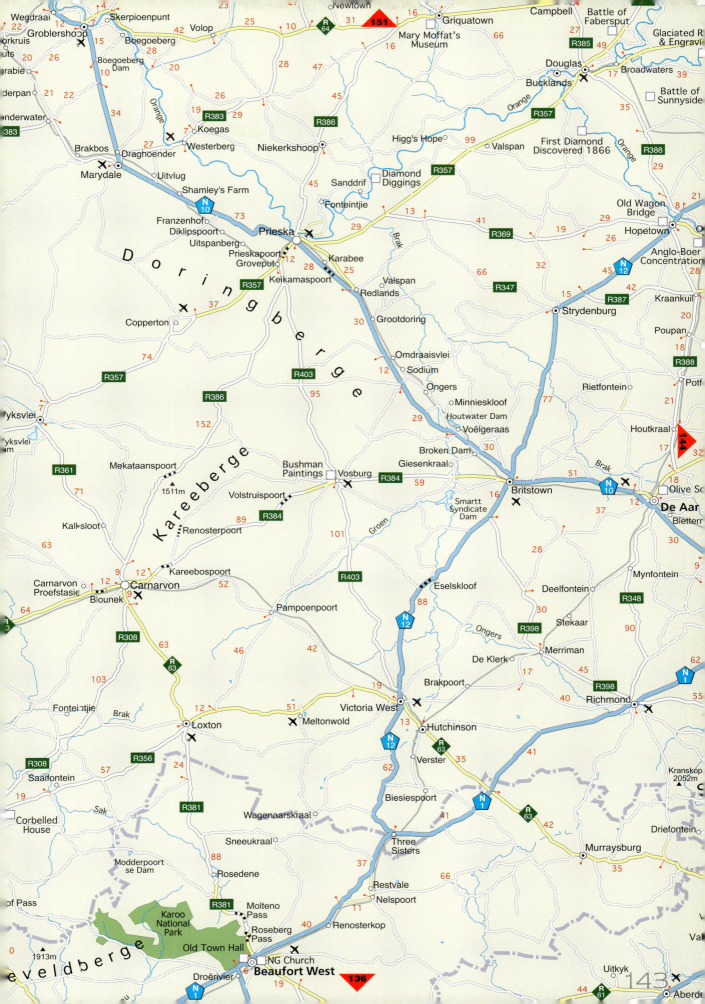

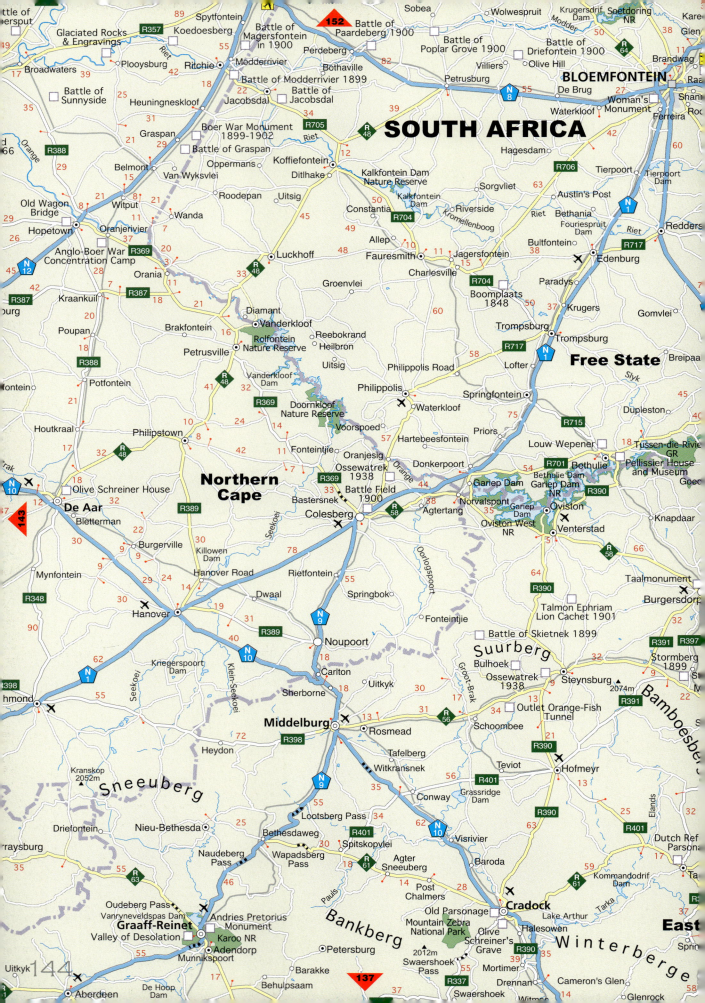

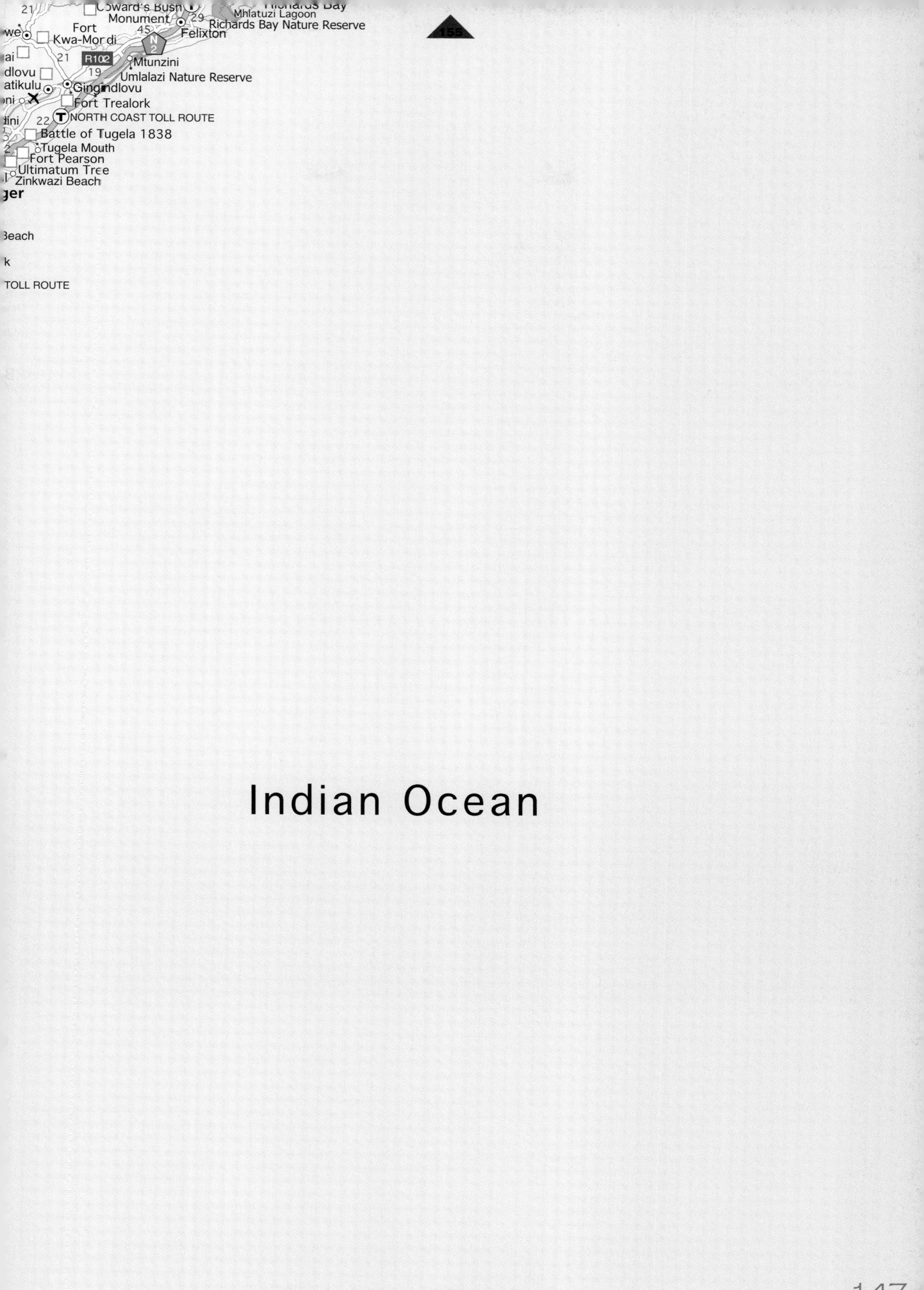

21 Coward's Bush Monument · Richards Bay
Fort Kwa-Mor di · 45 · Mhlatuzi Lagoon
· 29 · Richards Bay Nature Reserve
· Felixton
R102 · Mtunzini
21 · Umlalazi Nature Reserve
dlovu · 19
atikulu · Gingindlovu
· Fort Trealork
22 · T · NORTH COAST TOLL ROUTE
· Battle of Tugela 1838
· Tugela Mouth
· Fort Pearson
· Ultimatum Tree
· Zinkwazi Beach

ger

Beach

k

TOLL ROUTE

155

Indian Ocean

147

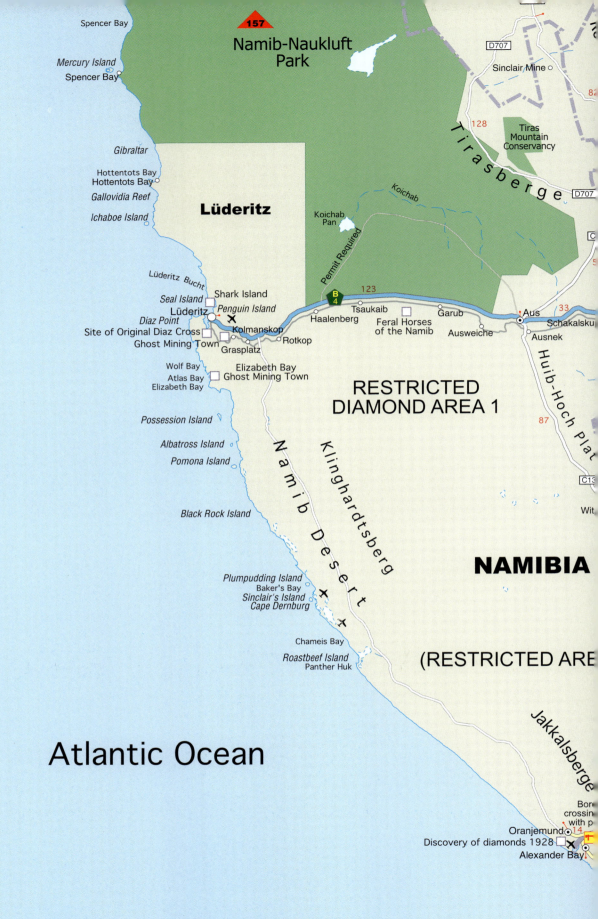

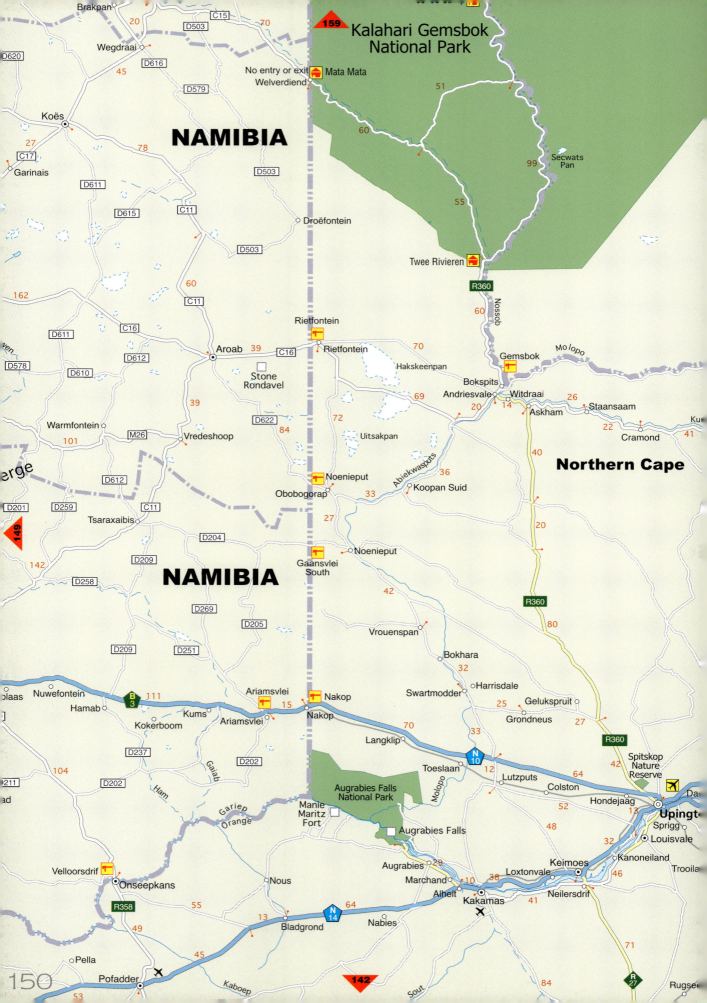

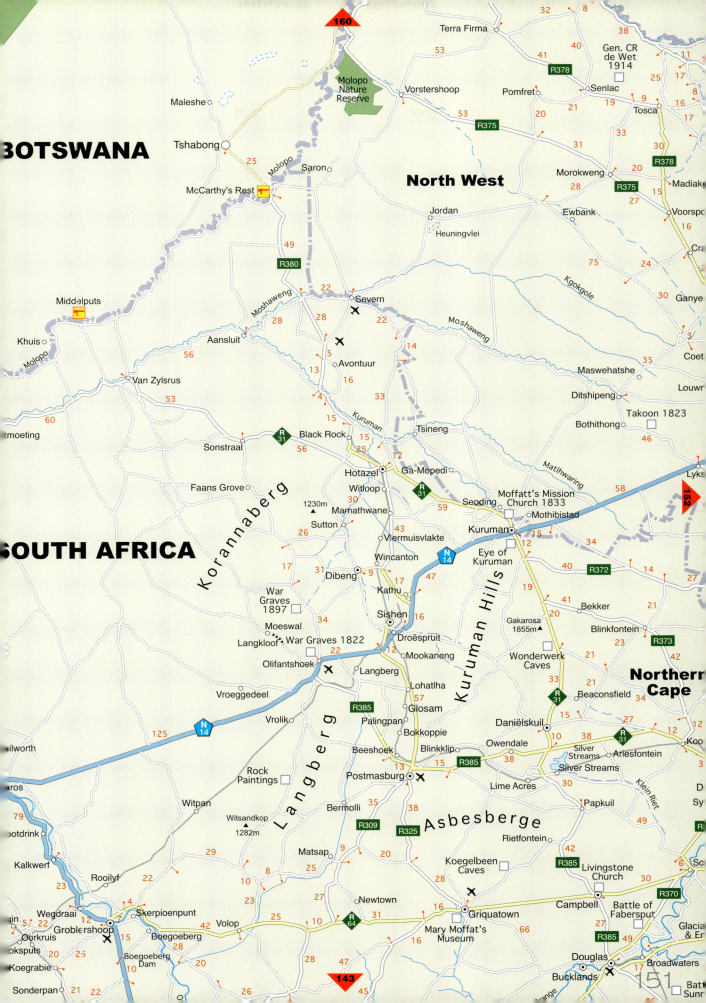

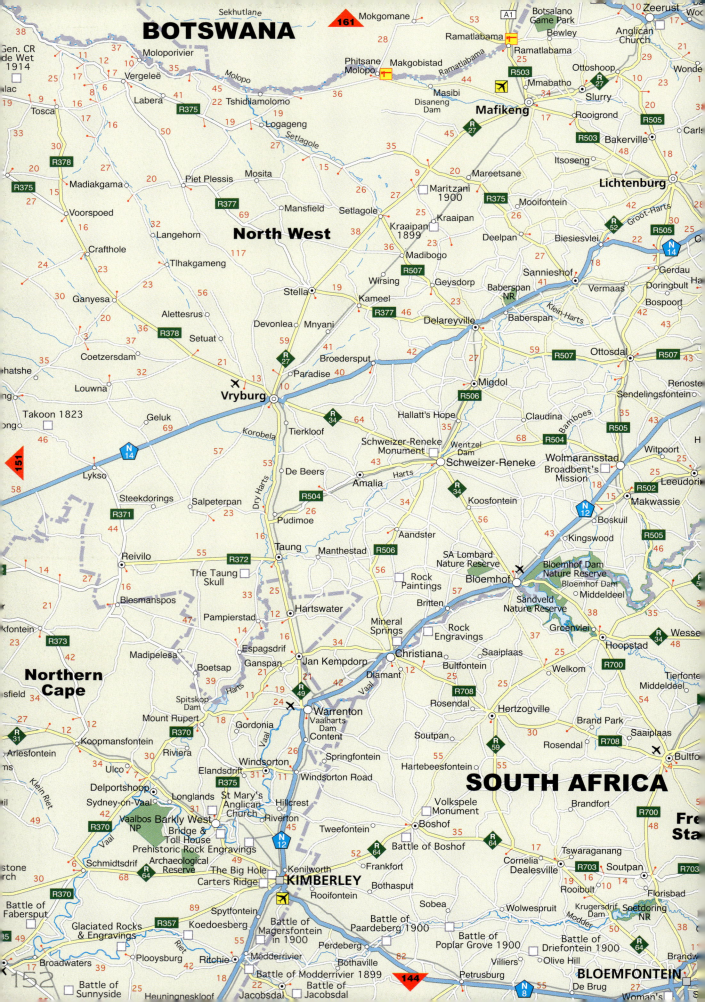

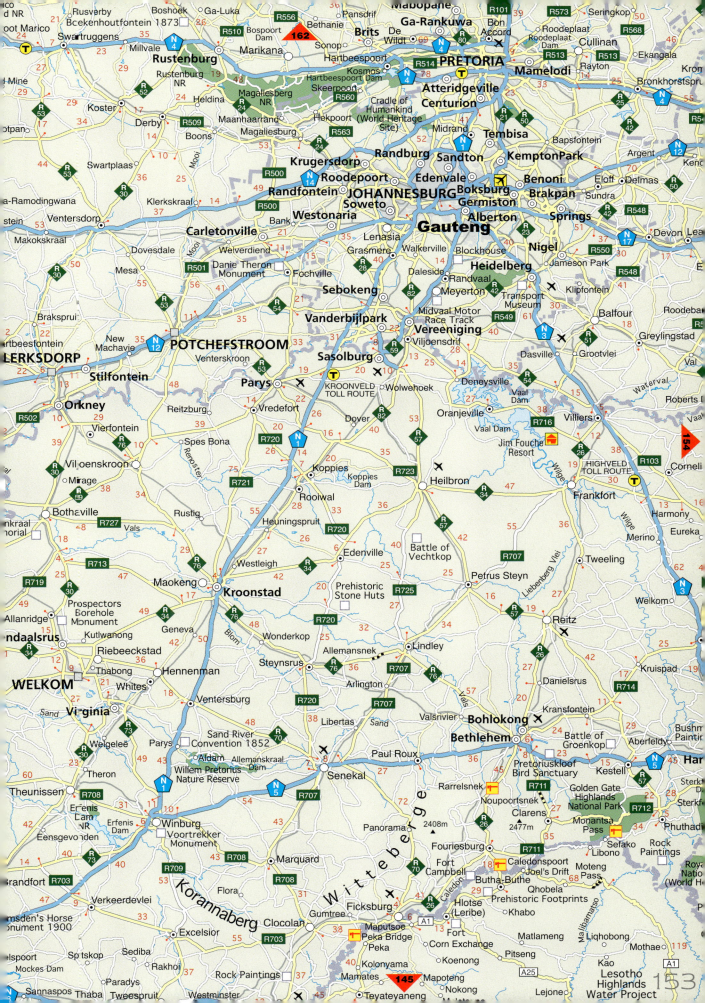

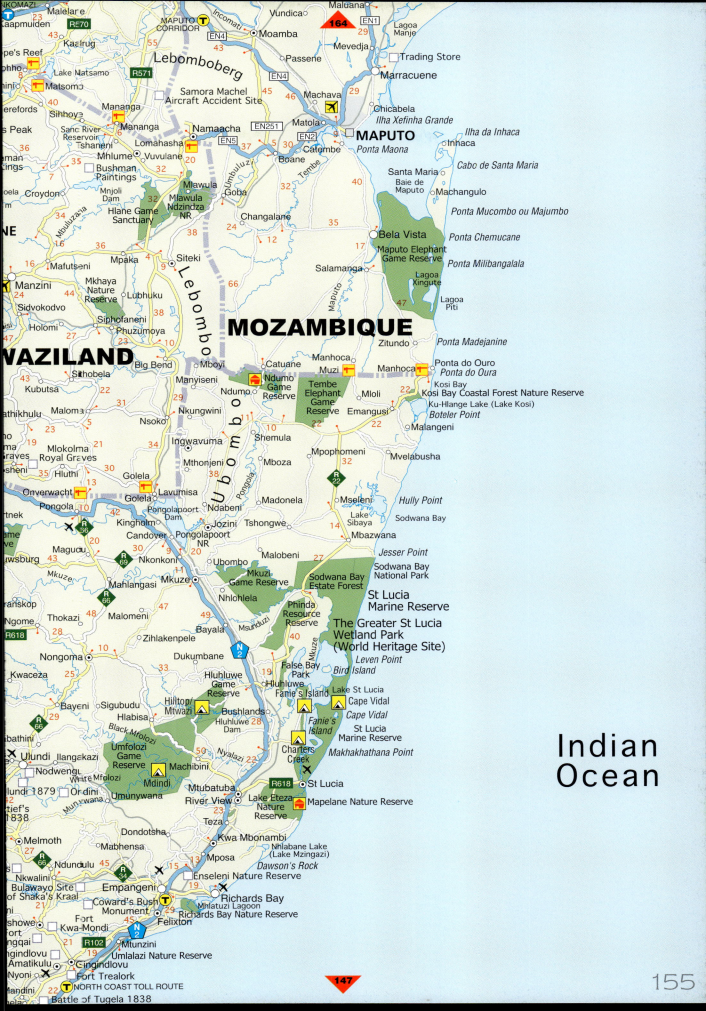

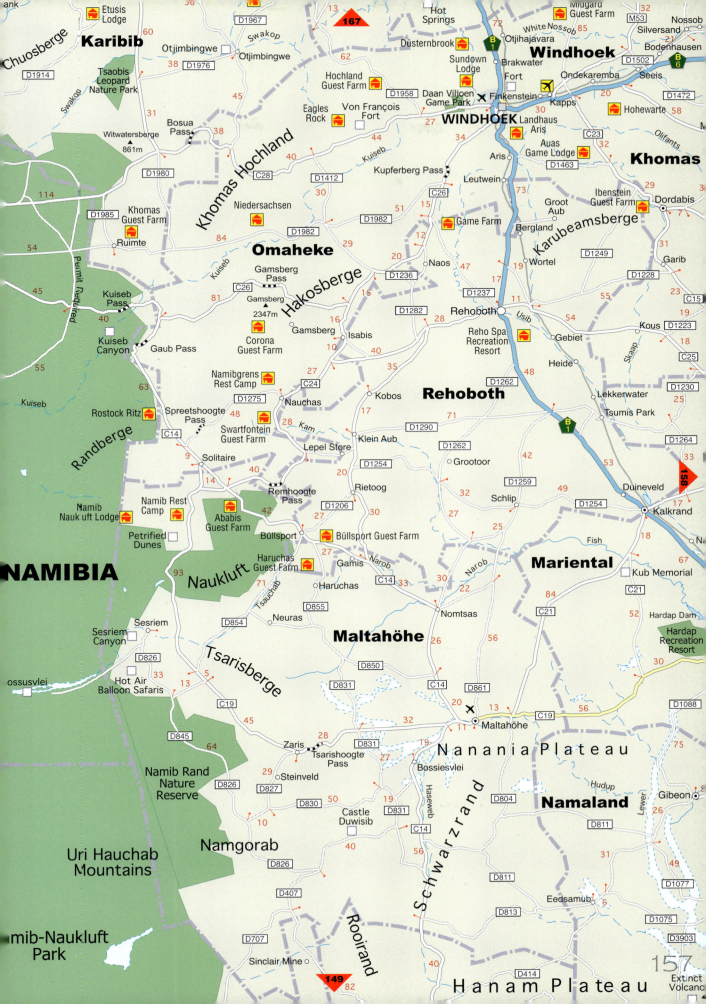

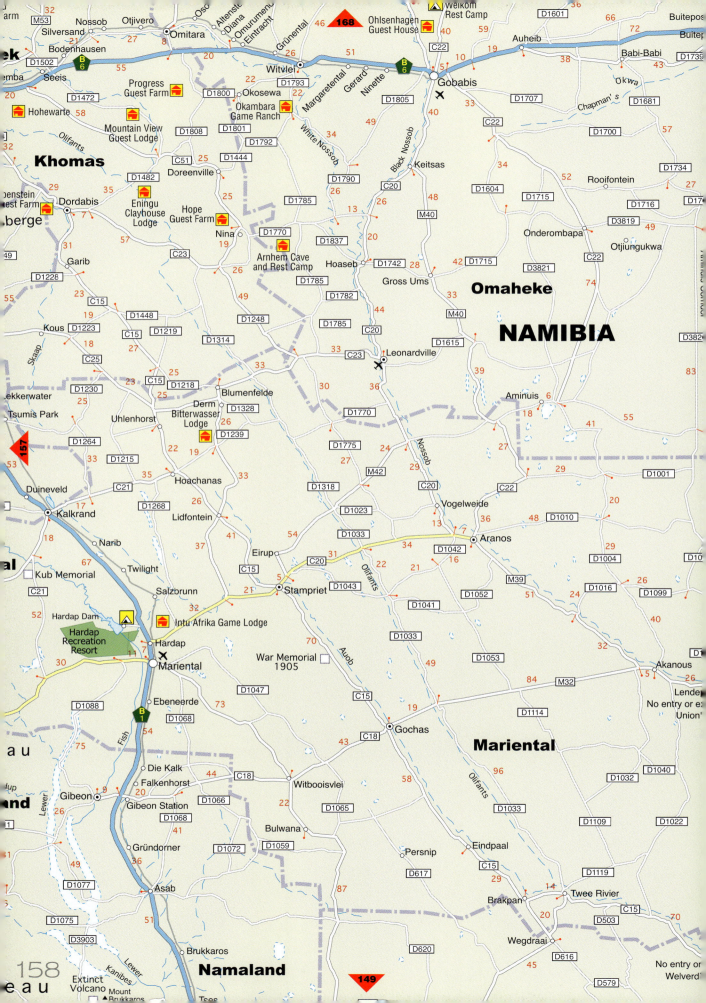

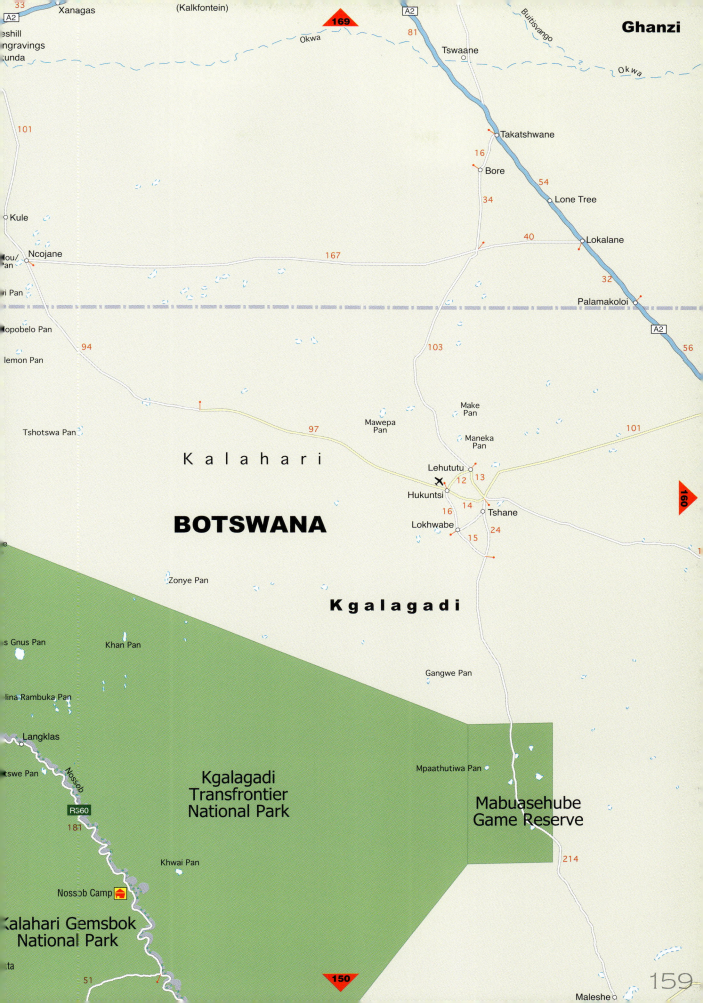

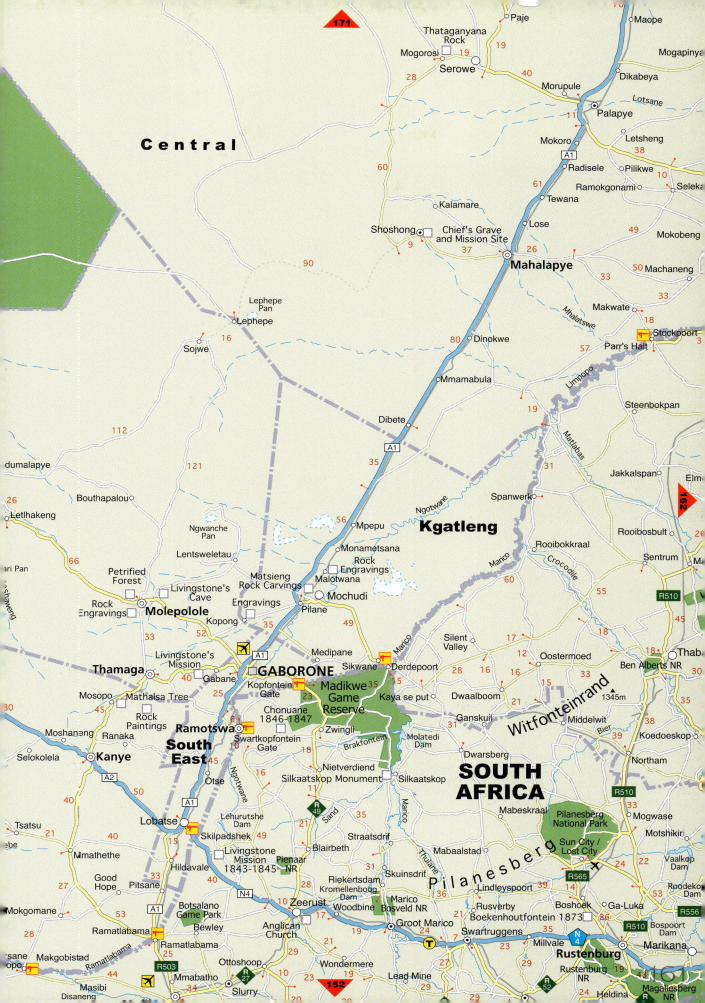

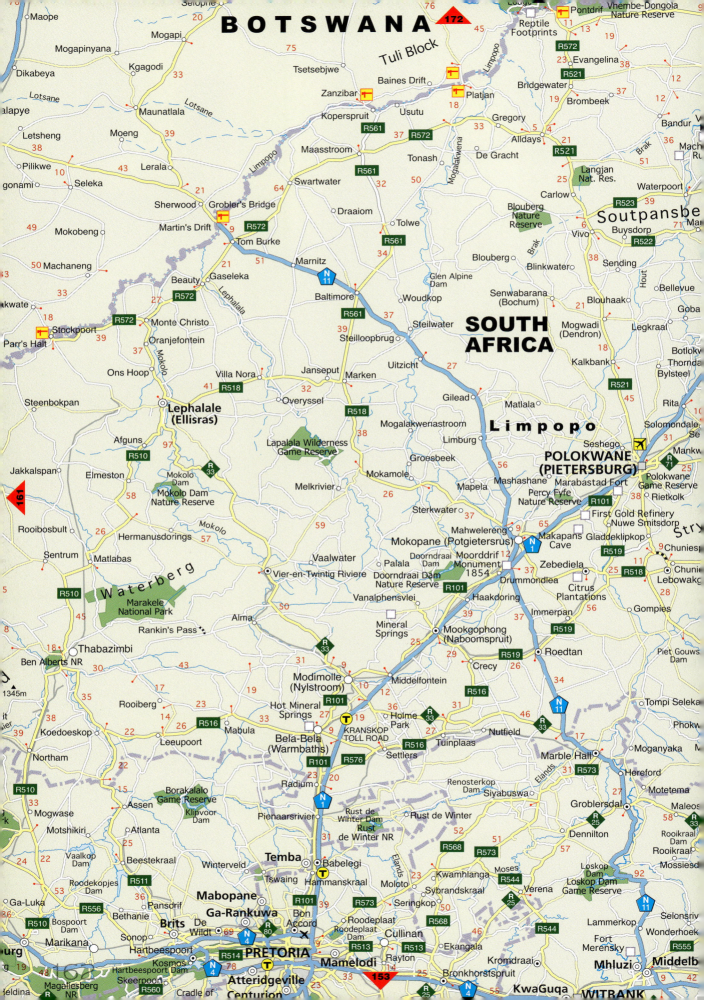

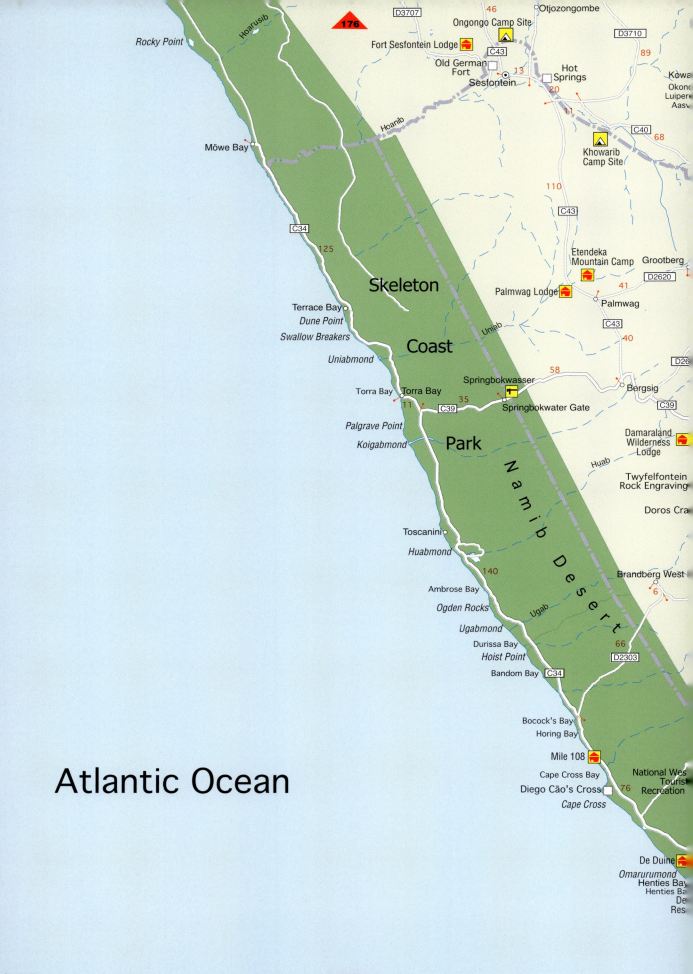

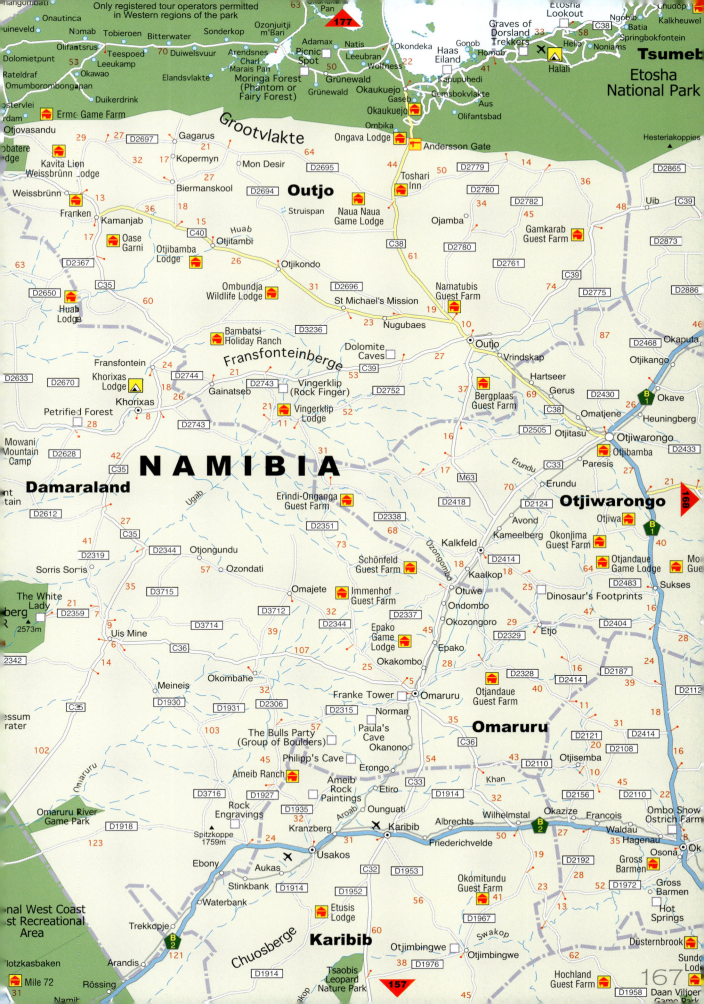

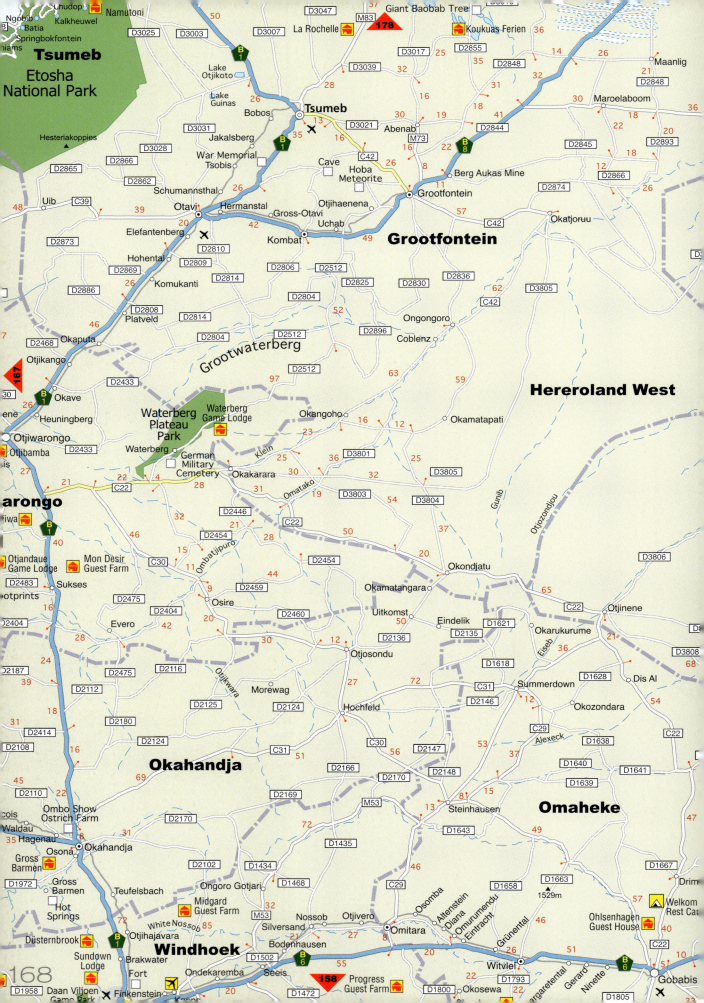

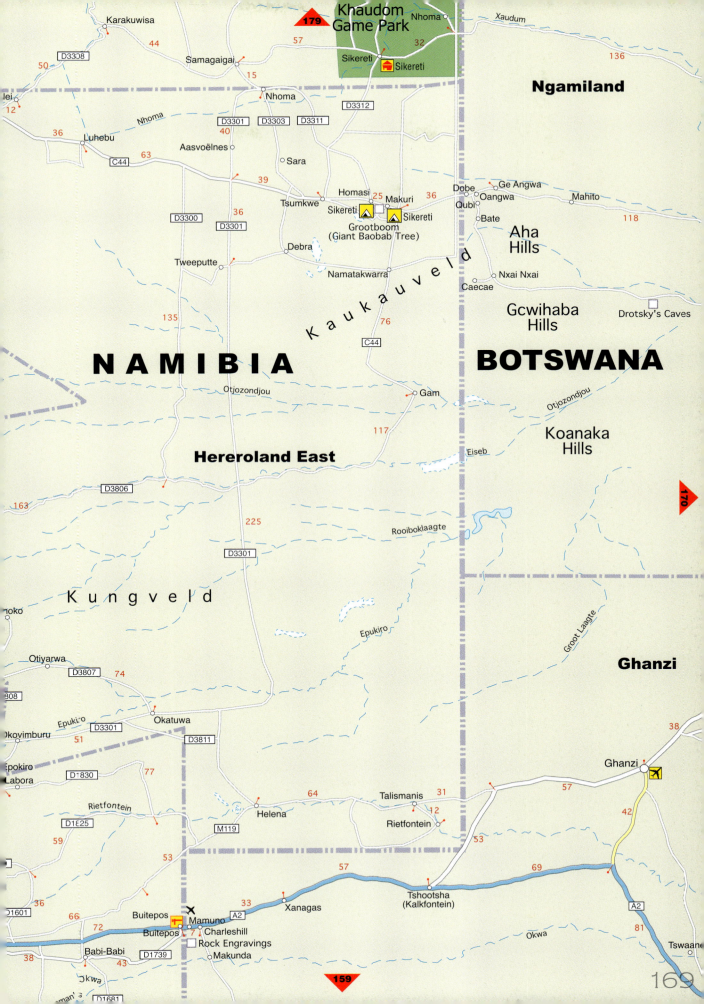

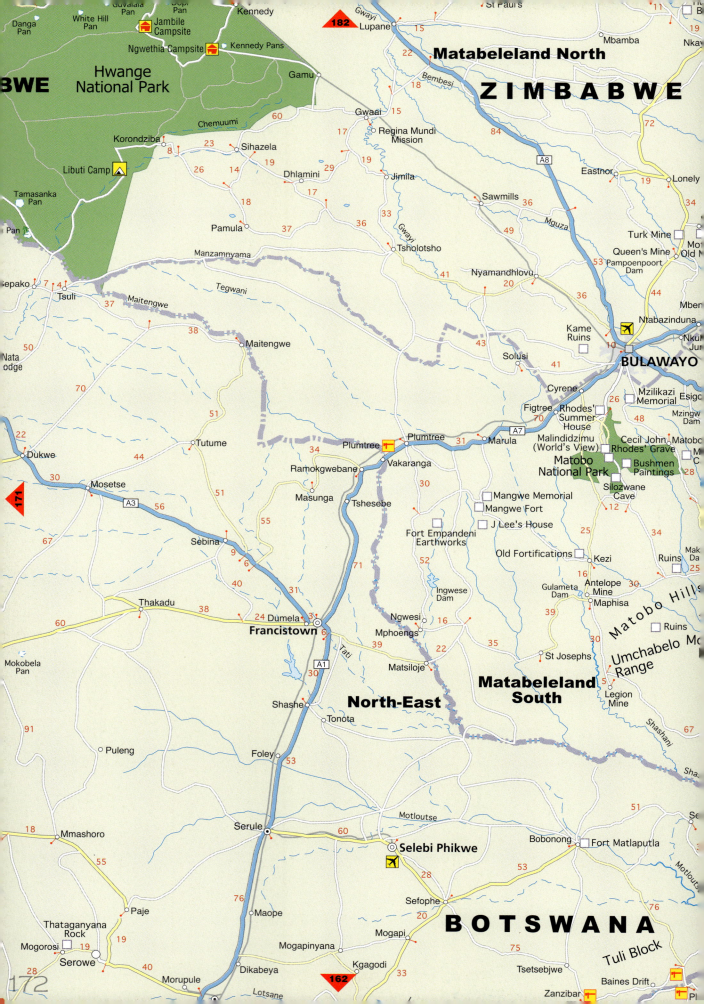

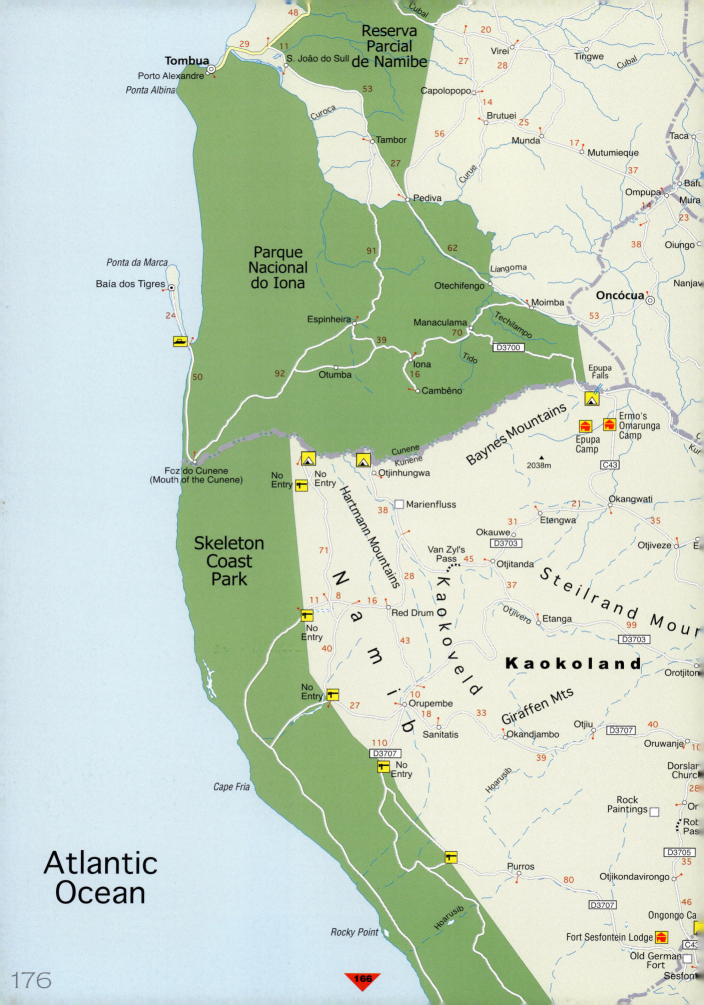

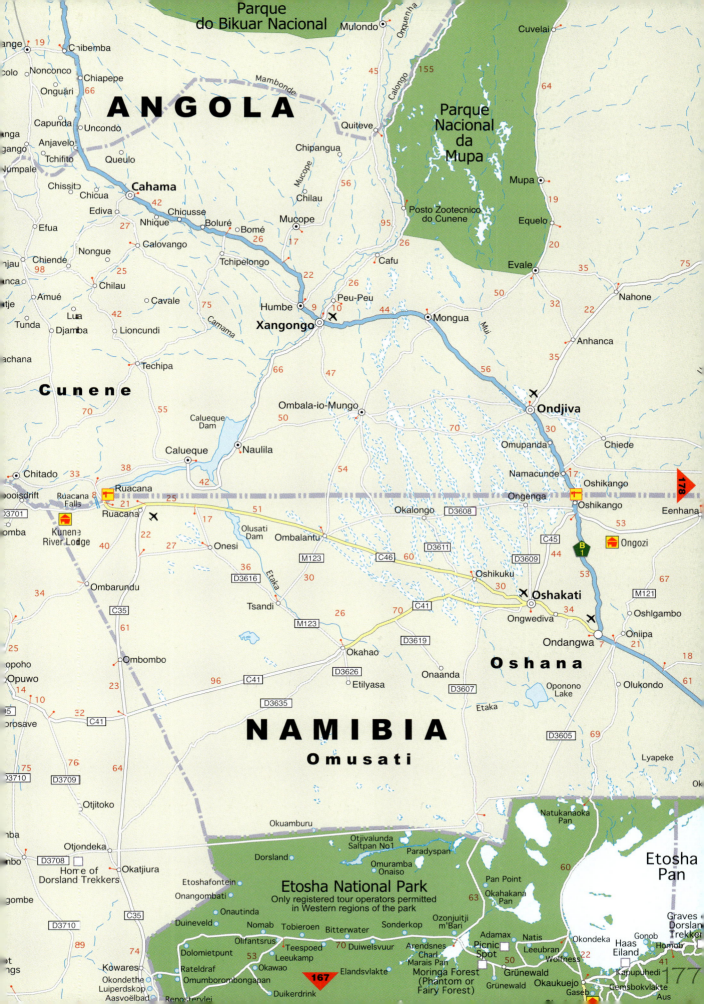

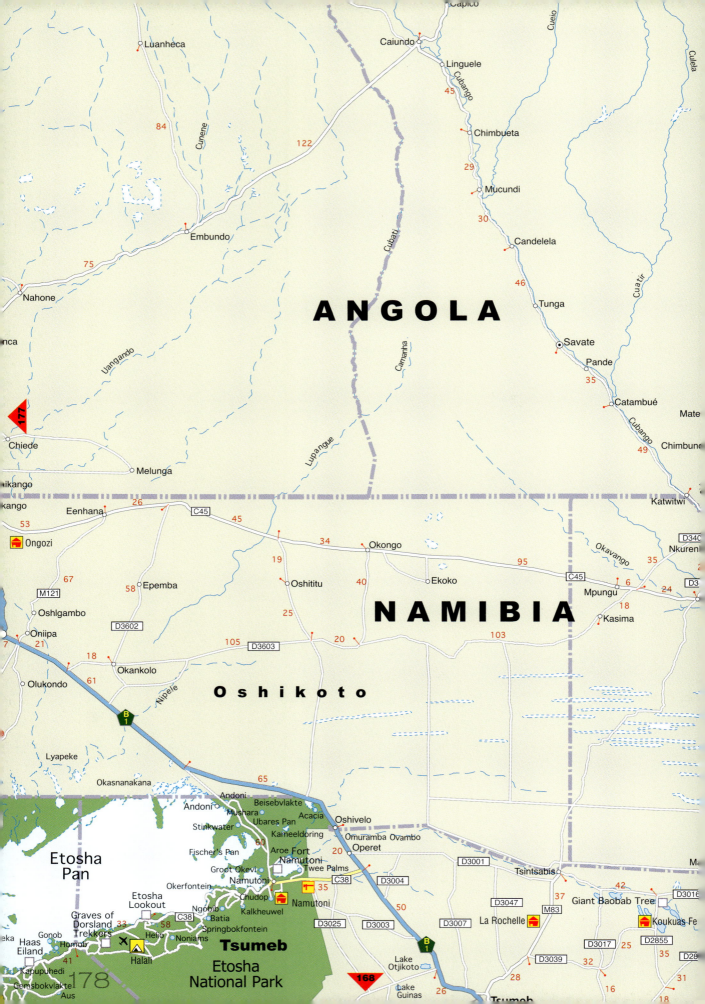

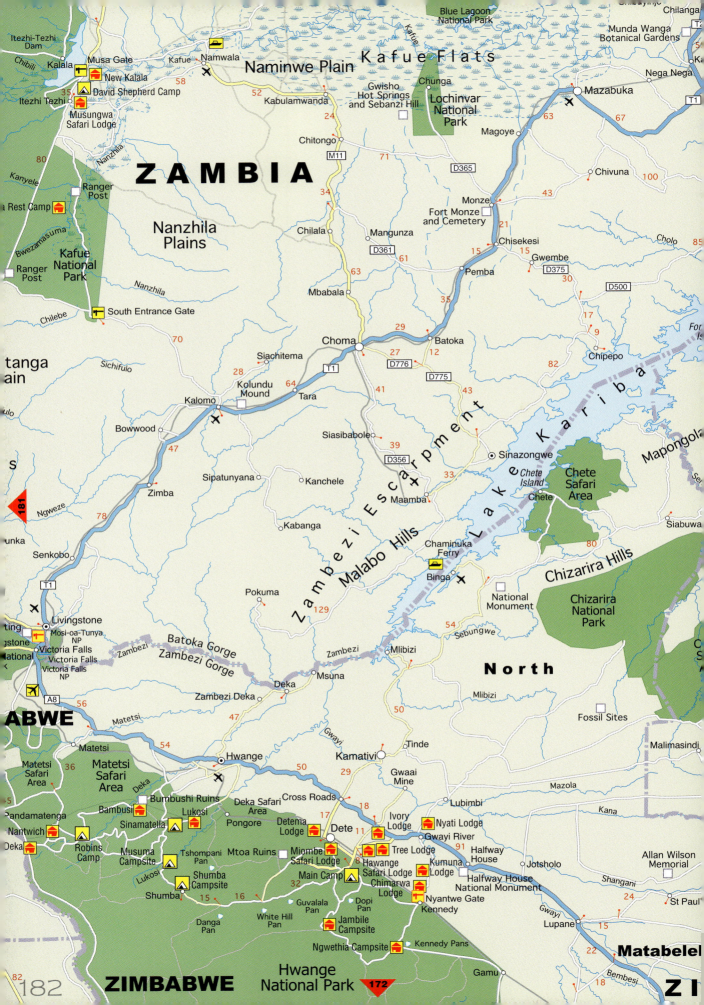

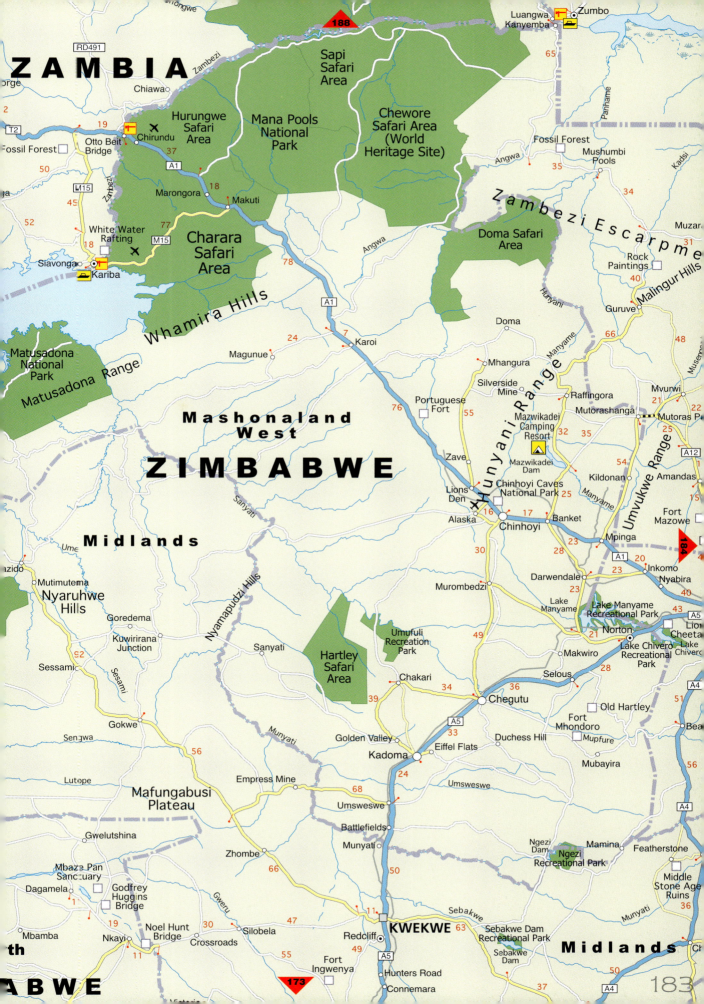

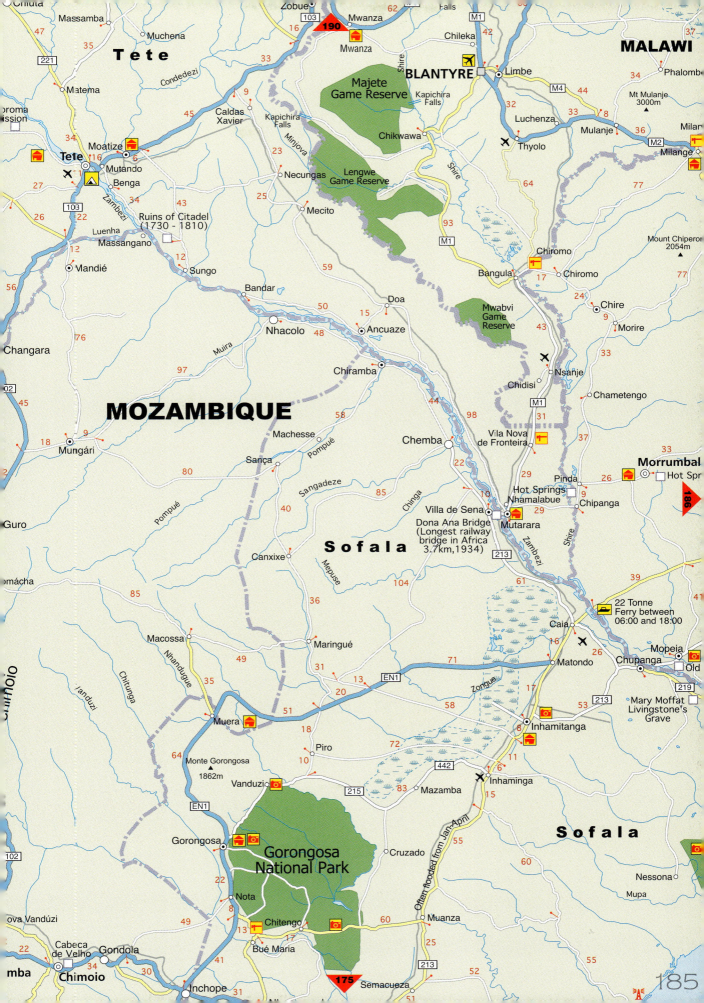

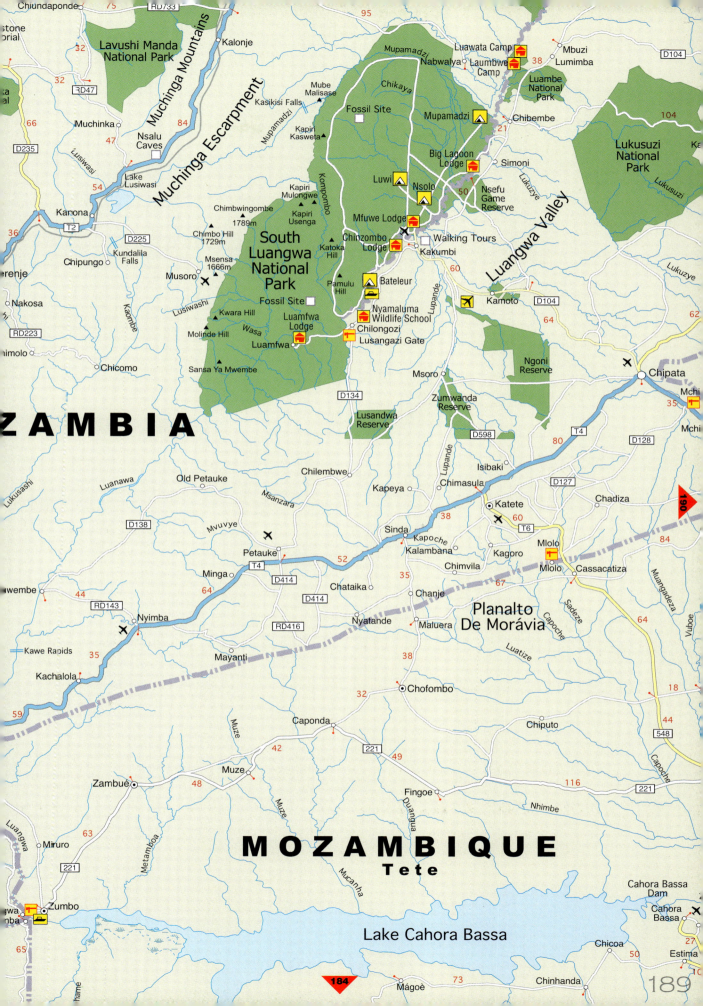

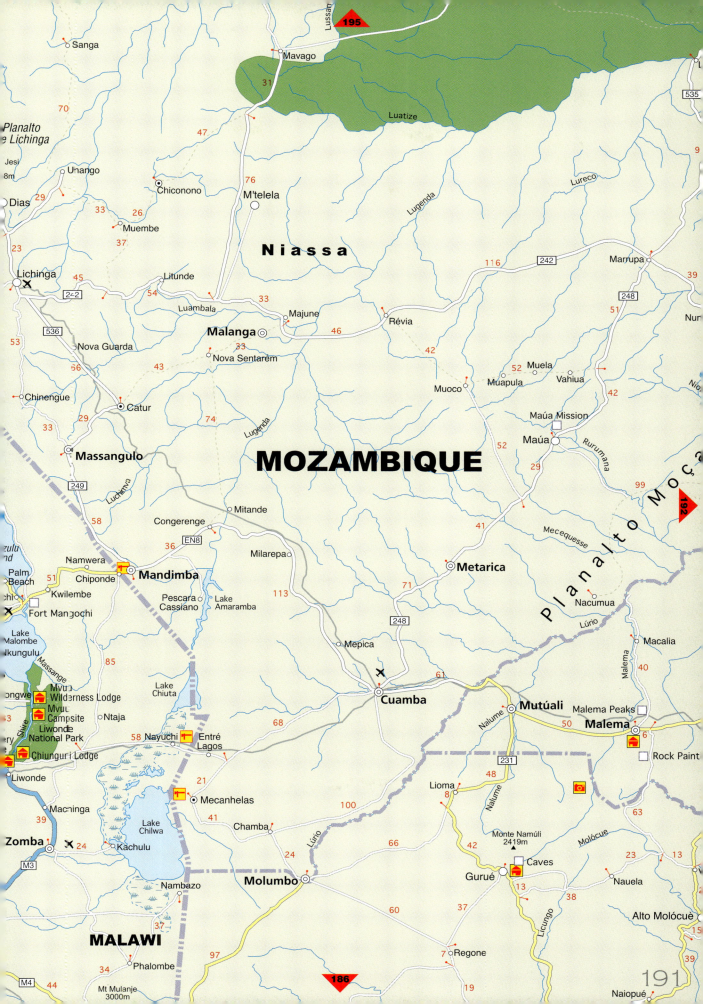

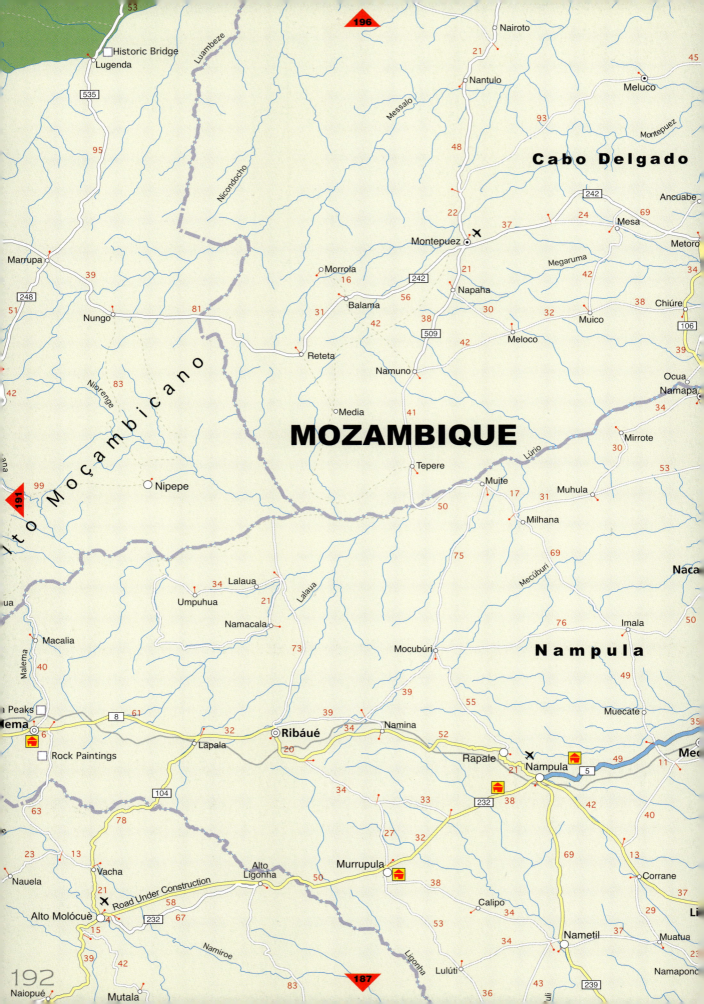

Resources

Route 1 - Pg 12-25
PG : COLUMN

PG 14 : 1 CAPE TOWN/ TABLE MOUNTAIN
Cape Town
Tel: 021 426 4260
info@cape-town.org
www.tourismcapetown.co.za
Table Mountain Aerial Cableway
Tel: 021 424 8181
www.tablemountain.net

PG 14 : 2 ROBBEN ISLAND
Tel: 021 419 1300
events@robben-island.org.za
www.robben-island.org.za

PG 14 : 3 MALMESBURY
Tourist Info
Tel: 022 487 1133
swartlandinfo@westc.co.za
swineroute@mbury.new.co.za
www.capewestcoast.org

PG 15 : 4 LANGEBAAN
Tourist Info
Tel: 022 772 1515
lbninfo@mweb.co.za
www.langebaaninfo.com

PG 15 : 5 CLANWILLIAM DAM
Tel: 027 482 8012/2133
Tourist Info
Tel: 027 482 2024
cederberg@lando.co.za
www.clanwilliam.info

PG 15 : 6 CEDERBERG
Cederberg Tourist Information
Tel: 027 482 2024/2812
cederberg@cnc.org.za
www.cederberg.co.za

PG 16 : 7 WEST COAST
West Coast Regional Tourism
Tel: 022 433 2380
tourism@capewestcoast.org
www.capewestcoast.org

PG 16 : 8 THE GIFBERG/ INLAND ISOLATION
Matzikama Tourism Office
Tel: 027 201 3376
tourism@matzikamamun.co.za
www.tourismmatzikama.co.za
Vanrhynsdorp Tourism
Tel: 027 219 1552
vanrhynsdorp@matzikamamun.co.za

PG 16 : 9 LÜDERITZ/KOLMANSKOP
Lüderitz Tourist Office
Tel: 09264 63 202 811
Municipality
Tel: 09264 63 202 041
Lüderitz Info Centre (Lüderitz Safaris)
Tel: 09264 63 202 719/622
ludsaf@africaonline.com.na
Elena Travel Services
Telefax: 09264 61 244 558/443
info@namibweb.com
www.namibweb.com
Kolmanskop Ghost Tours
www.outjo.com/ludtour.htm
Nacobta
Tel: 09264 61 250 558/5 977
office.nacobta@iway.na
www.nacobta.com.na

PG 17 : 10 BRUKKAROS VOLCANO/ QUIVERTREE FOREST AND GIANT'S PLAYGROUND
Keetmanshoop (Southern Tourist Forum)
Tel: 09264 63 221 266
Keetmanshoop Municipality
Tel: 09264 63 221 212
Mariental Tourist Info
Tel: 09264 63 245 661
Ministry of Environmental Affairs and Tourism
Tel: 09264 63 242 427
Mariental Municipality
Tel: 09264 63 245 600
Namibian Tourism Board
Tel: 09264 61 290 6000
info@namibiatourism.com.na
www.namibiatourism.com.na
Nacobta
Tel: 09264 61 255 977/250 558
office.nacobta@iway.na
www.nacobta.com.na
Namibia Helpdesk Cape Town
Tel: 021 422 3298
naminfo2@saol.com
www.namibiatourism.com.na

PG 17 : 11 DAAN VILJOEN GAME PARK
Daan Viljoen Game Park
Tel: 09264 61 226 806/232 393
Namibia Wildlife Resorts & Reservations
Tel: 09264 61 285 7000/200
reservations@nwr.com.na
info@nwr.com.na, ero@nwr.com.na
www.nwr.com.na

PG 17 : 12 OKAHANDJA TO OTAVI/ WATERBERG PLATEAU GAME PARK
Okahandja Tourist Info
Tel: 09264 62 501 051
okahandja@iway.na
Ministry of Tourism & Environment
Tel: 09264 62 501 925
Otavi Municipality (Tourist Info)
Tel: 09264 67 234 022
Waterberg Plateau Game Park
Tel: 09264 67 305 002

PG 22 : 1 ETOSHA (NAMUTONI FORT)
Namutoni Resort
Tel: 09264 67 229 300
Namibia Wildlife Resorts
Tel: 09264 61 285 7000/200

PG 22 : 2 TSUMEB/HOBA METEORITE
Tsumeb Tourist Office
Tel: 09264 67 220 728
travelnn@tsu.namib.com
www.namibiatourism.com.na
Hoba Meteorite
Tel: 09264 67 240 360

PG 22 : 3 DROTSKY'S CABINS
Tel: 09267 687 5035
drotskys@info.bw

PG 23 : 4 WEST AND EAST CAPRIVI
Namibia Wildlife Resorts
Tel: 09264 285 7000/200
reservations@nwr.com.na
ero@nwr.com.na, info@nwr.com.na
www.nwr.com.na
Caprivi Info Centre
Tel: 09264 66 686 802
bruno@iway.na

PG 23 : 5 TSODILO HILLS/GCWIHABA HILLS AND CAVES
Dept of Tourism, Botswana
Tel: 09267 395 3024
botswanatourism@gov.bw
www.botswanatourism.org
www.botswana-tourism.gov.bw
www.gov.bw/tourism

PG 23 : 6 LAKE NGAMI/GHANZI
Dept of Tourism, Botswana
Tel: 09267 395 3024
Dept of Wildlife and National Parks
Tel: 09267 318 0774/97 1405
dwnp@gov.bw
www.botswanatourism.org

Route 2 - Pg 26-39

PG 28 : 1 ORANGE RIVER/ RIVER RAFTING
South African Tourism
Tel: 011 895 3000
info@southafrica.net
www.southafrica.net
River Rafters
Tel: 021 712 5094
info@riverrafters.co.za
www.riverrafters.co.za
Felix Unite
Tel: 021 425 5181
info@felixunite.com
www.felixunite.com
Bushwacked Outdoor Adventures
Tel/Fax: 021 761 8953
info@bushwacked.co.za
www.bushwacked.co.za
Kalahari Adventure Centre
Tel: 054 451 0177
info@kalahari.co.za

www.kalahari.co.za
www.augrabies.co.za
Gravity Adventure Group
Tel: 021 683 3698
www.gravity.co.za

PG 28 : 2 AI-AIS/FISH RIVER CANYON
Ai-Ais Hot Springs Resort
Tel: 09264 63 262 045
Fax: 09264 63 262 047
reservations@nwr.com.na
info@nwr.com.na
www.nwr.com.na
Fish River and Löwen River Canyon
Tel: 09264 63 693 007/6
frgf@canyonnaturepark.com
www.canyonnaturepark.com

PG 28 : 3 UPINGTON
Upington Tourist Information Centre
Telefax: 054 332 6064
tourism@kharahais.gov.za
www.kharahasmunicipality.co.za
Green Kalahari Tourist Office
Tel: 054 337 2804
greenkal@webmail.co.za
greenkal@bodr.gov.za
www.greenkalahari.co.za

PG 29 : 4 AUGRABIES NATIONAL PARK
Tel: 054 452 9200
Fax: 054 451 5003
SA National Parks
Tel: 012 428 9111
reservations@parks-sa.co.za
www.parks-sa.co.za

PG 29 : 5 KALAHARI DESERT
Tel: 012 428 9111
reservations@parks-sa.co.za
www.parks-sa.co.za

PG 29 : 6 KGALAGADI TRANS-FRONTIER PARK
Kgalagadi Transfrontier Park (SA side)
Tel: 054 561 2000
Fax: 054 561 2005 (for 4x4 routes)
Dept of Wildlife, National Parks and Reservations Office, Botswana
Tel: 09267 318 0774
dwnp@gov.bw
www.botswanatourism.org
Dept of Wildlife and National Parks
Tel: 09267 397 1405
jbroekhuis@gov.bw

PG 30 : 7 THE 'GREEN' KALAHARI
Green Kalahari Tourist Office
Tel: 054 337 2826/04
greenkal@webmail.co.za
greenkal@bodr.gov.za
www.greenkalahari.co.za

PG 30 : 8 SISHEN/POSTMASBURG/KURUMAN
Mokala Safari Tourism (Sishen/Kathu)
Tel: 053 723 2391
info@mokala.co.za
www.mokala.co.za
Green Kalahari Tourist Office (Postmasburg)
Tel: 054 337 2804
Kalahari Tourist Office (Kuruman)
Tel: 053 712 1001
Fax: 053 712 2502
info@kalahari.org.za
www.kurumankalahari.co.za

PG 30 : 9 BARKLY WEST
Dikgatlong Municipality (Barkly West)
Municipal Manager (Tourist Info)
Tel: 053 531 0673/1
eilerd@lantic.net, dikgatlong@lantic.net
Northern Cape Tourism Authority
Tel: 053 833 1434/832 2657
tourism@northerncape.org.za
www.northerncape.org.za

PG 31 : 10 KIMBERLEY/THE BIG HOLE
Diamantfield Visitors Centre (Kimberley)
Tel: 053 832 7298
francoisbasson@fbdm.co.za
www.northerncape.org.za

PG 31 : 11 MASERU (LESOTHO)
Lesotho Tourism
Tel: 09266 22 312 427
touristinfo@ltdc.org.ls
www.lesotho.gov.ls/lstourism.htm

PG 31 : 12 KATSE DAM/WHAT TO DO IN LESOTHO
Katse Dam
Tel: 09266 22 312 442/2427
www.seelesotho.com/travel/info/waterproject
Hiking, horseriding, fishing -
Malealea Lodge & Ponytrek Centre
Tel: 051 447 3200
malealea@mweb.co.za
www.malealea.co.ls
Semonkong Lodge
Tel: 051 933 3106
bookings@placeofsmoke.co.ls
www.placeofsmoke.co.ls
Sani Top Chalet
Tel: 033 702 1158
sanitop@future.co.za
Hotel Mount Maluti - snowskiing
Tel: 09266 22 278 5224
mmh@leo.co.ls
Sani Tours - 4x4 trails
Tel: 033 701 1064
www.sanitours.co.za
Major Adventures
Tel: 033 701 1628
www.majoradventures.co.za
Trading Post - mountainbiking, quadbiking
Tel: 09266 22 340 202

tradingpost@leo.co.ls
www.africandream.org//malotiroute//Lesotho

PG 34 : 1 BLOEMFONTEIN
Tel: 051 405 8489
information@bloemfontein.co.za
www.bloemfontein.co.za

PG 34 : 2 JOHANNESBURG/NEWTOWN CULTURAL PRECINCT
Gauteng Tourism Authority
Tel: 011 327 2000
tourism@gauteng.net
www.gauteng.net
Newtown Cultural Precinct
Tel: 011 688 7834/327 2000
info@jda.org.za
www.jda.org.za
MuseumAfrika
Tel: 011 833 5624
Market Theatre Complex
Tel: 011 832 1641

PG 34 : 3 JOHANNESBURG SURROUNDS
Gauteng Tourism Authority
Tel: 011 327 2000
tourism@gauteng.net
www.gauteng.net
Gold Reef City
Tel: 011 248 6800

PG 35 : 4 PRETORIA
Pretoria Tourist Information Centre
Tel: 012 337 4430
andrewm2@tshwane.gov.za
www.tshwane.gov.za

PG 35 : 5 PRETORIA SURROUNDS
Pretoria Tourist Information Centre
Tel: 012 337 4430
Lesedi Cultural Village
Tel: 012 205 1394/433
enquiries@lesedi.com
www.lesedi.com
De Wildt Cheetah Research Centre
Tel: 012 504 1921, Fax: 012 504 1556
cheetah@dewildt.org.za
www.hartbeespoortdam.co.za

PG 35 : 6 HARTBEESPOORT/MAGALIESBERG
Hartbeespoort Dam
Tel: 012 253 1567
blackeagle@mweb.co.za
www.hartbeespoortdam.co.za
Magaliesberg Tourism
Tel: 014 577 1733
maginfo@mweb.co.za
www.magaliesinfo.co.za
www.magaliesburg.co.za

Resources

PG 36 : 7 POLOKWANE (PIETERSBURG)/BAKONE MALAPA MUSEUM
Polokwane Tourism
Tel: 015 290 7300/5 0483
info@golimpopo.com
www.golimpopo.com
www.limpopotourism.org.za
www.polokwane.org.za
Bakone Malapa Museum
Tel: 015 295 2432

PG 36 : 8 MARAKELE NATIONAL PARK/EASTWARD TO TZANEEN
Marakele National Park
Tel: 014 777 1745
info@golimpopo.com
www.golimpopo.com
www.limpopotourism.org.za
Limpopo Tourism and Parks Division
Tel: 015 288 9000
matibeke@mweb.co.za
khorommbim@golimpopo.com
www.golimpopo.com
Tzaneen Tourism
Tel: 015 307 6513/7244
reservations@tzaneeninfo.co.za
www.tzaneeninfo.co.za

PG 36 : 9 MUSINA (MESSINA)
Musina Tourism Information Centre
Tel: 015 534 3500
musinatourism@limpopo.co.za
www.limpopotourism.org.za

PG 37 : 10 GONAREZHOU NATIONAL PARK/MASVINGO
Zimbabwe National Parks and Wildlife
Tel: 09263 4 706 077/8, 707 624/9
natparks@africaonline.co.zw
www.zimparks.com
Zimbabwe Tourism Authority, Harare
Tel: 09263 4 758 730/12/24/34
info@ztazim.co.zw, gladys@ztazim.co.zw
www.zimbabwetourism.co.zw
Zimbabwe Tourism Authority, Bulawayo
Tel: 09263 9 74055/72358
ztabyo@africaonline.co.zw
www.arachnid.co.za/Bulawayo
Zimbabwe Tourist Office
Tel: 011 616 9534
zta@telkomsa.net
www.zimbabwetourism.co.zw
Great Zimbabwe Publicity Association (Masvingo)
Tel: 09263 39 62643
mgpa@webmail.co.za

PG 37 : 11 CHIMANIMANI NATIONAL PARK
Harare National Parks Central Reservations
Tel: 09263 4 706 077/8, 707 624/9
natparks@africaonline.co.zw
www.zimparks.com

PG 37 : 12 HIKING IN THE MOUNTAINS
Zimbabwe Tourism Authority, Harare
Tel: 09263 4 758 730/12/24/34
info@ztazim.co.zw, gladys@ztazim.co.zw
www.zimbabwetourism.co.zw

Route 3 - pg 40-53

PG 42 : 1 THE OVERBERG REGION
Overberg Tourism
Tel: 028 214 1466
info@capeoverberg.org
www.capeoverberg.org

PG 42 : 2 BONNIEVALE/SWELLENDAM
Bonnievale Tourism
Tel: 023 616 3753/422
info@bonnievale.co.za
www.bonnievale.co.za
Swellendam Tourism
Tel: 028 514 2770
infoswd@sdm.dorea.co.za
www.swellendamtourism.co.za

PG 42 : 3 DE HOOP NATURE RESERVE
Tel: 028 425 5020
capenature@tiscali.co.za
www.capenature.org.za

PG 43 : 4 THE GARDEN ROUTE/GARDEN ROUTE HIGHLIGHTS
Garden Route Klein Karoo Regional Tourism Organization
Tel: 044 873 6314
info@gardenroute.org.za
www.capegardenroute.org

PG 43 : 5 JEFFREYS BAY/PORT ELIZABETH TO GRAHAMSTOWN
Jeffreys Bay Tourism Bureau
Tel: 042 293 2923
Jbay-tourism@agnet.co.za
www.infojeffreysbay.com
Port Elizabeth (Nelson Mandela Bay Tourism)
Tel: 041 585 8884
info@nmbt.co.za
www.nmbt.co.za

PG 43 : 6 GRAHAMSTOWN/UMTATA
Grahamstown Tourism
Tel: 046 622 3241
info@grahamstown.co.za
www.grahamstown.co.za
Umtata Tourism
Tel: 047 531 5290/2
infomtata@ectourism.co.za
ectbw@ectourism.co.za
www.ectourism.co.za

PG 44 : 7 THE SOUTH COAST/COASTAL RESORTS
Hibiscus Coast Tourism (Uvongo, Margate)
Tel: 039 316 6139/2 2322
margate@venturenet.co.za
www.hibiscuscoast.kzn.org.za
Amanzimtoti Publicity Association
Tel: 031 903 7498/3
info@amanzimtoti.co.za
www.amanzimtoti.org.za
Oribi Gorge Nature Reserve
Tel: 039 679 1644
Port Edward Tourist Info
Tel: 039 311 1211
portedward@hibiscuscoast.org.za
www.hibiscuscoast.kzn.org.za

PG 44 : 8 DURBAN
KwaZulu-Natal Tourism Authority
Tel: 031 366 7500/04 7144
tkzn@zulu.org.za
www.zulu.org.za
Durban Africa
Tel: 031 304 4934
funinsun@iafrica.com
www.durbanexperience.co.za
www.durban.kzn.org.za

PG 44 : 9 THE NORTH COAST/RICHARDS BAY
Dolphin Coast Publicity Association
Tel: 032 946 1997/2434
info@dolphincoast.kzn.org.za
www.dolphincoast.co.za
Umhlanga Tourism information Centre
Tel: 031 561 4257
Richards Bay (uMhlathuze Tourism Office)
Tel: 035 901 5408/018/000
rbtour@ughungulu.co.za
rightb@richemp.org.za
www.tourismassociation.org.za
Mtunzini Tourism
Tel: 035 474 1141 ext 259

PG 45 : 10 KOSI BAY/MAPUTO
Elephant Coast Tourism Association
Tel: 035 562 0966
res@elephantcoastbookings.co.za
www.elephantcoastbookings.co.za
www.elephantcoast.kzn.org.za
Turtle Hotline
Tel: 035 590 1162
Camera Africa Adventures
Tel: 031 266 4172
camera-africa@iafrica.com
www.camera-africa.com
Ministry of Tourism, Mozambique
Tel: 09258 1 307 320/3, Fax: 307 324
info@futur.org.mz
www.futur.org.mz

PG 45 : 11 MORGAN'S BAY TO QOLORA MOUTH
Morgan's Bay Hotel
Tel: 043 841 1062
hotel@mweb.co.za
www.morganbay.co.za
Hiking, canoe trails, beach walks, rock climbing, abseiling, waterskiing,

4x4 adventures, horseriding -
Kei Mouth Beach Hotel
Tel: 043 841 1017
reservation@keimouthbeachhotel.co.za
www.keimouthbeachhotel.co.za
Fishing, hiking, horseriding, windsurfing, canoeing, gamerides, rock climbing -
Trennery's Hotel
Tel: 047 498 0004
trennerys@border.co.za
www.trennerys.co.za

PG 45 : 12 COFFEE BAY TO PORT ST JOHNS
Ocean View Hotel, Coffee Bay
Tel: 047 575 2005/6
oceanview@coffeebay.co.za
www.oceanview.co.za
Port St Johns Tourism
Tel: 047 564 1187/207/8
tourismpsj@wildcoast.co.za
www.portstjohns.org.za/tourism
Wild Coast District Council
Tel: 039 254 0320
Wild Coast Central Reservations
Tel: 047 531 1191
Wild Coast Holiday Reservations
Tel: 043 743 6181
www.wildcoastholidays.co.za

PG 48 : 1 ZULULAND
KwaZulu-Natal Tourism Authority
Tel: 031 366 7500/04 7144
tkzn@zulu.org.za
www.zulu.org.za

PG 48 : 2 HLUHLUWE-UMFOLOZI PARK
Tel: 033 845 1000/999
bookings@kznwildlife.com
www.kznwildlife.com

PG 48 : 3 GREATER ST LUCIA WETLAND PARK/LOGGERHEADS AND LEATHERBACKS
Tel: 033 845 1000, 035 590 1528
bookings@kznwildlife.com
www.kznwildlife.com
Loggerheads and Leatherbacks
Tel: 035 590 1162

PG 49 : 4 HLUHLUWE-UMFOLOZI NP
Tel: 012 428 9111, 021 423 8005
reservations@parks-sa.co.za
www.parks-sa.co.za

PG 49 : 5 MAPUTO'S MAPUTALAND
Ministry of Tourism, Mozambique
Tel: 09258 1 307 320/3
info@futur.org.mz
www.futur.org.mz

PG 49 : 6 PONTA DO OURO & INHACA
Tel: 011 803 9296/52
travel@mozambiquetourism.co.za
www.mozambiquetourism.co.za

PG 50 : 7 MAPUTO TO MUTARE
Ministry of Tourism, Mozambique
Tel: 09258 1 307 320/3
info@futur.org.mz
www.futur.org.mz
Mutare Publicity Association
Tel: 09263 20 64711
Harare Publicity Association
Tel: 09263 4 705 085/6
Zimbabwe Tourism Authority, Harare
Tel: 09263 4 758 730/4/40
info@ztazim.co.zw
www.zimbabwetourism.co.zw

PG 50 : 8 MANA POOLS NATIONAL PARK
Zimbabwe National Parks and Wildlife
Harare National Parks Central Reservations
Tel: 09263 4 706 077/8, 707 624/9
natparks@africaonline.co.zw
www.zimparks.com

PG 50 : 9 CAMPING AND CANOEING
Nyamepi Campsite
Tel: 09263 13 3371/2
Ruckomechi Luxury Camp
Tel: 09263 11 207 874
Cansaf Adventures & Canoeing Safaris
Tel: 011 803 5928
www.cansaf.com
Karibu Safaris
www.karibu.co.za
Natureways
Tel: 09263 4 861 766
www.natureways.co.za
Safari Par Excellence
Tel: 011 781 3851, 09260 33 20606

PG 51 : 10 LAKE KARIBA
Kariba Publicity Association
Tel: 09263 61 2328/3213
kpa@mweb.co.zw

PG 51 : 11 LUSAKA
Zambia National Tourism Board
Tel: 09260 1 229 087/9/90
Fax: 09260 1 225 174
zntb@zamnet.zm
www.zambiatourism.com
Zambia Wildlife Authority (ZAWA)
Tel: 09260 1 278 129
zawaorg@zamnet.zm

PG 51 : 12 LIVINGSTONE/ VICTORIA FALLS (ZAMBIA)
Tourist Centre Livingstone (Victoria Falls)
Tel: 09260 3 321 404/87
zntblive@zamnet.zm
www.zambiatourism.com

Route 4 - pg 54-67

PG 56 : 1 WORCESTER & HEX RIVER VALLEY
Worcester Tourism
Tel: 023 348 2795
damens@breedevalley.co.za
www.breedevalley.co.za
Hex River Valley Tourism
Tel: 023 356 2041
grapeescape@mweb.co.za

PG 56 : 2 THE LITTLE KAROO/ MATJIESFONTEIN
Central Karoo Regional Tourism Office
Tel: 023 449 1000
karootour@internext.co.za
www.centralkaroo.co.za
Matjiesfontein Tourism
Tel: 023 561 3011
milner2@mweb.co.za
www.matjiesfontein.com

PG 56 : 3 KAROO NATIONAL PARK
Tel: 023 415 2828
wendyj@parks-sa.co.za
www.parks-sa.co.za

PG 57 : 4 KIMBERLEY BATTLEFIELDS/ MAFIKENG
Kimberley Tourism
Tel: 053 832 7298, Fax: 053 832 7211
maryanne.snyders@fbdm.co.za
tourism@northerncape.org.za
www.northerncape.org.za
Mafikeng Tourism
Tel: 018 381 3155/6
tidcmf@yebo.co.za
www.tourismnorthwest.co.za

PG 57 : 5 GABORONE
Dept of Tourism, Botswana
Tel: 09267 395 3024

PG 57 : 6 TULI BLOCK
Dept of Tourism, Botswana
Tel: 09267 395 3024

PG 58 : 7 FRANCISTOWN
Tel: 09267 241 6279
Dept of Tourism, Botswana
Tel: 09267 395 3024

PG 58 : 8 MAKGADIKGADI & NXAI
Dept of Wildlife and National Parks, Botswana
Tel: 09267 397 1405
Parks & Reserves Reservations
Tel: 09267 318 0774
dwnp@gov.bw
www.botswanatourism.org

Resources

PG 58 : 9 TREACHEROUS PANS/ QUADBIKING
Dept of Tourism, Botswana
Tel: 09267 395 3024
botswanatourism@gov.bw
www.botswanatourism.org
Bush Bandits - quadbiking
Tel: 011 768 2040
bushbandits@intekom.co.za
www.bushbandits.co.za

PG 59 : 10 HWANGE NATIONAL PARK
Zimbabwe National Parks and Wildlife
Tel: 09263 4 706 077/8
natparks@africaonline.co.zw
www.zimparks.com
Zimbabwe Tourist Office
Tel: 011 616 9534
zta@telkomsa.net
www.zimbabwetourism.co.zw
Wilderness Safaris - gameviewing, walking safaris
Tel: 09263 70 7660
www.wilderness-safaris.com
Wild Horizons
www.wildhorizons.co.zw
Taggallong - 4x4 trails
Tel: 011 975 3293
www.tagalong.co.za

PG 59 : 11 SINAMATELLA & ROBINS CAMP
National Parks Central Reservations
Tel: 09263 4 706 077/8
natparks@africaonline.co.zw
www.zimparks.com

PG 59 : 12 MATOBO NATIONAL PARK
Zimbabwe Tourism Authority, Bulawayo
Tel: 09263 9 74055/2358
ztbyo@africaonline.co.za
www.zimparks.com
Bulawayo National Parks
Tel: 09263 9 63646/1018

PG 62 : 1 CENTRAL KALAHARI GAME RESERVE
Dept of Tourism, Botswana
Tel: 09267 395 3024
Dept of Wildlife and National Parks
Tel: 09267 397 1405
dwnp@gov.bw
www.botswanatourism.org
Parks and Reserves Reservations
Tel: 09267 318 0774

PG 62 : 2 THE GHANZI LANDSCAPE
Dept of Tourism, Botswana
Tel: 09267 395 3024
botswanatourism@gov.bw
www.botswanatourism.org

PG 62 : 3 BUITEPOS TO GOBABIS
Buitepos Border Post (open 24 hours)
Tel: 09264 62 560 419

Gobabis Tourism
Tel: 09264 62 562 428/1 284 2111
www.met.gov.na

PG 63 : 4 WINDHOEK
Namibian Tourism Board
Tel: 09264 61 290 6000
info@namibiatourism.com.na
www.namibiatourism.com.na
Namibia Helpdesk, Cape Town
Tel: 021 422 3298
Namibia Wildlife Resorts
Tel: 09264 61 285 7000
reservations@nwr.com.na
info@nwr.com.na, ero@nwr.com.na
www.nwr.com.na

PG 63 : 5 SWAKOPMUND/ SPITZKOPPE
Swakopmund Tourism (Namib-i)
Tel: 09264 64 404 827
namibi@iway.na
www.namibi.org.na
Nacobta
Tel: 09264 61 250 558
Nacobta Booking Office
Tel: 09264 61 255 977
office.nacobta@iway.na
www.nacobta.com
Spitzkoppe Campsite
Tel: 09264 64 530 879
Walkers Rock and Rope Adventures - rock climbing & abseiling
Tel: 09264 64 403 122
walkers@iafrica.com
Guided Ascents in Africa
Tel: 021 788 3894
www.southscape.co.za
Blue Mountain Adventures
Tel: 021 439 8199
tonyblue@iafrica.com

PG 63 : 6 ACTION IN SWAKOPMUND
Swakopmund Tourism (Namib-i)
Tel: 09264 64 404 827
namibi@iway.na
www.namibi.org.na
Okakambe Trails - horse trails
Tel: 09264 64 402 799
www.okakambe.de
Dare Devil Advent - quadbiking
Tel: 09264 64 401 183
www.namplaces.com
Namibia Quadbike Adventures
Tel: 09264 64 462 686
bpwcs@mweb.com.na
Laramon Tours - angling
Tel: 09264 64 402 359
laramontours@mweb.com.na
Ocean Adventures & Angling Tours
Tel: 09264 64 404 281
oceanadv@iway.na
Mola Mola - marine cruises
Tel: 09264 64 205 511
www.mola-mola.com.na

Levo Tours
Tel: 09264 64 207 555
www.levotours.com
Skydive Swakopmund
Tel: 09264 64 404 500
www.pleasureflights.com.na

PG 64 : 7 HENTIES BAY
Tel: 09264 64 501 143
info@hentiesbay.com
www.hentiesbay.com

PG 64 : 8 SKELETON COAST
Namibia Reservations
Tel: 09264 67 304 716
ulrika@namibiareservations.com
info@namibiareservations.com
www.namibiareservations.com
Namibia Wildlife Resorts
Tel: 09264 61 285 7000/200
reservations@nwr.com.na
www.nwr.com.na
Skeleton Coast National Park
Tel: 09264 64 694 004/402 172
www.e-tourism.com.na
Skeleton Coast National Park Terrace Bay Resorts and Torra Bay Camping Sites:
Tel: 09264 64 694 004/402 172
Fax: 09264 64 694 003/402 796
reservations@nwr.com.na
www.nwr.com.na
Skeleton Coast Camp
Tel: 09264 61 274 500
info@nts.com.na
www.skeleton-coast.com
www.e-tourism.com.na

PG 64 : 9 NAMIB-NAUKLUFT PARK
Namibia Wildlife Resorts
Tel: 09264 61 285 7000/200
reservations@nwr.com.na
www.nwr.com.na
Naukluft Hiking Trails - Tok Tokkie Trails
Tel: 09264 63 693 011
toktokki@iway.na

PG 65 : 10 SANDWICH HARBOUR & KUISEB/SESRIEM CANYON
Namibia Wildlife Resorts
Tel: 09264 61 285 7000/200
Sesriem Campsite
Tel: 09264 63 693 247, Fax: 693 249
Sossusvlei Eco Quad - quadbiking, balloon safaris
Tel: 09264 63 293 293
Le Mirage Desert Lodge and Spa (Sossusvlei)
mirage@mweb.com.na
www.sossusvlei-mirage.com

PG 65 : 11 THE DRIVE
Namibian Tourism Board
Tel: 09264 61 290 6000
info@namibiatourism.com.na

www.namibiatourism.com.na

PG 65 : 12 THE SPECTACLE
Namibian Tourism Board
Tel: 09264 61 290 6000
info@namibiatourism.com.na
www.namibiatourism.com.na

Route 5 - pg 68-79

PG 70 : 1 BRANDBERG NATURE RESERVE
Namibia Wildlife Resorts
Tel: 09264 61 285 7000/200
reservations@nwr.com.na
www.nwr.com.na

PG 70 : 2 THE WHITE LADY/ DAMARALAND
Nacobta
Tel: 09264 61 255 977/0 558
Namibia Wildlife Resorts
Tel: 09264 61 285 7000/200
Namibian Tourism Board
Tel: 09264 61 290 6000
info@namibiatourism.com.na
www.namibiatourism.com.na

PG 70 : 3 TWYFELFONTEIN & BURNT MOUNTAIN
Nacobta
Tel: 09264 61 255 977/0 558
office.nacobta@iway.na
www.nacobta.com.na

PG 71 : 4 PETRIFIED FOREST/ VINGERKLIP
Nacobta
Tel: 09264 61 255 977/0 558
office.nacobta@iway.na
www.nacobta.com.na
Vingerklip Lodge
Tel: 09264 61 255 344
vingerkl@mweb.com.na
The Cardboard Box Travel Shop
Tel: 09264 61 256 580
norelle@namibian.org
www.namibian.org

PG 71 : 5 SOUTH OF ETOSHA
Huab Lodge
Tel: 09264 67 697 016
huab@iway.na
www.huablodge.com
Kavita Lion Lodge
Tel: 09264 67 330 224
kavita@iway.na
www.kavitalion.com
Hobatere Lodge
Tel: 09264 67 330 261
hobatere@mweb.com.na
www.discover-africa.com.na

PG 71 : 6 SESFONTEIN
Fort Sesfontein Lodge
Tel: 09264 65 275 534
fort.sesfontein@mweb.com.na
www.fort-sesfontein.com
The Cardboard Box Travel Shop
Tel: 09264 61 256 580
norelle@namibian.org
www.namibian.org
Namibia Wildlife Resorts
Tel: 09264 61 285 7200/000

PG 72 : 7 THE DORSLAND TREKKERS/ DORSLAND MONUMENTS
Tel: 021 850 0010
janjoubertsafaris@absamail.co.za

PG 72 : 8 RUACANA FALLS/RAFTING ON THE KUNENE
Ruacana Eha Lodge
Elena Travel Services
Tel: 09264 61 244 558/443
The Cardboard Box Travel Shop
Tel: 09264 61 256 580
norelle@namibian.org
www.namibian.org
Gravity Adventure Group - whitewater rafting
Tel: 021 683 3698
www.gravity.co.za
Kunene River Lodge
Tel: 09264 65 274 300
info@kuneneriverlodge.com

PG 72 : 9 EPUPA FALLS/ OWAMBOLAND
Epupa Camp
Tel: 09264 61 232 740
epupa@mweb.com.na
www.epupa.com.na
Nacobta
Tel: 09264 61 255 977/0 558
Namibian Tourism Board
Tel: 09264 61 290 6000

PG 73 : 10 CROSSING THE DESERT
Opuwo Tourism
Tel: 09264 65 273 003/105
www.met.gov.na
Namibian Tourism Board
Tel: 09264 61 290 6000

PG 73 : 11 THE HIMBA
Namibian Tourism Board
Tel: 09264 61 290 6000
info@namibiatourism.com.na
www.namibiatourism.com.na

PG 73 : 12 KHOMAS HOCHLAND/ VON FRANÇOIS FORT
Namibian Tourism Board
Tel: 09264 61 290 6000

PG 76 : 1 KHAUDOM GAME RESERVE
Namibia Wildlife Resorts
Tel: 09264 61 285 7000/200
reservations@nwr.com.na
www.nwr.com.na
Ministry of Environment & Tourism
Tel: 09264 61 284 2111/63 131
www.met.gov.na

PG 76 : 2 MAHANGO GAME RESERVE/CAPRIVI & COMMUNITY
Mahango Lodge
Tel: 09264 66 259 037
Namibia Wildlife Resorts
Tel: 09264 61 285 7200/000
info@nwr.com.na
reservations@nwr.com.na
www.nwr.com.na
Caprivi Info Centre
Tel: 09264 66 686 802
bruno@iway.na

PG 76 : 3 MUDUMU NP/MAMILI NP
Namibia Wildlife Resorts
Tel: 09264 61 285 7000/200

PG 77 : 4 KATIMA MULILO
Tel: 09264 66 253 027/5 403
Namibian Tourism Board
Tel: 09264 61 290 6000
info@namibiatourism.com.na
www.namibiatourism.com.na

PG 77 : 5 LIVINGSTONE/MOSI-OA-TUNYA NATIONAL PARK
Livingstone Tourism
Tel: 09260 3 321 404/87
zntblive@zamnet.zm
www.zambiatourism.com
Mosi-oa-Tunya National Park
Zambia Wildlife Authority (ZAWA)
Tel: 09260 1 278 129
zawaorg@zamnet.zm
Zambia National Tourism Board
Tel: 09260 1 229 087/90
zntb@zamnet.zm
www.zambiatourism.com

PG 77 : 6 ZAMBIAN FALLS VIEWS/ LIVINGSTONE ISLAND PICNICS
Zambia Tourist Centre (Livingstone)
Tel: 09260 3 321 404/87
zntblive@zamnet.zm
Zambia National Tourist Board (Lusaka)
Tel: 09260 1 229 087/90
zntb@zamnet.zm
www.zambiatourism.com

Route 6 - pg 80-91

PG 82 : 1 DURBAN
KwaZulu-Natal Tourism Authority
Tel: 031 366 7500/04 7144
tkzn@zulu.org.za
www.zulu.org.za

Resources

Durban Africa
Tel: 031 304 4934
funinsun@iafrica.com
www.durbanexperience.co.za
www.durban.kzn.org.za

**PG 82 : 2 SALT, SURF AND SAND/
BE ENTERTAINED**
Durban Beach Tourism Office
Tel: 031 332 2595
funinsun@iafrica.com
beach@durbansouthafrica.co.za
www.durbanexperience.co.za
Natal Maritime Museum
Tel: 031 311 2230
BAT Centre
Tel: 031 332 0451
The Wheel (uShaka stretch)
Tel: 031 332 4324

**PG 82 : 3 uSHAKA MARINE
WORLD/PIETERMARITZBURG**
Tel: 031 328 8000/1
znobandla@ushakamarineworld.co.za
www.ushakamarineworld.co.za
Pietermaritzburg Tourism
Tel: 033 345 1348/9/451
info@pmbtourism.co.za
www.pmbtourism.co.za
www.pietermaritzburg.co.za

PG 83 : 4 HOWICK
Howick Tourism Office
Tel: 033 330 5305
nr@futurenet.co.za
www.howick.org.za
Alberts Falls Area
Tel: 033 569 0010, 082 708 4246

PG 83 : 5 FARMING COUNTRY
Midlands Meander Association
Tel: 033 330 8195
info@midlandsmeander.co.za
www.midlandsmeander.co.za

PG 83 : 6 A SLOW MEANDER
Midlands Meander Association
Tel: 033 330 8195
info@midlandsmeander.co.za
www.midlandsmeander.co.za

PG 84 : 7 DUNDEE/VRYHEID
Tel: 034 212 2121 ext 2262
tourism@dundeekzn.co.za
www.tourdundee.co.za
Talana Museum
Tel: 034 212 2654
Vryheid Information Bureau
Tel: 034 2133 ext 2229
information@vhd.dorea.co.za
www.vryheid.co.za

PG 84 : 8 HARRISMITH
Tourism Info
Tel: 058 672 1044

montrose@telkomsa.net
www.zulu.org.za

**PG 84 : 9 BASOTHO CULTURAL
VILLAGE/GOLDEN GATE HIGHLANDS**
Tel: 058 721 0300
basotho@dorea.co.za
www.dorea.co.za/ecotourism
Golden Gate National Park
Tel: 058 255 0075
names@sanparks.org
www.sanparks.org

PG 85 : 10 VAAL DAM
Gauteng Tourism Authority
Tel: 011 327 2000
tourism@gauteng.net
www.gauteng.net
Johannesburg Tourism Company
Tel: 011 214 0700

PG 85 : 11 THE RESISTANCE YEARS
Gauteng Tourism Authority
Tel: 011 327 2000
Johannesburg Tourism Company
Tel: 011 214 0700
info@joburgtourism.com
www.joburgtourism.com

PG 85 : 12 SOWETO TOURS
Tel: 011 886 1822
richard@soweto.co.za
www.soweto.co.za

**PG 88 : 1 WINDHOEK/
WINDHOEK'S 'CASTLES'**
Namibian Tourism Board
Tel: 09264 61 290 6000
info@namibiatourism.com.na
www.namibiatourism.com.na
Namibia Helpdesk, Cape Town
Tel: 021 422 3298
naminfo2@saol.com
www.namibiatourism.com.na

PG 88 : 2 WINDHOEK TO BUITEPOS
Buitepos Border Post (open 24 hours)
Tel: 09264 62 560 419
Namibia Tourism Board
Tel: 09264 61 290 6000
Dept of Tourism, Botswana
Tel: 09267 395 3024

PG 88 : 3 TROPIC OF CAPRICORN
Dept of Tourism, Botswana
Tel: 09267 395 3024
Lobatse Border Post
Tel: 09267 533 0225

PG 89 : 4 MADIKWE GAME RESERVE
Tel: 018 3672 ask 2411, 083 629 8282
madikweadmin@wol.co.za
www.parksnorthwest.co.za

**PG 89 : 5 GROOT MARICO/ON THE
ROAD TO PRETORIA**
Groot Marico Tourism
Tel/Fax: 014 503 0085, 083 272 2958
info@marico.co.za
www.marico.co.za
Pretoria Tourist Information Centre
Tel: 012 337 4430
andrewm2@tshwane.gov.za
www.tshwane.gov.za

PG 89 : 6 PRETORIA/MAPUTO
Ministry of Tourism, Mozambique
Tel: 09258 1 307 320/3
info@futur.org.mz
www.futur.org.mz
Mozambique Consulate, Cape Town
Tel: 021 426 2944, Fax: 426 2946

Route 7 - pg 92-99

**PG 94 : 1 HARARE/SHONA
SCULPTURE**
Harare Publicity Association
Tel: 09263 4 705 085/6
Zimbabwe Tourism Authority (Harare)
Tel: 09263 4 758 730/4/40
info@ztazim.co.zw
www.zimbabwetourism.co.zw
Zimbabwe Tourism Authority
Tel: 09263 4 758 712/4/24/34
info@ztazim.co.zw, gladys@ztazim.co.zw
marketing@ztazim.co.zw
www.zimbabwetourism.co.zw

**PG 94 : 2 LAND OF OPHIR/
NYAMAPANDA TO TETE**
Zimbabwe Tourism Authority
Tel: 09263 4 758 712/4/24/34
info@ztazim.co.zw
www.zimbabwetourism.co.zw
*Great Zimbabwe Publicity Association
(Masvingo)*
Tel: 09263 39 62643
mgpa@webmail.co.za
Kariba Publicity Association
Tel: 09263 61 2328/3213, Fax: 2880
kpa@mweb.co.zw
Tete Tourism
Tel: 09258 52 23762
Fax: 09258 52 24225
dpturism.mz@hotmail.com
www.futur.org.mz

**PG 94 : 3 LIWONDE NATIONAL PARK/
LAKE MALAWI**
Dept of Tourism, Malawi
Tel: 09265 1 620 902, Fax: 621 923
tourism@malawi.net
www.tourismmalawi.com

**PG 95 : 4 CUAMBA TO NIASSA/
NIASSA RESERVE**
Ministry of Tourism, Mozambique
Tel: 09258 1 307 320/3

info@futur.org.mz
www.futur.org.mz
Niassa Reserve
Tel: 09258 1 499 937
anarodmoz@hotmail.com
www.niassa.com

PG 95 : 5 MOZAMBIQUE ISLAND
Mozambique Tourism
Tel: 011 803 9296/52
travel@mozambiquetourism.co.za
www.mozambiquetourism.co.za

PG 95 : 6 PEMBA & QUIRIMBA
Quilalea Sales Office
Tel: 011 447 9422
quilaleaisland@iafrica.com
www.quilalea.com

PG 96 : 1 A PRISTINE COASTLINE/ BILENE & XAI-XAI
Ministry of Tourism, Mozambique
Tel: 09258 1 307 320/3
info@futur.org.mz
www.futur.org.mz
Mozambique Consulate, Cape Town
Tel: 021 426 2944, Fax: 426 2946
Mozambique Tourism (Bilene & Xai-Xai)
Tel: 011 803 9296/52
travel@mozambiquetourism.co.za
www.mozambiquetourism.co.za

PG 96 : 2 TIME FOR BREEDING.../ INHAMBANE
Ministry of Tourism, Mozambique
Tel: 09258 1 307 320/3
Inhambane Province Tourism
Telefax: 09258 23 20216
turismo.inhambane@teledata.mz
www.futur.org.mz

PG 96 : 3 VILANKULO/BAZARUTO ARCHIPELAGO
Vilankulo Info
Tel: 09258 23 82031/2
information@vilanculos.org
www.vilanculos.org
Vilanculo Tourist Services
Tel: 09258 23 82228
margie@teledata.mz
Vilanculos Camping
Tel: 015 516 1427
vilanculos@mweb.co.za
www.vilanculoscamping.co.za
Vilanculos Beach Lodge
Tel: 09258 23 82388, 021 706 0517
beachlodge@teledata.co.za
www.vilanculos.co.za
Mozambique Tourism (Bazaruto Achipelago)
Tel: 011 803 9296/52

PG 97 : 4 NORTH OF BAZARUTO TO INCHOPE & BEIRA/BEIRA
Ministry of Tourism, Mozambique
Tel: 09258 1 307 320/3

Mozambique Tourism
Tel: 011 803 9296/52
travelmozambiquetourism.co.za
www.mozambiquetourism.co.za
Beira Tourism
Tel: 09258 3 27282

PG 97 : 5 A REHABILITATED RESERVE
Gorongosa National Park
Tel: 09258 1 499 937
anarodmoz@hotmail.com

PG 97 : 6 DEFINITELY FOR THE BIRDS
Ministry of Tourism, Mozambique
Tel: 09258 1 307 320/3

Cities & Towns - pg 101

PG 101 PRETORIA
Tourist Information Centre
Tel: 012 337 4430, Fax: 337 4485
andrewm2@tshwane.gov.za
www.tshwane.gov.za

PG 102 CAPE TOWN
Cape Town Tourism
Tel: 021 426 4260
info@cape-town.org
www.tourismcapetown.co.za

PG 103 WINDHOEK
Namibian Tourism Board
Tel: 09264 61 290 6000
info@namibiatourism.com.na
www.namibiatourism.com.na

PG 104 GABORONE
Dept of Tourism, Botswana
Tel: 09267 395 3024
botswanatourism@gov.bw
www.botswanatourism.org
www.botswana-tourism.gov.bw

PG 105 MAPUTO
Ministry of Tourism, Mozambique
Tel: 09258 1 307 320/3
info@futur.org.mz
www.futur.org.mz
www.mocambiqueturismo.co.mz

PG 106 MASERU/MBABANE
Lesotho Tourism
(Lesotho Development Corporation)
Tel: 09266 22 312 213
ltdc@ltdc.org.ls
www.ltdc.org.ls
Swaziland Tourism Authority, Mbabane
Tel: 09268 404 9693
Swaziland Tourism, Mbabane
Tel: 09268 404 4556
www.swazi.com/tourism

PG 107 HARARE
Harare Publicity Association
Tel 09263 4 705 085/6

Zimbabwe Tourism Authority, Harare
Tel: 09263 4 758 730/12/24/34/40
info@ztazim.co.zw, gladys@ztazim.co.zw
www.zimbabwetourism.co.zw

PG 108 JOHANNESBURG
Gauteng Tourism Authority
Tel: 011 327 2000, Fax: 327 7000
tourism@gauteng.net
www.gauteng.net
South African Tourism
Tel: 011 895 3000
info@southafrica.net
www.southafrica.net

PG 109 PORT ELIZABETH/ EAST LONDON
Nelson Mandela Bay Tourism
Tel: 041 585 8884, Fax: 585 2564
info@nmbt.co.za
www.nmbt.co.za
East London Tourism
Tel: 043 722 6015, Fax: 743 5091
info@tourismbuffalocity.co.za
www.visitbuffalocity.co.za
Eastern Cape Tourism Board
Tel: 043 701 9600
info@ectourism.co.za
www.ectourism.co.za

PG 110 DURBAN/ PIETERMARITZBURG/KIMBERLEY
KwaZulu-Natal Tourism Authority
Tel: 031 366 7500/304 7144
tkzn@iafrica.com
www.zulu.org.za
Durban Africa
Tel: 031 304 4934
funinsun@iafrica.com
www.durbanexperience.co.za
www.durban.kzn.org.za
Pietermaritzburg Tourism
Tel: 033 345 1348/9, Fax: 394 3535
info@pmbtourism.co.za
www.pmbtourism.co.za
www.pietermaritzburg.co.za
Kimberley Information Centre
Tel: 053 832 7298, Fax: 832 7211
maryanne.snyders@fbdm.co.za
www.northerncape.org.za

PG 111 BLOEMFONTEIN/ POLOKWANE/BISHO
Bloemfontein Publicity
Tel: 051 405 8111/30 8206
information@bloemfontein.co.za
www.mangaung.co.za
Polokwane Tourism
Tel: 015 290 7300
info@golimpopo.com
www.golimpopo.com
www.limpopotourism.org.za
Polokwane Municipality
Tel: 015 290 2010
www.polokwane.org.za

Resources

Bisho Tourism
Tel: 043 722 6015, Fax: 743 5091
info@tourismbuffalocity.co.za
www.visitbuffalocity.co.za

PG 112 NELSPRUIT/MAFIKENG/ KEETMANSHOOP/WALVIS BAY
Tel: 013 755 1988
nelspruit@soft.co.za
www.lowveld.info
Mpumalanga Tourism Association
Tel: 013 752 7001
mtanlpsa@cis.co.za
www.mpumalanga.com
Mafikeng Tourism Information & Development Centre
Tel: 018 381 3155
tidcmf@yebo.co.za
www.tourismnorthwest.co.za
Southern Tourist Forum (Keetmanshoop)
Tel: 09264 63 221 266
Keetmanshoop Municipality
Tel: 09264 63 221 212
Walvis Bay Tourism
Tel: 09264 64 209 170
walvisinfo@iway.na
www.walvisbay.com.na

PG 113 MAUN/BULAWAYO/ BEIRA/INHAMBANE
Maun Tourism
Tel: 09267 686 0492
Dept of Tourism, Botswana
Tel: 09267 395 3024
botswanatourism@gov.bw
www.botswanatourism.org
Zimbabwe Tourism Authority (Bulawayo)
Tel: 09263 74055/2358
bpa@netconnect.co.zw
ztabyo@africaonline.co.zw
www.arachnid.co.zw/bulawayo
Beira Tourism
Tel: 09258 3 322 985
Ministry of Tourism, Mozambique
Tel: 09258 1 307 320/3
Inhambane Province Tourism
Telefax: 09258 23 20216
turismo.inhambane@teledata.mz
www.futur.org.mz

PG 114 BEAUFORT WEST/ BETHLEHEM/CITRUSDAL/ CLANWILLIAM
Beaufort West Tourism
Tel: 023 415 1488
bwtbinfo@xsinet.co.za
www.beaufortwestsa.co.za
Bethlehem Tourism
Tel: 058 303 5732/4993
info@bethlehem.org.za
www.dihlabeng.org.za
Citrusdal Tourist Info
Tel: 022 921 3210
info@citrusdal.info
www.citrusdal.info

Clanwilliam Tourist Info
Tel: 027 482 2024
cederberg@lando.co.za
www.clanwilliam.info

PG 115 COLESBERG/GEORGE/ ESTCOURT/GRAAFF-REINET
Colesberg Tourism
Tel: 051 753 0777
belinda@mjvn.co.za
George Tourism
Tel: 044 801 9295/73 5228
info@georgetourism.co.za
www.georgetourism.co.za
Estcourt (Umtshezi Municipality)
Tel: 036 352 3000/6253
umtshezitourism@lantic.net
www.mtshezi.co.za
Graaff-Reinet Publicity
Tel: 049 892 4248
info@graaffreinet.co.za
www.graaffreinet.co.za

PG 116 GRAHAMSTOWN/KNYSNA/ KROONSTAD/LADYSMITH
Grahamstown Tourism
Tel: 046 622 3241, Fax: 622 3266
info@grahamstown.co.za
www.grahamstown.co.za
Knysna Tourism
Tel: 044 382 5510
knysna.tourism@pixie.co.za
www.knysna-info.co.za
Kroonstad Tourism
Tel: 056 212 3611
krdchamber@ict.co.za
Ladysmith Tourism
Tel: 036 637 2992
info@ladysmith.co.za
www.ladysmith.co.za

PG 117 LAMBERTS BAY/ LYDENBURG/MOSSEL BAY/MUSINA
Lamberts Bay Tourism
Tel: 027 432 1000
lambertsinfo@mweb.co.za
www.lambertsbay.com
Lydenburg Tourist Info
Tel: 013 235 2121/213
sportartcul@lantic.net
www.lydenburg.org
Mossel Bay Tourism
Tel: 044 691 2202/0 3077
mbtb@mweb.co.za
www.visitmosselbay.co.za
Musina Tourism
Tel: 015 534 3500
musinatourism@limpopo.co.za
www.limpopotourism.org.za

PG 118 NEWCASTLE/OUDTSHOORN/ PILGRIMS REST/PORT SHEPSTONE
Newcastle Tourism
Tel: 034 315 3318
info@newcastle.co.za

www.tourismnewcastle.co.za
Oudtshoorn Tourism
Tel: 044 279 2532/2 8226
otb@mweb.co.za
www.oudtshoorn.co.za
Pilgrims Rest Tourist Info
Tel: 013 768 1060
sagpa@absamail.co.za
www.mpumalanga.com
Hibiscus Coast Tourism Office
Tel: 039 316 6139/2 2322
Port Shepstone Tourism
Tel: 039 682 2455
portshepstone@hibiscuscoast.org.za
www.hibiscuscoast.kzn.org.za

PG 119 RICHARDS BAY/ RUSTENBURG/SISHEN/SPRINGBOK
Richards Bay (uMhlathuze Tourism Office)
Tel: 035 901 5408/000
rbtour@ughungulu.co.za
rightb@richemp.org.za
www.tourismassociation.org.za
Rustenburg Tourism
Tel: 014 597 0904
tidcrust@mweb.co.za
www.tourismnorthwest.co.za
Mokala Safari Tourism - Sishen
Tel: 053 723 2391/1501
info@mokala.co.za
www.mokala.co.za
Springbok Namaqua Tourist Office
Tel: 027 718 2985/6
tourismsbk@namakwa-dm.co.za
www.northerncape.org.za
www.namakwa-dm.co.za

PG 120 STELLENBOSCH/ST LUCIA/ STRAND/SWELLENDAM
Stellenbosch Tourism
Tel: 021 883 3584, Fax: 883 8017
info@stellenboschtourism.co.za
www.stellenbosch.co.za
St Lucia Information Centre
Tel: 035 550 4059, 590 1247/047
leisure@telkomsa.net
www.stlucia.co.za
Helderberg Tourism Bureau (Strand)
Tel: 021 851 4022
helderberg@tourismcapetown.co.za
www.tourismcapetown.co.za
Swellendam Tourist Info
Tel: 028 514 2770
infoswd@sdm.dorea.co.za
www.swellendamtourism.co.za

PG 121 TZANEEN/UMTATA/ UPINGTON/VRYBURG
Tzaneen Tourism
Tel: 015 307 6513/7244
reservations@tzaneeninfo.co.za
www.tzaneeninfo.co.za
www.limpopotourism.org.za
Umtata Tourism
Tel: 047 531 5290/2

infomtata@ectourism.co.za
ectbw@ectourism.co.za
www.ectourism.co.za
Upington Tourist Information Centre
Tel: 054 332 6064
tourism@kharahais.gov.za
www.kharahaismunicipality.co.za
Green Kalahari Tourism (Upington)
Tel: 054 337 2804
greenkal@webmail.co.za
greenkal@bocr.gov.za
www.greenkalahari.co.za
Vryburg Tourism
Tel: 053 927 1434
lecoge@bophrima.co.za
www.bophirima.co.za

PG 122 VRYHEID/WITBANK/ WORCESTER/GOBABIS
Vryheid Tourism
Tel: 034 982 2133 ext 2229
information@vhd.dorea.co.za
www.vryheid.co.za
Witbank Tourism
Tel: 013 656 2327
infotour@netactive.co.za
Worcester Tourism
Tel: 023 348 2795
jcdamens@breedevalley.gov.za
www.breedevalley.gov.za
Gobabis Tourism
Tel: 09264 62 562 428
Ministry of Environment and Tourism
Tel: 09264 61 284 2111
www.met.gov.na

PG 123 HENTIES BAY/KATIMA MULILO/KOLMANSKOP/LÜDERITZ
Henties Bay Tourism
Tel: 09264 64 501 143
info@hentiesbay.com
www.hentiesbay.com
Katima Mulilo Tourism
Tel: 09264 66 253 027/5 403
Namibia Tourism Board (Kolmanskop)
Tel: 09264 61 290 6000
info@namibiatourism.com.na
www.namibiatourism.com.na
Lüderitz Tourism
Tel: 09264 63 202 719/622
ludsaf@africaonline.com.na

PG 124 MARIENTAL/OKAHANDJA/ OPUWO/OSHAKATI
Mariental Tourism
Tel: 09264 63 245 661/2 427
www.met.gov.na
Okahandja Tourism
Tel: 09264 501 051/91
okahandja@iway.na
www.met.gov.na
Opuwo Tourism
Tel: 09264 65 273 003/105
Oshakati Tourism
Tel: 09264 61 290 6000

PG 125 OTJIWARONGO/RUNDU/ SESFONTEIN/SWAKOPMUND
Otjiwarongo Tourism
Tel: 09264 67 302 645
www.met.gov.na
Rundu Tourism
Tel: 09264 66 255 749
csikopo@hotmail.com
www.met.gov.na
Fort Sesfontein Lodge (Sesfontein)
Tel: 09264 65 275 534
fort.sesfontein@mweb.com.na
www.fort-sesfontein.com
Swakopmund Tourism (Namib-i)
Tel: 09264 64 404 827
namibi@iway.na
www.namibi.org.na

PG 126 TSUMEB/FRANCISTOWN/ GHANZI/JWANENG
Travel North Namibia (Tsumeb)
Tel: 09264 67 220 728
travelnn@tsu.namib.com
Francistown
Tel: 09267 241 6279
Dept of Tourism, Botswana (Ghanzi, Jwaneng)
Tel: 09267 395 3024
botswanatourism@gov.bw
www.botswanatourism.org

PG 127 KANYE/MAHALAPYE/ NATA/SELEBI PHIKWE
Dept of Tourism, Botswana (Kanye)
Tel: 09267 395 3024
Motse Lodge (Kanye)
Tel: 09267 548 0370
Tel: 021 680 6767/8
motselodge@botsnet.bw
Mahalapye Hotel
Tel: 09267 471 0200
Nata Lodge
Tel: 09267 621 1260
natalodge@inet.co.bw
www.natalodge.com

PG 128 CHIMANIMANI/CHINHOYI/ GWERU/KARIBA
Harare National Parks Central Reservations
Tel: 09263 4 706 077/8, 707 624/9
natparks@africaonline.co.zw
www.zimparks.com
Dept of Tourism, Botswana (Chinhoyi)
Tel: 09267 395 3024
Gweru Publicity Association
Tel: 09263 54 224 071/230
Kariba Publicity Association
Tel: 09263 61 2328/3213, Fax: 2880
kpa@mweb.co.zw

PG 129 KWEKWE/MASVINGO/ MUTARE/VICTORIA FALLS
Zimbabwe Tourism Authority (Kwekwe)
Tel: 09263 4 758 712/4/24/30/34
info@ztazim.co.zw
www.zimbabwetourism.co.zw
Great Zimbabwe Publicity Association (Masvingo)
Tel: 09263 396 2643
mgpa@webmail.co.za
Mutare Publicity Association
Tel: 09263 20 64711, Fax: 67728
Victoria Falls Publicity Association
Tel: 09263 13 44202
vfpa@mweb.co.zw
www.geosites.com/vicfallspublicity

PG 130 BLANTYRE/MOZAMBIQUE ISLAND/NAMPULA
Dept of Tourism, Malawi (Blantyre)
Tel: 09265 1 620 902, Fax: 621 923
tourism@malawi.net
www.tourismmalawi.com
Ministry of Tourism, Mozambique (Mozambique island/Nampula)
Tel: 09258 1 307 320/3, Fax: 307 324
info@futur.org.mz
www.futur.org.mz

PG 131 QUELIMANE/TETE/ VILANKULO/XAI-XAI
Zambézia Province Tourism
Tel: 09258 4 215 822/3 689
Fax: 09258 4 212 004
dpictventura@teledata.mz
Vilankulo Tourist Services
Tel: 09258 23 82228
margie@teledata.mz
Vilankulo Info
Tel: 09258 23 82031/2
information@vilanculos.org
www.vilanculos.org
Ministry of Tourism, Mozambique (Quelimane, Tete, Xai-Xai)
Tel: 09258 1 307 320/3, Fax: 307 324
info@futur.org.mz
www.futur.org.mz
www.mocambiqueturismo.co.mz
Mozambique Tourism
Tel: 011 803 9296/52
travel@mozambiquetourism.co.za
www.mozambiquetourism.co.za
Quilalea Sales Office
Tel: 011 447 9422
quilaleaisland@iafrica.com
www.quilalea.com
Rani Resorts
Tel: 011 467 1277
enquiries@raniresorts.com
www.raniresorts.com

MapStudio

This edition first published in 2005 by **MapStudio** South Africa

ISBN 1 86809 807 9

Author – Mariëlle Renssen
Publishing manager – John Loubser
Designer – Geraldine Cupido
Senior cartographer – Elaine Fick
Project cartographer – Ryan Africa
Researcher – Deniellé Lategan
Design concept – Maryna Beukes

Map Studio
80 McKenzie Street, Cape Town
PO Box 1144, Cape Town, 8000
Tel – 021 462 4360
Fax – 021 462 4378
www.mapstudio.co.za
Images of Africa
www.imagesofafrica.co.za
Reproduction by
Resolution Colours (Pty) Ltd, Cape Town, South Africa
Printed and bound by
Tien Wah Press (Pte) Ltd, Singapore

Text & maps © 2005: Map Studio
Photos © 2005: Listed on this page

The author would like to acknowledge writers Paul Tingay and Peter Joyce, whose descriptions, in some cases, of certain sites in Southern Africa simply couldn't be topped! Thanks for their inspiration.

The information contained herein is derived from a variety of sources. While every effort has been made to verify the information contained in such sources, the publisher assumes no responsibility for inconsistencies or inaccuracies in the data nor liability for any damages of any type arising from errors or omissions. Reproduction or recording of any maps, text, photographs, illustrations, or other material contained in this publication in any manner including, without limitation, by photocopying and electronic storage and retrieval, is prohibited.

Pages from left to right

8/9
- SHAEN ADEY
- HEIN VON HORSTEN
- SHAEN ADEY
- GERHARD DREYER
- NIGEL DENNIS

10/11
- IAN MICHLER
- ARIADNE VAN ZANDBERGEN
- ARIADNE VAN ZANDBERGEN
- NIGEL DENNIS
- ROGER DE LA HARPE
- IAN MICHLER
- ARIADNE VAN ZANDBERGEN

12/13
- SHAEN ADEY
- JÉAN DU PLESSIS
- GERALD CUBITT
- MARTIN HARVEY
- HEIN VON HORSTEN
- THE CARDBOARD BOX
- OFF2 AFRICA

14/15
- SHAEN ADEY
- SHAEN ADEY
- KEITH YOUNG
- SHAEN ADEY
- SHAEN ADEY
- WALTER KNIRR

16/17
- SHAEN ADEY
- IMAGES OF AFRICA
- JÉAN DU PLESSIS
- HEIN VON HORSTEN
- JÉAN DU PLESSIS
- WALTER KNIRR

18/19
- SHAEN ADEY
- SHAEN ADEY
- SHAEN ADEY
- KEITH YOUNG

20/21
- HEIN VON HORSTEN
- GERHARD DREYER
- PETER PICKFORD
- SHAEN ADEY

22/23
- TONY CAMACHO
- WILLIE & SANDRA OLIVIER
- TONY CAMACHO
- CHANAN WEISS
- ILLUSTRATIVE OPTIONS
- DARYL BALFOUR

24/25
- MARTIN HARVEY
- MARTIN HARVEY
- MARTIN HARVEY
- PETER PICKFORD

26/27
- ROGER DE LA HARPE
- ARIADNE VAN ZANDBERGEN
- WALTER KNIRR
- ROGER DE LA HARPE
- ROGER DE LA HARPE
- COLOUR LIBRARY
- WALTER KNIRR

28/29
- ARIADNE VAN ZANDBERGEN
- MARTIN HARVEY
- SAM J BASCH
- LANZ VON HORSTEN
- NIGEL DENNIS
- NIGEL DENNIS

30/31
- ARIADNE VAN ZANDBERGEN
- WALTER KNIRR
- COLOUR LIBRARY
- KEITH YOUNG
- DIRK SCHWAGER
- SHAEN ADEY

32/33
- MARTIN HARVEY
- SHAEN ADEY
- SHAEN ADEY
- PETER PICKFORD
- WALTER KNIRR
- DAVID ROGERS

34/35
- WALTER KNIRR
- WALTER KNIRR
- WALTER KNIRR
- WALTER KNIRR
- SHAEN ADEY
- WALTER KNIRR

36/37
- LIMPOPO TOURISM & PARKS
- NIGEL DENNIS
- WALTER KNIRR
- KEITH BEGG

38/39
- WALTER KNIRR
- HEIN VON HORSTEN
- DOUGLAS BLACK
- ROGER DE LA HARPE

40/41
- KEITH BEGG
- KEITH BEGG
- ERHARDT THEIL
- ROGER DE LA HARPE
- IAN MICHLER
- ROGER DE LA HARPE
- WALTER KNIRR
- IAN MICHLER
- DAVID ROGERS

42/43
- SHAEN ADEY
- HEIN VON HORSTEN
- LANZ VON HORSTEN
- GERHARD DREYER
- SHAEN ADEY
- LANZ VON HORSTEN

44/45
- ROD HAESTIER
- WALTER KNIRR
- ROGER DE LA HARPE
- SHAEN ADEY
- SHAEN ADEY
- WALTER KNIRR

46/47
- GERHARDT DREYER
- GERHARDT DREYER
- GERHARDT DREYER
- CHANAN WEISS

48/49
- SHAEN ADEY
- LEONARD HOFFMAN
- MARTIN HARVEY
- IAN MICHLER

50/51
- ROGER DE LA HARPE
- KEITH BEGG
- KEITH BEGG
- ROGER DE LA HARPE
- DAVID ROGERS
- PETER BLACKWELL

52/53
- PETER PICKFORD
- ARIADNE VAN ZANDBERGEN
- ROGER DE LA HARPE
- ROGER DE LA HARPE

54/55
- SHAEN ADEY
- CAROL POLICH
- NIGEL DENNIS
- DARYL BALFOUR
- COLOUR LIBRARY
- DARYL BALFOUR
- DARYL BALFOUR

56/57
- KEITH YOUNG
- KEITH YOUNG
- WALTER KNIRR
- KEITH YOUNG
- DARYL BALFOUR
- DARYL BALFOUR

58/59
- ILLUSTRATIVE OPTIONS
- MARTIN HARVEY
- MARTIN HARVEY
- ROGER DE LA HARPE
- ROGER DE LA HARPE

60/61
- IAN MICHLER
- MARTIN HARVEY
- MARTIN HARVEY
- DARYL BALFOUR

62/63
- ARIADNE VAN ZANDBERGEN
- ARIADNE VAN ZANDBERGEN
- ROGER DE LA HARPE
- ROGER DE LA HARPE
- CHANAN WEISS
- JÉAN DU PLESSIS

64/65
- GERALD CUBITT
- MARTIN HARVEY
- CHANAN WEISS
- JÉAN DU PLESSIS
- CAROL POLICH
- WALTER KNIRR

66/67
- CHANAN WEISS
- ARIADNE VAN ZANDBERGEN
- CHANAN WEISS
- JÉAN DU PLESSIS
- CHANAN WEISS
- JÉAN DU PLESSIS

68/69
- JÉAN DU PLESSIS
- JÉAN DU PLESSIS
- MARTIN HARVEY
- DAVID ROGERS
- ROGER DE LA HARPE
- JÉAN DU PLESSIS
- WILLIE & SANDRA OLIVIER
- JÉAN DU PLESSIS

70/71
- GERHARDUS DU PLESSIS
- JÉAN DU PLESSIS

- JÉAN DU PLESSIS
- JÉAN DU PLESSIS
- JÉAN DU PLESSIS
- JÉAN DU PLESSIS

72/73
- WILLIE & SANDRA OLIVIER
- PATRICK WAGNER
- JÉAN DU PLESSIS
- IAN MICHLER
- PETER PICKFORD
- JÉAN DU PLESSIS

74/75
- TONY CAMACHO
- MARTIN HARVEY
- MARTIN HARVEY
- MARTIN HARVEY

76/77
- JÉAN DU PLESSIS
- JÉAN DU PLESSIS
- PATRICK WAGNER
- WILLIE & SANDRA OLIVIER
- DAVID ROGERS
- ARIADNE VAN ZANDBERGEN

78/79
- ARIADNE VAN ZANDBERGEN
- ARIADNE VAN ZANDBERGEN
- ARIADNE VAN ZANDBERGEN
- JÉAN DU PLESSIS
- WILLIE & SANDRA OLIVIER
- GERALD CUBITT

80/81
- KEITH YOUNG
- ROGER DE LA HARPE
- WALTER KNIRR
- MARK VAN AARDT
- ROGER DE LA HARPE
- HEIN VON HORSTEN
- IAN MICHLER

82/83
- JOY HAESTIER
- SHAEN ADEY
- JOHN ROBINSON
- WALTER KNIRR
- PETER PICKFORD
- ROD HAESTIER

84/85
- ROGER DE LA HARPE
- WALTER KNIRR
- WALTER KNIRR
- SHAEN ADEY
- SHAEN ADEY
- SHAEN ADEY

86/87
- ROGER DE LA HARPE
- ROGER DE LA HARPE
- WALTER KNIRR
- WALTER KNIRR

88/89
- JÉAN DU PLESSIS
- IAN MICHLER
- ILLUSTRATIVE OPTIONS
- PETER PICKFORD
- SHAEN ADEY
- WALTER KNIRR

90/91
- WALTER KNIRR
- CAROL POLICH
- SHAEN ADEY
- LANZ VON HORSTEN
- LANZ VON HORSTEN
- KEITH YOUNG

92/93
- KEITH BEGG
- ANTHONY JOHNSON
- IAN MICHLER
- IAN MICHLER
- IAN MICHLER
- IAN MICHLER

94/95
- KEITH BEGG
- IAN MICHLER
- ARIADNE VAN ZANDBERGEN
- IAN MICHLER
- ARIADNE VAN ZANDBERGEN
- ARIADNE VAN ZANDBERGEN

96/97
- IAN MICHLER
- IAN MICHLER
- IAN MICHLER
- IAN MICHLER
- IAN MICHLER
- IAN MICHLER

98/99
- IAN MICHLER
- IAN MICHLER
- NIGEL DENNIS
- IAN MICHLER